SUPERDADS

Superdads

How Fathers Balance
Work and Family
in the 21st Century

Gayle Kaufman

NEW YORK UNIVERSITY PRESS

New York and London

NEW YORK UNIVERSITY PRESS
New York and London
www.nyupress.org

References to Internet websites (URLs) were accurate at the time of writing.
Neither the author nor New York University Press is responsible for URLs
that may have expired or changed since the manuscript was prepared.

Library of Congress Cataloging-in-Publication Data
Kaufman, Gayle.
Superdads : how fathers balance work and family in the 21st century / Gayle Kaufman.
pages cm
Includes bibliographical references and index.
ISBN 978-0-8147-4915-9 (cl : alk. paper) -- ISBN 978-0-8147-4916-6 (pb : alk. paper)
1. Fathers. 2. Fatherhood. 3. Work and family. 4. Work-life balance. I. Title.
HQ756.K375 2013
306.874'2--dc23
2012049434

New York University Press books are printed on acid-free paper,
and their binding materials are chosen for strength and durability.
We strive to use environmentally responsible suppliers and materials
to the greatest extent possible in publishing our books.

Manufactured in the United States of America

c 10 9 8 7 6 5 4 3 2 1
p 10 9 8 7 6 5 4 3 2 1

To Emily and David's superdad, Kevin

CONTENTS

ACKNOWLEDGMENTS

There are so many people I would like to thank for helping me as I wrote this book. First, I must thank all the fathers who shared their stories with me. Many men met with me during their lunch hour, after work, or on their first day off in weeks, and the time they took to speak with me was time away from their families. I am so thankful that these men poured their hearts out to me, sharing personal joys and hardships of parenting and life. Thanks also to Toshiba Conner, Kristen Fortin, Don Grady, Elisa Moreno, Nannie Potts, Vivian Rogers-Cannon, Connie Scher, Aimee Symington, Larry Taylor, Verde Torrence, and several community organizations for help in recruiting fathers. A special thanks to Judith and Jay Schreider for opening their home to me to conduct many of my California interviews.

I am also grateful for grant support from the American Sociological Association's Fund for the Advancement of the Discipline, which is supported by the American Sociological Association and the National Science Foundation. This grant is intended to fund "small, groundbreaking research" and it certainly helped me get this project started. Other funding from the Economic and Social Research Council (ESRC), the Social Science Research Council (SSRC), several Davidson College Faculty Study and Research grants, and the Centre for Research in the Arts, Social Sciences and Humanities (CRASSH) at the University of Cambridge was instrumental in fostering this research.

This project also benefited from my involvement with other scholars. I owe a great deal to Fran Goldscheider, who introduced me to family sociology and has inspired me for twenty years now, first as my professor and mentor and later as my colleague and friend. Through comparative research with British colleagues Clare Lyonette and Rosemary Crompton I have been better able to see the important tendencies in my American data. Working with Swedish colleagues Eva Bernhardt, Livia Oláh, and Anna-Lena Almqvist has also made me want to push harder for change in American policies. I have also had the good fortune of working with my frequent collaborator and friend Hiromi Taniguchi, who pushes me in the research realm and entertains me in the personal realm. Thanks for early comments to Andrea Doucet, Linda Haas, and Margaret O'Brien.

At Davidson College, thanks to Mary Muchane and Beverly Winecoff for grant support and thanks to Cheryl Branz for administrative support. I am very thankful for having such a fine departmental colleague in Gerardo Marti, who provided invaluable advice and support through the entire process. Thanks to all my undergraduate research assistants, Georgie Ahrendt, Allie Christ, Katie Hamilton, Justin Hartanov, Ryan Hubbard, Shantay Mobley, Eric Reeves, Paul Sayed, and Damion White, for help with literature searches, data transcription, and coding. A very special thanks to Damian White for reading, thinking, commenting, and talking through every detail of the book. After "super" July, I will always see you as a trusted colleague.

Ilene Kalish has been a great editor, expressing interest in my book project right away and helping me to think through important issues such as the title. The reviewers provided positive and useful feedback, encouraging me to focus more on superdads. Thanks also to Aiden Amos, who helped with the very practical matters of the book publishing process.

For listening to me work through all sorts of details, I am grateful to my running partner and friend Suzanne Cooper-Guasco. Thanks also to Lynda Stark, Kristie Foley, and Angela Willis. Finally, I am truly thankful for having such a great family. Hugs and kisses to Mary Ann and Victor Jung, Fred and Lori Kaufman, Robert and Frances Bell, Rick and Vee Kaufman, Kai and Suji Jung, Chris and Kindra Bell, John Bell and Hilary Spiegelman, and my adorable nieces and nephews—Aleksei, Noah, Hannah, Elliot, and Quinn. I find it difficult to describe the incredible joy of having two amazing kids, Emily and David, who make my world brighter. And never-ending thanks to my husband, Kevin Bell, who is my reader and rock, the one who has supported and nurtured me from beginning to end. As the model for "superdads," this book simply would not be possible without you.

ONE

Introduction

More Dads at the Bus Stop

A few days ago I was at the afternoon bus stop. The bus from the elementary school comes anytime between 3:50 and 4:05, dropping off somewhere around 15 children. What I noticed this day was that there were more fathers at the bus stop than mothers. This is not completely unusual for our block, but rather you could see it coming if you paid attention to the ups and downs of the market and the individual job changes within this particular group of fathers. I suppose I should qualify my observation by noting that two of the fathers are professors, one is a pilot who mainly works weekends, and one is recently unemployed. Not to mention my husband, a writer who works from home. But we have had other, more occasional, fathers, ones whose schedules are not quite as flexible but who still make the effort to move things around at work if they need to be at home. The point is that fathers are no longer an anomaly at the bus stop. There are more dads holding hands, tossing balls, and talking with children as they wait for the bus. One local dad plays "rock, paper, scissors" with his young daughter through the bus window as other children board the morning bus.

Sociologists such as myself call these men "new" dads or "involved" dads, a sign that times are changing and men's roles as fathers are changing too. But we have been talking about new dads for a while now. They have become an accepted and perhaps expected part of our culture. Most dads today want to be involved and are actively seeking ways to spend more time with their children. And men are expected to be more and more involved with their families. The new father takes time to eat with his family, read to his children, throw a ball around, and even change diapers. At the same time, however, men are not routinely offered options when it comes to negotiating issues of work-family balance. Instead, after becoming fathers, they are expected to continue on with their work lives as if they had experienced a minor blip on their family radar screens. Given these contrasting expectations, I became interested in discovering if fathers feel conflicted between their work and family lives. Moreover, I wanted to find out what issues are important to fathers and what kinds of strategies they use in order to balance work and family obligations and expectations.

Although there has been growing research on work and family suggesting that not only women but also men experience work-family conflict, less is known about the strategies working fathers use in an attempt to balance their work and family lives. With dramatic changes in work and family life over the past few decades, including increases in women's labor force participation, especially mothers' labor force participation, and increases in divorce and nonmarital childbearing, families consisting of a breadwinner husband/father and homemaker wife/mother are fairly uncommon. Instead, dual-earner families and single-parent families are the more standard family forms of today. These working parents often struggle to balance the time commitments involved in performing work and family roles.

Superdads provides a glimpse into the lives of American fathers in the 21st century as they attempt to be more involved fathers while fulfilling the more traditional role of provider for their families. Today's dads want to spend more time with their children and yet struggle with how they will spend that time with their kids while still being responsible workers. They may think and plan before their child arrives. Or it may not occur to them until they are holding their newborn. But more often than not fathers come to the realization that they want to be more than financial providers—they want to be dads.

While expectations for father involvement have risen, the societal supports to make greater involvement possible have not kept pace. The workplace still sees men as men and not as fathers. This book offers a picture

2

of men's experiences and struggles as they make the transition to fatherhood. It begins with the very real feelings of stress that are often wrapped up with a sense of work/life imbalance. This often starts with (or is exacerbated by) the birth of a child. Fathers find themselves scrambling to take time off as their options for family leave are limited. But here is where the story becomes more complicated. While some fathers accept their situation for what it is, others make changes. They do this in a variety of ways, some extreme (changing jobs) and some more tame (cutting back hours, working from home, using flex time). Out of this emerges what I call superdads, fathers who significantly adjust their work in order to have more time with their families. We might not think this would be so revolutionary if we were talking about mothers, but these fathers are a step in the direction of better families and greater gender equality.

Old Dads, New Dads, and Superdads

Erik[1] is a 34-year-old, white landscape architect. He is married with a 2-year-old son and a second child on the way at the time of our interview. When we talked, he was working at a small firm but had accepted a position with a larger firm, one that would provide more opportunities for career development and a higher income. While Erik liked working at the small firm, he also felt like a failure because his wife wanted to stay home and raise their children. She often complained about having to drop their son off at daycare, and this contributed to Erik's stress. His new, higher-paying job will enable his wife to stay home, but it also involves longer hours and more travel, a sacrifice he is willing to make for his family.

Kenan is a 25-year-old, black merchandising assistant for a large home-improvement company. He is married with a 7-year-old stepson and a 4-year-old son, and he makes it clear that he treats both sons the same. Kenan's wife works in a medical office full-time and also has a second job cleaning the same office building in the evenings every other week. This means that Kenan is solely responsible for picking up the kids, helping with their homework, cooking, and getting the kids to bed half the time. While Kenan has not had to make large changes to his work schedule, he does leave work a little early every other week. At this point, Kenan feels as though he can get away with not staying late and not taking work home, but he does expect certain changes as he attempts to climb the ladder in his company.

Luis is a 29-year-old, Mexican American, married father of two who was working his way through college when we met. He is completely devoted to his family, and it was clear that all his decisions about education and work stemmed from his efforts to be a better father. In fact, Luis was adamant that he did not want to balance work and family but would rather spend as much time with his family as possible while working enough to pay the bills. This attitude led to his decision to quit his job at a casino and work in real estate, which has allowed him to spend two to three hours each morning with his children.

Larry is a 42-year-old, white, divorced father. He is a fabricator, but this was not always his dream job. When he and his wife separated, he felt he was at a crossroads. On the one hand, he could continue down his career path on his way to being a crew chief and be a "one-day-a-week daddy." Or, he could choose to be a real parent to his then 18-month-old daughter, which would require stepping off the fast track and into a more stable position that would not require traveling but instead offer shorter and more flexible work hours. Larry chose the latter path, moving into the shop, sharing custody equally with his ex-wife, and cherishing the relationship he now has with his daughter.

While these fathers all experience some amount of work-family conflict, their solutions differ. Erik is an "old" dad, one who sees his primary role as provider and will sacrifice his own family time in order for his wife to stay at home with their children. Kenan is a "new" dad, an involved father who makes minor adjustments to his work schedule in order to balance work and family but who nevertheless sees more constraints than solutions. Luis and Larry are "superdads," men who specifically change their work lives in order to accommodate their families.

In *No Man's Land*, sociologist Kathleen Gerson suggests that men are in "a territory of undefined and shifting allegiances, in which they must negotiate difficult choices between freedom and commitment, privilege and sharing, and dominance and equality."[2] The book begins with a description of three men, an uninvolved husband, a "well-dressed bachelor," and a young, involved father. These men represent the concepts of breadwinning, autonomy, and family involvement. A few years after Arlie Hochschild's now-classic *The Second Shift*, in which she wrote about the stalled revolution in which changes in men's behavior, particularly regarding household responsibilities, were lagging behind women's changes, most notably their flooding of the labor force,[3] Gerson was saying that a growing number of men were more involved, placing family commitments above work commitments. Yet two-thirds of the men she interviewed were turning not toward family involvement but instead toward breadwinning or autonomy (having no children and forgoing or leaving marriage).[4] Certainly, these concepts are still relevant, as there continue to be childless men and uninvolved fathers, but a lot has changed since Gerson's book was published. Since Gerson's book, the breadwinners have declined in number, the involved group has grown, and I argue that a new group, superdads, has emerged.

Discussion over the past decade has turned to the "new father" and whether the reality of involved fatherhood has caught up with the ideology of new dads. In the book *Halving It All*, social psychologist Francine Deutsch showed that some fathers "undo" traditional gender roles, and even challenge masculinity, as they seek to become equal parents.[5] In examining men's work and family reconciliation in Europe, prominent Norwegian scholar Oystein Holter revealed a shift in men's gender ideal from breadwinner, in which men act as primary or sole earners in their families, to caring masculinities, in which men fully participate in caregiving. Of key importance is the idea that initial changes are more likely to occur at home rather than at work. In other words, new fathers may adjust their domestic role by adding childcare responsibilities during nonworking hours while leaving their work role relatively unchanged. In addition, Holter posits two models: the "new man" model, in which change occurs because men are dedicated to gender equality, and the "new circumstances" model, in which change occurs because of particular circumstances. Here we see that some men commit to change because they believe they are equally responsible for their children as their female partners, while other men do not necessarily plan to change their behavior but take on new roles because their situation requires it (e.g., partner's working hours or lack of childcare availability).[6] At the 2010 International Sociological Association World Congress,

Canadian sociologist Gillian Ranson argued that there is a small, seldom-discussed group of men that she refers to as "working fathers." She defines these fathers as "men who *do* take advantage of workplace initiatives most commonly used by mothers, and who in other ways explicitly organize their working lives around family responsibilities they are committed, or obliged, to assume." Ranson uses the term "working fathers" as an equivalent to "working mothers" in that the emphasis is on *fathers* who happen to work rather than workers who happen to be fathers. In her study of Canadian fathers, she finds that "working fathers" generally have employed partners, low career aspirations, and jobs that are not privileged within the family.[7] I build on Ranson's conceptualization to develop what I call superdads.

In this book, I distinguish between three types of dads—"old" dads, "new" dads, and superdads. "Old" dads refers to those fathers who are more traditional or old-fashioned in their outlook and behavior. This term does not refer to age, though fathers who are older in age are more likely to be characterized as old dads than younger fathers are. Old dads see their primary role as father to be a breadwinner, and some are consumed by work, earning the label workaholic. These fathers tend to see their children little during the week but may try to make up for this deficit by spending extra time with their children on weekends. They tend to feel moderate amounts of stress related to work-family conflict because they would like to see their children more, but they also know that they are providing for their families, and often they have stay-at-home wives. For the purpose of my study, *old dads make little change to their work lives upon becoming fathers*, and in fact may increase their time on, and attention to, work. About 20 percent of the fathers I talked with fit into this group (see chapter 4).

"New" dads refers to those fathers who are less traditional in their outlook and behavior. They identify strongly with their role as father. New dads place a high priority on the issue of balancing work and family and attempt to fill both the breadwinner and caregiver roles. They spend a good deal of time with their children, though weekend time still far outweighs weekday time. New dads experience the greatest amount of stress because they would like to spend more time with their children and have not achieved a desired balance between work and family. *New dads may alter some of their work practices*, but changes are limited and only provide partial solutions for their work-family dilemmas. This was the most common group of fathers, representing half the men I interviewed (see chapter 5).

"Superdads" refers to those fathers who see their role as caregiver as more important than breadwinner. They want to spend as much time with their children as possible and feel that they have an equal responsibility for raising their children. They experience lower stress levels than the other two types of dads, mainly because they have found a way of balancing work and family. Indeed, some superdads specifically resist the idea of balance, placing more importance on the family side of the scale. Importantly, *superdads deliberately adjust their work lives to fit their family lives*, rather than vice versa. About 30 percent of the fathers I spoke with fit my description of superdads (see chapters 6 and 7).

Let me take some time right now to address the concerns of some readers about the particular terminology I have chosen. The use of "super," after all, suggests that these dads are special and perhaps more special than many working mothers who make similar choices without such recognition. Here I would make two points. First, if we go back to the 1970s and 1980s, we see that the term "supermom" was used in popular discourse to refer to mothers who "did it all."[8] The "super" part of being a supermom was the addition of paid employment to a woman's usual mom duties. For superdads, the "super" part comes from their role as dads and how this affects their decisions regarding work. It is, therefore, not a completely parallel concept because it relies on the interaction between domains rather than the simple addition of a role. Second, while some readers may be incredulous at the seeming coronation of superdads over moms who do the same thing, societal expectations for men and women have been and continue to be different. To give an example, when a woman becomes a CEO or senator, we applaud her in a way we would not applaud a man doing the same thing. That is because the big change for women has been to enter the previously male-dominated world of work and politics. Likewise, men tend to be applauded when they do something they have not done before. In other words, the big change for men is to enter the previously female-dominated world of childrearing. To give credit where credit is due, new dads have entered the home realm with great enthusiasm, contributing much to their children's and partners' needs. Nevertheless, the varied structural and situational constraints they face have limited any major changes in their work lives. In this regard, they have made more changes at home than at work. In contrast, superdads respond to their family's needs by changing their work lives.

Table 1.1: Three types of fathers

	OLD	NEW	SUPERDAD
Primary role	Breadwinner	Breadwinner/caregiver	Caregiver
Stress level	Medium	High	Low
Time with children	Weekends	Occasional time	As much as possible
Change	No change	Small change	Large change

Changing Work and Family Roles

In 1950, 82 percent of men and 42 percent of women age 18 and older were in the labor force. In 2007, 66 percent of men and 57 percent of women age 18 and older were in the labor force. Men's labor force participation had decreased slowly over this time period, while women's participation increased until the 1990s (the latest decrease for both women and men may be due to increases in postsecondary school enrollment among young adults). The change in mothers' labor force participation has been even more dramatic, with 47 percent participation rates for women with children under age 18 in 1975 compared with 71 percent in 2007. Women are contributing more income, 44 percent of family income among dual-earner couples in 2008, an increase of 5 percent in the past decade. There has also been an increase in couples in which the female partner earns more. In 1997, 15 percent of dual-earner couples had wives who earned at least 10 percent higher incomes than their husbands, compared with 26 percent in 2008.[9]

Attitudes have changed, too. A common attitudinal statement in work-family surveys is "it is better for all involved if the man earns the money and the woman takes care of the home and children." In 1977, a slight majority of women (52 percent) and a large majority of men (74 percent) agreed with this statement, resulting in a significant gender difference in attitudes. In

2008, about two-fifths of both women and men agreed with this statement, showing that there has been a particularly strong shift in men's attitudes that has brought convergence in beliefs about work and family roles.[10]

Other signs of convergence include employed parents' time with children. Today employed fathers spend more time with young children on workdays than they did 30 years ago, but employed mothers spend about the same amount of time with children. In 1977, employed fathers spent an average of 2 hours per workday with their children under 13. This increased by one hour so that fathers now spend 3 hours, on average, with their preteen children. During the same time period, employed mothers' time with children remained steady at 3.8 hours per workday. While there is still a gender difference, the trend is one of convergence. Another study found that fathers spend an average of 2.5 hours per day with their children on weekdays and 6.3 hours per day on weekends. Furthermore, about half of employed fathers now say they take an equal share or more of the responsibility for the care of their children, which includes the management of childcare arrangements as well as daily caregiving.[11]

It is also important to note that over the past few decades, there has been a more general intensification of parenting, which is particularly prevalent among middle-class parents. Legal scholars Gaia Bernstein and Zvi Triger assert that intensive parenting is a "socio-technological trend" because it requires the use of technology in order to fully cultivate and monitor children's progress.[12] Indeed, the desire to offer children a range of opportunities and the need to transport children to an increasing number of activities results in parenting taking more time and energy. This often creates a sense among parents that more time with children is better. Because of fathers' greater likelihood to work and to work longer hours, their feelings of a time deficit with children are even greater than mothers'.[13]

Why Care about Fathers, Work, and Family?

The Families and Work Institute recently reported that a higher percentage of fathers than mothers experience work-family conflict. In 1977, 35 percent of men said they experienced work-family conflict. Today that number is 59 percent.[14] Some people might read this as bad news. After all, nobody wants to feel conflict between what are arguably the two most important and time-consuming domains in one's life. But there is another way to read these results, and that is to emphasize the changing role of fathers. First, men were just not that involved in family life back in the 1970s. Second, most men viewed their primary role as breadwinner, and so going to work was what they did for their families. However, change was on its way back then, and while some people were impatient during the 1980s and 1990s, it is more and more clear that involved fatherhood is the new norm in the early 21st century. And this means that, just like mothers, fathers are struggling with the task of providing economically for their families, which has not disappeared, while spending more time with their children. Accomplishing all facets of involved fatherhood is "becoming more challenging" for men.[15]

Ulrich Beck, a German sociologist who has influenced a great deal of thinking on modernization, globalization, and individualization, asks, "What happens in a society where, on the one hand, fealty is forever being sworn to *family values*, and to motherhood and fatherhood and parenthood, while on the other it is preached with equally doctrinaire zeal that everyone must always place him- or herself at the absolute disposal of a labor market that offers fewer and fewer zones of protection and long-term security?"[16] Beck pinpoints the current dilemma that so many parents face and wonders how a society can do justice to family values when its mothers and fathers must answer to the demands of a labor market that is not family friendly.

The focus on work-family conflict started with a focus on working mothers. As women entered the workforce and continued to care for their homes and families—what Arlie Hochschild called the second shift[17]—they found it difficult to advance in their careers while being good mothers. On one hand, this created a great deal of stress for working mothers. On the other hand, this created a situation in which employers questioned women's, and particularly mothers', work commitment and ability to be productive employees. A spotlight was also shone on working mothers as the general public expressed concerns about children's welfare. Through this all, men were never questioned about their continued emphasis on work, but they were also rarely given the choice of whether to emphasize work or family more.

While work-family issues are certainly important for women, I argue that it is no longer solely a women's issue. Balancing work and family is also essential for men. In turn, these issues are important for children and society at large. In a study of IBM workers, a large majority of employed fathers experienced work-family conflict. In addition, fathers were just as likely to experience work-family conflict as mothers.[18] Not surprisingly, extended work hours are associated with work-family strain for men as well as women.[19] Job pressure and having an employed partner also contribute to fathers' work-family conflict. However, there are some factors that can reduce men's work-family conflict. Men who hold family-centric (more focused on family than work) or dual-centric attitudes (focused on work and family about the same) experience less conflict than those who hold work-centric views (more focused on work than family). Also, having supervisor support and more autonomy at work improve work-family balance.[20]

While men who work more hours are less likely to experience work-family balance, men whose wives work more hours report greater work-family balance. One study found that men and women make an equal number of sacrifices at work for family life, but men's sacrifice is most likely to come in the form of working additional hours rather than cutting back. Men tend to make more sacrifices at home than women, most often by missing a family occasion.[21] Family life may also have an impact on work life. For example, one study found that men who had arguments with a spouse or child one day experienced higher levels of work stress the following day.[22]

Fathers who are more engaged with their children have higher levels of psychological well-being.[23] Fathers say that they learn more about themselves, their values, and their ability to express emotions from children. In learning how to care for their children, fathers develop important skills and gain more self-assurance.[24] Children also benefit from contact with fathers. Children who live with their father generally have better outcomes in terms of grades and delinquent behavior. However, all residential fathers are not equal. When adolescents live with their father and have a close relationship with him, they have higher self-esteem and less depression, indicating the importance of father relationship as well as presence.[25] Kyle Pruett, an internationally known child psychiatrist and expert on fathers, argues that fathers are just as essential as mothers for children's development, noting an association between high levels of father involvement and child development outcomes such as exploration, problem solving, and confidence.[26]

While I cannot argue that either a mother or father, based solely on their sex, is essential for children, as there is mounting evidence that children raised by same-sex parents have as good or better outcomes as those raised by opposite-sex parents,[27] I do hope to raise awareness of the importance of fathers in debates concerning work and family.

Historical Context and Men's Changing Roles

It is important to provide some historical context for men's changing work and family roles before unpacking the current study's findings. While many politicians and groups focused on family values like to make comparisons to the 1950s, this is a false comparison. Seeing the shift in fathers' roles—how they have gone from overlapping work-family domains to separate spheres (with an emphasis on breadwinning) to blurred spheres (with a greater emphasis on fathering)—is crucial to understanding the current dynamics of work and family for men.

When someone says he or she grew up in a traditional family or conservative political groups talk about bringing back traditional family values, they are referring to a family form with corresponding values that developed in the 19th century and reached its prime in the mid-20th century. In this respect, it is more modern than traditional, a relatively recent phenomenon in the long history of humankind. For much of this country's history, from the time of colonization until the mid-19th century, there was an agricultural economy and a corresponding family in which everyone, including women and children, was expected to contribute to the household economy. The family was responsible for producing just about everything it consumed. While men and women in the nonslave population had somewhat different roles, with men doing most of the farm work and women doing most of the "light manufacturing" and household work, the family was seen as an economic unit, and both women and men worked at home. Among the slave population, there was even less distinction in gender roles as both men and women performed field work.[28]

With the industrial revolution, large structural changes in the economy led to large changes in family life. As factories replaced farms, production moved out of the household. This meant that men too left the household to engage in paid employment, while most women stayed at home. With the decreased need for piecework at home (clothing production, laundering, etc.), women's roles began to focus primarily on housework and childcare. And thus separate spheres—men at work and women at home—and the traditional family were born. Yet this traditional family was not completely institutionalized among minority, immigrant, and lower-class families, which often could not get by on one income. While only 5 percent of married women were employed at the beginning of the 20th century, this number was much higher for African American married women, with almost one-quarter employed in domestic or farm work.[29]

Still, the model was one of breadwinner and homemaker, and these roles were mutually reinforcing. Just as male breadwinners made it possible for women to stay at home, female homemakers made it possible for men to fully focus on work. So while the traditional family was relatively short-lived, it was the dominant family form during the crucial initial stages of the modern workplace. This meant that workplaces and employers came to rely on having what is called an ideal worker, one who could focus entirely on work, with the assumption that someone else (a wife) would be able to take care of any household needs. This is what most sociologists refer to as an "institutionalized" assumption, because organizational practices reinforce the ideology.[30] Louise Marie Roth, author of *Selling Women Short*, has argued, "Modern organizations have institutionalized employment practices that treat workers as though they have no family responsibilities, implicitly assuming that most families have a breadwinner-homemaker division of labor even though this is no longer the statistical norm."[31] There is evidence that employer expectations reinforce a long-hours culture.[32] In *Competing Devotions*, Mary Blair-Loy refers to female executives as falling into either a "devotion to work" schema or a "devotion to family" schema. The former workers fit well within the ideal worker image as they wanted to work long hours. Yet these workers' actions influenced the more structured expectations that other workers would also have an unencumbered devotion to work.[33] Roth further suggests that assumptions about gendered care work, that women are primarily responsible for caregiving, result in unequal treatment of female employees.[34]

While I do not argue against the existence of differential treatment of female and male employees, I assert that women are not the only ones who are disadvantaged by these outdated assumptions. Men, too, are harmed by these assumptions. Surely, one could argue that women would prefer to be treated the same as male employees, which would result in more equal pay and promotions. We rarely if ever hear that men want to be treated the same as female employees. Why would they? Less pay, fewer promotions, questions about their commitment to the job. However, one could also argue that women are not held up to the ideal worker image in the same way that men are. On the one hand, while this may lead to some of the more negative outcomes just mentioned, it also provides a little more freedom and in some cases differential policies that positively impact women (e.g., maternity policies versus paternity policies). On the other hand, the pressure on men to be breadwinners and ideal workers is enormous and increasingly difficult to successfully accomplish in today's economy. In addition, it ignores the question of what men want. While women, at least middle-class women, are faced with options, men are told that they have one acceptable pathway. And so men may not lose out in the concrete economic ways that women do, but they seem to lose out when it comes to time with children. Therefore, men either miss family commitments for work or try to conceal the fact that they are taking time off for family reasons.[35]

In the second half of the 20th century, the traditional family was on the decline, and by the end of the century, it was no longer the norm. Women's roles changed first as they entered the labor force in droves. In 1940, 28 percent of women were in the labor force. In 2000, 60 percent of women were in the labor force. Even more remarkable was the increase in maternal employment.[36] Initially, this increase in female labor force participation was due to changing ideas about women's roles, first driven by their experiences working during World War II and then by rising education levels, the movement toward a service economy, and the women's movement. However, starting in the 1970s, there was also a greater need for women to work, as male wages decreased throughout the 1980s and into the mid-1990s. In fact, studies suggest that family incomes would have fallen in the 1980s if not for wives' earnings.[37]

When it was so obvious that women's roles were changing, what happened to men's roles? On the one hand, men's economic provider role became less important or, at least, less complete, with the often necessary supplementation, and occasionally replacement, of women's earnings. While many men may still consider their economic contribution to the family an important one, more and more do not want it to be their only contribution. Furthermore, an increasing number of men want partners who will also share the financial responsibility of providing. We can see this with the greater likelihood of men to marry more educated women and women with jobs.[38] On the other hand, men's domestic roles have also changed. This first occurred in the ideology of fatherhood. In the late 20th century, the "new nurturant father role" emerged and resulted in greater expectations for fathers' involvement.[39] Cultural ideals shifted, and the new father was expected to be involved in every aspect of a child's life.[40] There was some indication that ideas about fathers were changing faster than fathers' actual behavior.[41] While some scholars noted little or slow change in the 1980s and into the 1990s,[42] the most recent evidence shows that men today spend much more time with their children than they did in the past. Among married parents, fathers' time with children has increased considerably, while mothers' time has remained more stable. Between 1977 and 1997, fathers' time with children increased by five hours per week, and fathers' proportion of childcare increased by 5 percent from 38 percent to 43 percent. Another study found that fathers' share of childcare was close to half (47 percent) on weekends.[43]

As noted earlier, Gerson found that a substantial number of men in her study wanted to share the role of caregiver, but she also found that they faced social and economic constraints that made it difficult for them to cut back at work in order to spend more time parenting.[44] Likewise, in *More Equal than Others*, Rosanna Hertz found that many of the dual-earner couples in her study felt that men had been "shortchanged as nurturers."[45] Nevertheless, some fathers challenge the status quo by prioritizing their family responsibilities and making their work lives fit their family lives.[46]

Father Identity and Involvement

Identity theory, originally formulated by Sheldon Stryker, can further our understanding of fathers' role expectations, how they identify with these roles, and how they actually enact these roles. Derived from symbolic interactionism, which emphasizes the way individuals construct their selves through their interactions with others, identity theory focuses on the relationship between identities, hierarchies, and behaviors. According to

Stryker, identities are "internalized sets of role expectations, with the person having as many identities as roles played in distinct sets of social relationships."[47] Identities can also be seen as the meanings one attaches to a role.[48] These identities are influenced by societal expectations and in turn form hierarchies based on the salience of various identities. In other words, some identities are more salient and thus higher up on the hierarchy than others. These identity hierarchies, in turn, influence behavior.[49]

Applied to fathers and father involvement, we can see that men occupy various statuses, such as father, husband, and employee. In a study of the relative importance of statuses, parent status had the highest mean rating among fathers, followed by worker status and spouse status. Most fathers consider their father role to be their most rewarding and the one that has the most influence on their lives.[50] Within each status, there can also be multiple roles; for example, a father may be a provider, nurturer, companion, and disciplinarian.[51] Michael Lamb, a prominent developmental psychologist and editor of the definitive reference book *The Role of the Father in Child Development*, identified three dimensions of paternal involvement: engagement, accessibility, and responsibility.[52] Rob Palkovitz, another development psychologist who has been active in the conceptualization of father involvement, expanded Lamb's categories of involvement to include 15 categories, only one of which is providing.[53]

In a recent study of men's perceptions of their father role identity, researchers found seven role identities within the father status: provider, protector, teacher, supporter, disciplinarian, caretaker, and co-parent. The provider role was one of the most prominent for the fathers in their study.[54] Others argue that it is still particularly salient to many men's identity as fathers.[55] Still, it is clear that fathers take on several roles beyond providing. Recent studies have found a positive relationship between father role salience, or the desire to enact a role, and father involvement.[56] However, fathers who see their parental status as central do not necessarily involve themselves in caregiving. Rather, fathers who feel that their nurturing role is central are significantly more involved than fathers who do not identify with the nurturing role.[57] Therefore, men's incorporation of a specific view of parenting is important in increasing father involvement. Fathers who have a more flexible view of their family roles have higher rates of paternal involvement.[58]

While there is often a great deal of attention paid to the transition to fatherhood, it is important to note that there are also transitions within fathering that affect father identity and the relative weight of various father roles. Transitions can lead to restructuring of both inner self and outward behavior, can involve disequilibrium and resolution of conflict, and can occur at any stage of fatherhood.[59] I apply this concept to work-family conflict in considering how challenges arise through not only individual change but also family development and family changes and how fathers seek to achieve a new equilibrium.

A Note on Masculinity and Class

Ideas about masculinity and "masculinity orientation" influence ideas about fathering. A more traditional view of masculinity may be associated with the breadwinning role (chapter 4), while a more modern view, one that redefines the father role as more nurturing, may highlight the need to adjust work roles (chapters 5–7). It is difficult to write about masculinity without mentioning Raewyn Connell, an Australian sociologist who has been profoundly influential in shaping our notions of this concept. In *Gender and Power*, she described hegemonic masculinity as a cultural ideal of masculinity that is "constructed in relation to various subordinated masculinities as well as in relation to women."[60] While this ideal need not represent a majority of men, most men support it or are at least complicit in its dominance. Furthermore, Connell's text *Masculinities*, which is often seen as a foundational work for the field of "men's studies," argued for the construction of multiple masculinities.[61] More recently, Connell teamed up with criminologist James Messerschmidt to offer a reconceptualization of hegemonic masculinity. They remind us, "Gender is always relational, and patterns of masculinity are socially defined in contradistinction from some model (whether real or imaginary) of femininity."[62]

Therefore, traditional constructions of fatherhood are bound to incorporate notions of masculinity, which emphasize provider, protector, and disciplinarian roles. These traditional constructions also actively avoid behaviors that appear feminine or those associated with mothering. However, there are multiple masculinities, and these are being constructed and reconstructed continually. Furthermore, hegemonic masculinity often creates internal conflict as individual men attempt to take on multiple roles. For fathers, this may take the form of work-family conflict as the traditional provider role and ideal worker norm clash with newer ideas of father as nurturer. Again, Connell and Messerschmidt suggest that "hegemonic masculinity does not necessarily translate into a satisfying experience of life."[63] A focus on men as providers reveals particular pressures on men on the one hand and an absence or reduction of an emotionally rewarding role as caregiver on the other. Connell and Messerschmidt assert that gendered power differentials can be eliminated if we focus on both the organizational level and the individual level.[64] At the organizational level, this will require more family-friendly workplace policies. At the individual level, this might be a change initiated by superdads.

The notion of multiple masculinities suggests that men with different class backgrounds may have different ideas about masculinity, fatherhood, and the emphasis on various father roles. Further, different work experiences are likely to shape ideas about parenting as well as opportunities regarding work and family. There are mixed findings regarding class, employment, and fathers' involvement. Fathers who are not employed have higher rates of paternal involvement, while fathers who spend more time at work spend less time as the primary caregiver. However, when mothers work more hours, fathers' participation in childcare increases. Although fathers in poor families are less involved with their children, father involvement can reduce the negative effects of poverty on children's delinquency.[65]

While complicated, class is an important factor that distinguishes fathers' work-family experiences. Certainly working-class and lower-middle-class men have fewer options when it comes to balancing work and family, and this difference will be highlighted more in the book.

Who Are the Dads?

I began looking for fathers of young children who might be facing work-family conflict by going to the most practical place I could think of—daycare centers. This strategy resulted in my finding a wide range of fathers in terms of age, race, and occupational status. However, most of these fathers were married to employed wives. Therefore, I broadened the search by posting information at or making contact with community centers and churches, which increased racial diversity and the number of men with stay-at-home wives. In order to recruit more unmarried fathers, I contacted single-parent and single-father groups. Finally, I relied on some personal contacts and snowball sampling, obtaining a few names from fathers I had already interviewed (see the appendix for more information about research methodology).

I personally conducted interviews with 70 fathers, 44 in the Charlotte, North Carolina, area and 26 in Northern California.[66] Most interviews took place in my office, a colleague's office, or the father's workplace, which ranged from a business office to a medical building to a barbershop. Before starting any interview, I went through the informed-consent process and gave each father a copy of his signed consent form. All interviews were recorded and transcribed word for word. Interviews generally took between an hour and an hour and a half. The interviews were semistructured, which means I started with a list of topics and questions related to work, family, and work-family issues and allowed for other areas of conversation depending on the father's interest and experiences.

In order to be considered for my study, men had to be employed and reside with at least one child under 18 years of age. Children did not have to be biological. Single fathers had to have custody of their children on at least some workdays, though most had 50/50 custody. Although the men currently reside in one of two states, about 40 percent grew up in a different region from where they now live. The average age of the sample is 40, with 81 percent of fathers in their 30s or 40s. The sample is relatively diverse, with 19 minority fathers (13 black, 4 Asian, and 2 Hispanic). While a majority are college educated (24 with bachelor's degrees and 20 with graduate degrees), another 26 have not completed college (18 with some college and 8 with a high school diploma). Fifty-five are married and 15 are single, most of whom are divorced. Only one father openly identified as gay. The average number of children is two, though 20 men were first-time fathers. Twelve fathers had stepchildren or children with multiple partners. There was a wide range of children's ages, with 57 percent of fathers having their youngest child under 6, 31 percent having their youngest child between 6 and 12, and 11 percent having their youngest child 13 years or older.

About This Book

The rest of this book tells these fathers' stories about work-family conflict and their attempts to balance these two important domains. It draws heavily on direct quotes from the fathers themselves. Chapter 2 focuses on the transition to fatherhood. It presents the experience of becoming a father, focusing on both changes in attitudes about the importance of work and decisions regarding family leave around the time of birth. In becoming a father, men considered this transition to be more than simply having a baby. Rather, many fathers expressed how being a dad is a choice, a role that is not simply passive but requires active involvement. This realization often changed men's attitudes concerning the relative importance of work versus family. Decisions regarding family leave are most notably affected by what is available. Because the United States does not offer paid leave, most fathers use accumulated vacation days, which favors men in occupations with benefits such as paid vacation days and sick leave. Other fathers rely on the goodwill of their immediate supervisor and informal practices, and yet others experience resistance from employers and co-workers. The discrepancy between employer-offered maternity leave and paternity leave is noted, and the chapter ends by describing California's paid family leave policy and the experiences of men who have benefited from this policy.

Chapter 3 explores men's work-family dilemmas and feelings of stress in trying to balance work and family. It presents the struggles that men face in combining their roles as father and worker. There are subsections on multiple roles and role strain, feelings of imbalance, conflict due to work, and conflict due to family. Since fathering has become a more involved role, several fathers consider themselves as having two full-time jobs, one as worker and one as father. Other fathers add the role of husband, which often takes a backseat. The attempt to take on these roles fully and the reality of working full-time often lead to feelings of imbalance. While it can be difficult to disentangle a single cause of stress, fathers often point the finger at work requirements and less often turn the blame on family.

The next four chapters go into detail about the three types of dads described earlier in this chapter and the strategies they use to balance work and family. Chapter 4 describes the experiences of the old dads, who often meet the dictionary definition of workaholics and are compulsive about work. This chapter focuses on those men who work long hours and fit (mainly) into more traditional notions of fatherhood. Old dads' work decisions are based mainly on financial obligations rather than childcare aspects of fathering. The chapter further breaks down these fathers' reasoning, considering work as rewarding versus work as a means to supporting one's family. Many of these old dads are characterized by a high work commitment and experience feelings of stress more from not getting work done than from not being with family. There is a definite emphasis on the provider role, particularly for those with stay-at-home wives and for blue-collar workers who have increased financial need. There is also a sense of responsibility to family, with some fathers increasing their work hours in order to make it possible for their wives to stay home. Because of their long work hours, most rely on wives to care for their children either because they do not want their children in daycare or because they think it does not make sense given the cost of daycare. When it comes to wives' ambitions, if the wife works or wants to go back to work, there is an assumption that his career is more important than hers. Many old dads do not feel a lot of conflict between their work and family roles, and some who acknowledge an imbalance have accepted it. These fathers often focus on the positive, for example, that they are at home nights and weekends. Finally, there is limited talk of change.

Chapter 5 describes the experiences of the new dads and their partial solutions. New dads do not identify themselves solely, or even mainly, as breadwinners and are often intentional in their efforts to avoid work consuming them. In fact, several new dads describe themselves as not being career driven, and others talk of moderation in their career ambitions. New dads draw their identity more from their role as involved dads. Although they are not completely indifferent to the breadwinner role and the importance of their financial contributions, they are more likely than old dads to also embrace their wife's career, which often means making adjustments to their own schedule. New dads tend to struggle more than old dads or superdads in their pursuit of work-family balance. This is due to the fact that they emphasize family involvement more than old dads but make fewer work adjustments than superdads. These fathers make other attempts at balancing work and family through either their separation or blending of these two domains. Fathers who separate work and family talk about the physical and mental separation of these roles and their decision not to bring work home. Fathers who blur the lines between these two domains often bring work home and occasionally bring children to work. Those who keep a strict separation between work and family argue that they are equal partners when at home, while those who blend their roles as worker and father argue that they are maximizing their time with family. Finally, some men make little change to their work lives but talk about how their job is already well suited to being a dad, while others find themselves as new dads after an unanticipated change at work.

Chapters 6 and 7 highlight the new phenomenon of superdads. Chapter 6 focuses on married superdads, while chapter 7 focuses on single superdads. Superdads are those fathers who go above and beyond to spend as much time with their children as possible, making changes to their work lives *because* of their father role. Each chapter presents several case studies that illustrate different strategies these superdads employ in order to balance work and family. Chapter 6 provides examples of superdads who quit their jobs, changed their careers, changed their jobs or positions within a work organization, became self-employed, assembled flexible working arrangements including part-time work, arranged shift work, and started to work from home. All of these work adjustments allowed these fathers to spend more time with their children, which underscores the theme of rearranging priorities and kid-centered decision-making. These fathers often took on the primary caregiving role or shared caregiving equally with their partners. Married superdads arrange their work schedules around their children's schedules and wife's work schedule. Some trade off with their wives in order to reduce or eliminate daycare costs. These fathers generally see these adjustments as a good resolution to work-family dilemmas, although there are some financial costs. Also, class becomes important in determining fathers' strategies, as professional men are better able to take advantage of flexible work arrangements, while working-class men more often use shift work to balance work and family demands. Chapter 7 shines attention on residential single fathers, an often neglected group in the work-family literature. Single fathers face unique challenges as they

attempt to gain custody or raise children on their own. Like married superdads, these single superdads view their father role as central. However,
both their need to provide economically and their need to care for their
children are more expansive as they take on these roles alone. Therefore,
single superdads often differ from married fathers in their route to becoming a superdad and their performance of the role. Several of these fathers
were not superdads when they were married but rather took on more traditional roles. For these men, divorce directly led to career changes. Some
fathers made decisions about work based on being physically close to their
children. Others realized they needed to change their work lives in order
to be a good single dad. This chapter describes how single superdads make
it all work. The need for daily management of work and family schedules
is critical for single fathers, and this shows in the ways these single dads
actually handle day-by-day work decisions regarding work hours, workplace, and work effort. There is a general sense of satisfaction with the work
changes that these fathers have made, though a couple of fathers note a
greater sense of sacrifice. In enacting the role of single superdad, gender
lines sometimes blur as these fathers take on tasks traditionally associated
with mothers.

The final chapter summarizes the main findings of the book and explores the policy implications raised by these findings. Most workplace
policies are drafted with an emphasis on retaining female employees who
become mothers. This study provides a greater understanding of fathers'
needs and therefore can be used to suggest policy changes that might be
more relevant to men.

TWO

Becoming a Father

What I've learned out of this is raising a child if you're doing it, let me put it this way, if you're doing the best you can, genuinely the best you can, you put that child before your needs, and it's truly the toughest job you'll ever have. . . . It's also in my heart the most rewarding thing I've ever done. It beats out anything I've ever done. (Claude, barber)

Today's fathers are expected to do more than fathers in times past. Surely, fathers have had different responsibilities throughout history—moral teachers in the 17th and 18th century, economic providers in the 19th and 20th century—and to some extent these expectations remain.[1] But today fathers are also expected to be there, present from day one. Of course, most new fathers are present at the birth of their child.[2] But men are expected to be more actively involved in caring for their children as well, and fathers do spend more time with their children now than in the past.[3] Indeed, modern men with kids strongly identify themselves as fathers, and recent surveys indicate that men "accept the notion that they should see themselves as fathers first and workers second."[4] So it is no surprise that fathers, like mothers, must make some hard choices when it comes to work and family. Becoming a father generally leads to some reevaluation of priorities, a process that involves the changing of attitudes toward work and family.

In *Family Man*, published in the mid-1990s when scholars and activists were becoming impatient with the relatively slow change in men's family roles, Scott Coltrane predicted that the future would bring an increasing number of actively involved fathers.[5] Now is the future Coltrane was talking about, and current fathers are in fact more involved than past fathers.[6] In American two-parent households, there has been an increase since 1965 in fathers' time spent caring for children.[7] By the end of the 20th century, fathers spent five more hours per week with their children than they had 20 years earlier. In addition, fathers' proportion of total parental time spent on childcare surpassed 40 percent.[8] Another study found that while fathers were responsible for 40 percent of childcare during the week, they took on a full 47 percent of childcare on weekends.[9] Today being a good father means more than providing financially for one's children. It also means directly caring for children.[10]

This chapter explores changes in attitudes about work and family brought on by becoming a father and men's options regarding family leave around the time of birth. I first focus on how men adapt their attitudes toward work and family as they become fathers, transitioning from a greater focus on work to a greater focus on family. Two themes are important. The first is that fathers recognize that their priorities have changed as kids take over the top spot that work once occupied. The second is that men realize that being a dad is a choice, one that involves actively choosing to make time for their children. The first choice fathers must make is how much time to take off when their baby is born. The fathers in this study demonstrate a range of options concerning family leave. However, fathers can generally be placed in one of three categories: no or limited time off, one to two weeks leave, and extended leave. The choices they make concerning family leave are strongly linked to financial considerations, their perceived flexibility and security within the workplace given employer attitudes, gender-role attitudes and expectations, and leave policies.

"I Am My Kids' Father"—Changing Priorities

Several men I interviewed mentioned how their attitudes toward work changed once they had children. Before children, they clearly saw work as a priority, both in terms of time and commitment. Once they had children, they realized that their kids were more important than their work. Adam, a divorced consultant, talks about this change in priorities:

> There comes a point in your life when your job is a priority, and you go
> to work a lot and do a lot of things for work, but then there's a point

when you just gotta say that it's kids time. . . . My job is not a passion as it was beforehand. It's now a job more. I guess I let kids kinda trump the opportunity to go to a meeting and better myself. But I feel that if it has to do with spending time with them, then it's worth it. I would say I let them trump what I am doing 98 percent of the time.

Likewise, Brandon, a transportation manager, also describes how his priorities have changed:

I think I have altered my priorities when it comes to my job. As important as my job is for my livelihood, my kids are just more important. . . . Where before when I was a kid and just a free spirit, a job was a job, and the job seemed more important than anything that I had to do. But now it is more important that my kids know that I am there for them for anything that they have to do.

Both of these men describe changing priorities as a result of where they were in their life cycle.[11] When they were younger and did not have children, work seemed more important than anything else. It consumed their time and passion. But now that they have children, "kids are just more important." Work has become more of a job rather than a passion or perhaps career. And when it is a choice between a work opportunity and spending time with kids, almost every time, kids trump work.

Based on work patterns in the past, these men could work more, but they choose not to. Gary, a service manager, describes his reaction to his workaholic boss:

I've had a boss that was a workaholic, and they expect you to be one too, and that doesn't work out for me. It's not that I can't. It's just that now I won't. There are other—there's some other things going on that, frankly, I need to be at home taking care of my wife and my kid—not taking care of them, but with them.

Here Gary is focused on the amount of time his boss works. While he continues to work hard, he does not feel that compulsive need to work that defines workaholics. Now that he has a kid, his focus is on his family, which takes top priority. Other men have found that it has been difficult in the past to tear themselves away from work at the end of the day. But the arrival of children can bring about profound changes of feeling. Erik, a landscape architect, finds himself wanting to get home to his son:

> The biggest change, like, emotionally is that I want to get home as soon as possible to spend time with my son, whereas before I would just, you know, I'd—I really like what I'm doing, I like, you know, my work and everything, so I'll tend to stay there a little longer than I should, but now I'm like, you know, out the door right at 5.

For those who like their work and feel compelled to stay after their shift officially ends, few things can seem more important. But a child is one thing that seems to work its magic on new fathers, drawing them away from work, converting former workaholics into average guys who want to get home. Sometimes fathers build up a commitment to involved fatherhood after they become fathers.[12] In this sense becoming a father makes one aware of the importance of being a father and instills a desire to be a good father. The arrival of a child can also alter one's feelings about certain jobs. Duane was a police officer when his first child was born. He describes how his feelings about his work changed with children:

> The funny thing about police work—before my firstborn, I felt invincible. I thought that I was top dog. I didn't have a fear in the world. Then when my firstborn came, I started wondering, and I said, "Boy, you know, there's someone else depending on me, and I need to be there." I wanted to make sure that—well, a friend of mine was killed in the line of duty. He was younger than I was. So that made me look at life—you know, if I was gone, my family would be taken care of. But I kept having this image of me giving my daughter away when she gets married. So this just changed—the job changed.

Feeling different about his job, he found it easier to retire from the police force when he found out he had a hearing disability. He wound up staying home with his second child for two years before starting his current job as a school security guard, which is safer and has similar hours as his children.

Some men mentioned the influence their own father had on them. Sometimes men felt as though their fathers had been there for them and were good models now that they were fathers. However, more often men remembered their fathers not being there and reacted against this. These men do not want to be like their fathers and often contrast their experiences as dads with how their own fathers were.[13] Barry, a gardener, talks about his father's absence as an influence on his ideas of fatherhood:

> I think part of it is, is the fact that my dad, being a farmer, I never saw my dad, ever. My dad never did anything with us—occasionally, a family vacation here and there. But most of the time my dad didn't come to any of my school events because he was working. And I never felt that that was right. I feel I am my kids' father, and I need to spend time with them and around them. So I have just changed, just made sure that it's a top priority to take care of my kids.

Barry uses his father as a model of what not to be. Instead he identifies himself as his "kids' father," and to him that means being there. Similar to Gary, he demonstrates his conviction through his use of the word "need" when saying he needs to spend time with his children. It is not that he does not like his work. In fact, he claims he could work many more hours, given his interest and physical ability, but his priorities have shifted more toward his children.

Most fathers experienced some change in their attitudes about work. Those fathers who are highly involved are particularly likely to reconsider work as a top priority. "Fatherhood may encourage men to seek regular, responsible employment, but moderate their desire to 'overcommit' to their jobs or careers. Perhaps fatherhood provides men with an alternative source of identity to one's occupation."[14] While some completely shifted attitudes from being workaholics to being daddies, others witnessed smaller changes but generally in the direction of putting more emphasis on family life. Throughout my discussions with fathers, choice was an overarching theme. For some, shifting attitudes meant choosing fatherhood.

Being a Dad Is a Choice

Several men used the language of choice when talking about being a dad while working. Todd makes a distinction between being a father, which anyone, or any man, can do, and being a dad, which requires making a choice:

> Being a father is a choice. Anyone, I guess anyone can be a father. You have to be a dad by choice. And that's by being active in your kids' lives. Being there for them. Being there when they—they're singing at school or getting an award at school or in a play somewhere. Those are the things that kids remember. It's a choice to be at those things, and that's a lot of times a decision. I could be working, because I'm paid by the hour. I could be home or be here at the office and not have to leave during the day to do things like that. And I could be making more money. But no, it's a choice that I make that it's more important to be there for the kids than to make money. And it's very literally for me—I could put a dollar figure at every minute that I'm gone from work. But I don't think about it in those terms. But yeah, it's a choice.

Todd uses the word "choice" five times in this excerpt—the choice to be at school events, the choice to be at home with his children, the choice to make less money, the choice to be a dad. He views "being there" as the main requirement for being a dad. This means being at children's activities or the important events "that kids remember." The issue is that being there often means making a choice between work and family. For this particular father, missing work costs him since he is paid by the hour. He realizes that he could be at work more and make more money, but again he feels it is more important to be there for his kids than to be at work. And by emphasizing the idea of choice, he feels he has more control over his work-family situation.

Others also make the choice to focus on kids and feel they are reducing stress and tension brought on by conflicting responsibilities. When faced with a choice, Marshall, a college administrator, chooses his kid's activity over work or church:

I think it's pretty balanced because I won't allow it to be a strain. If I feel a strain, I'll pull back off the work stuff. Because I just feel that that's important. . . . If I got a conflict with, say, an organizational meeting [at work] or my son's game or an auxiliary meeting at the church and something that my kid's involved in, I'm not doing the other stuff. I'm just not. And I don't make any excuses for it, you know. My son's got this going on, I'm gonna do that. You know, so and that's kinda the way I do that.

He feels that work-family balance is under his control because he "won't allow it to be a strain." He is fortunate in that he has considerable autonomy in his job and can rearrange things on his schedule in order to attend his kid's activities (as well as the everyday tasks of being there before and after school). But he also frames the balance he experiences as a choice. Ross, a school psychologist, is another father who sees prioritizing family as a means of balancing work and family:

You can say, "my priority is family," and it's very easy not to have any conflicts with that. I don't *have* to put in those extra hours to make that extra money to make sure that he can go to space camp, you know, all those things. We have a comfortable lifestyle. . . . I get to spend a lot of time with my family. And I think that's when you start seeing how important things are, and it's fun.

Ross feels "it's very easy" to avoid conflict because he chooses to limit his time at work and to focus the rest of his time on his family. Although he has the option to work extra hours, something that could pay for extra activities for his child, he chooses not to do that, and he emphasizes the choice in saying, "I don't have to put in those extra hours." For him, it is more important, and fun, to be at home with his family. Leo, a cable maintenance technician, proposes making an even earlier decision:

You have to determine now, especially now, with everything that's going on now, is that job feasible for you and your child? Because you look at today—like, I think I've been blessed in that aspect, to have the job that I've had, where I've been able to—kid's sick, go pick them up. Or just I can pick them up early and take them to the dentist. I've been blessed in that aspect to be able to do that. Any other job, I'd been fired. A couple times over. So I think, when you look at a career, you've gotta make sure, if you decide you gonna have a family, it's gonna be family oriented.

Again, he is making a choice, a decision to take a job that is family oriented. He realizes that other jobs, or employers, would not be "family oriented" and instead would fire him for leaving work to care for his children.

All of these fathers have focused on choices that they can or have made rather than what they expect their jobs or employers to provide for them. In this sense, these fathers take individual responsibility for the choices they make. They look to themselves and no one else to make sure they can find time to be dads. The theme of individual choice recurs throughout these fathers' narratives and allows us to make sense of how fathers manage work and family. One of the first choices or decisions that fathers make concerns family leave.

Family Leave and Fathers

When it comes to family leave, the United States is in stark contrast to other developed countries.[15] According to a 2011 Human Rights Watch report, paid maternity leave is nearly universal. Of the 190 countries studied, "just three countries definitively offer no legal guarantee of paid maternity leave: Papua New Guinea, Swaziland—and the United States."[16] It goes without saying that the United States does not have paid paternity leave either, at a time when most Western countries have added paid leave for fathers to their family policies. In fact, 66 countries now offer paid paternity or parental leave.[17] Countries that offer paternity leave have been successful in achieving high levels of use among new fathers. For example, Norway introduced a four-week fathers' quota in 1993, a period of leave that can only be used by fathers. By 2003, most eligible fathers (89 percent) used this leave.[18] In Iceland, changes in leave policy have led to increases in fathers' use of leave; 90 percent of fathers take parental leave for an average of three months.[19] Overall, a majority of fathers in countries that offer paid paternity leave take leave.[20]

The United States, on the other hand, is one of the few countries that do not offer paid leave for mothers or fathers. Instead the United States tends to encourage informal or private arrangements.[21] The first federal legislation addressing family leave was the Family and Medical Leave Act (FMLA) of 1993. This legislation requires employers to allow new parents to take up to 12 weeks of unpaid leave. There are some limitations, such as the requirement that one be employed for one year and work in a company of 50 or more employees. With FMLA, close to half of all new fathers are guaranteed the right to unpaid leave.[22] In 2002, California was the first state to offer paid family leave. Eligible parents can take up to six weeks at 55 percent salary.[23]

How Much Time Do New Fathers Take?

By the early 1990s, most new fathers took at least some time off work around the time of their child's birth. A study of fathers in Minnesota, Oregon, Rhode Island, and Wisconsin found that between 70 and 75 percent of fathers took leave. Another study in southeastern Massachusetts found that 87 percent of fathers took time off, and yet another study in Wisconsin found that 91 percent of fathers took leave. At the beginning of the 21st century, the percentage of fathers taking some time off after having a child remained high but less than 100 percent.[24] Based on a large national sample from the early 2000s, researchers found that 89 percent of fathers took some time off after having a child.[25]

While the number of fathers taking leave seemed to change little between the 1990s and 2000s, there is some evidence that the amount of leave has increased. In the early 1990s, new fathers took an average of five days (or one week) of leave for a new child.[26] In 2001, the average length of leave was one and a half weeks. While one week was the most common length (42 percent), more fathers took two or more weeks off (36 percent) than less than one week (22 percent).[27] Other smaller studies have found that most fathers took one or two weeks leave.[28] In one exploratory study, fathers who took leave averaged 12 days, longer than fathers in previous studies.[29]

Among the fathers I talked with, one to two weeks was the most common length of leave following the birth of a child. However, there was quite a bit of variation, with a few fathers taking no time and a handful taking several weeks. At one extreme, there were fathers who did not take any time off when their partner had a baby. There were a few reasons for this decision, and most of these involved limited choice on the part of the new fathers. The most important reason for blue-collar workers was the immediate financial consequences of not working. Barry, the gardener, was constrained by financial reasons and as a result could only take off two days:

> She was born in the middle of the week, went in at 5 o'clock in the afternoon or 8 o'clock in the afternoon—I guess she was born at 5 the next morning. So I took the next day off, and I think I may have taken the next one off when I brought my wife home. But then I, you know, went back to work. I didn't take any time off other than that.

As a hired gardener, he did not have vacation or sick days but was paid by the hour. Not only each day but each hour not working meant less money for the family. He felt fortunate to fit time in with his family at lunchtime but knew he had to keep working to support his family. This is a common experience for low-income fathers, who are less likely to take leave than higher-income fathers.[30]

A second reason for not taking time, which was more common among professional men, was the potential repercussions for one's career, and this was directly related to workplace resistance (see the section later in this chapter). Finally, some fathers mentioned their wife's maternity as a reason they could limit their leave. Erik, the landscape architect, focused on his wife's role: "I didn't take any time off, and you know, she got a pretty good maternity leave—I want to say six months—but I think she compiled her vacation and sick leave and all that, so I don't think she put Logan in daycare until he was like six months. So that worked out very well." The lack of paternity leave reinforces gender-role expectations. Linda Haas and Philip Hwang, noted for their prolific research on parental leave and family policy in Sweden, refer to a "gender contract" in which women are expected to be more oriented toward the family and men are expected to be oriented more toward work.[31] Because these expectations are taken for granted, there may be little discussion within couples about who will take parental leave. In these cases, the assumption translates into mothers taking leave and fathers taking little, if any. Therefore, couples who have a more traditional outlook and view fathers as secondary caregivers do not find decisions about work and leave-taking as difficult to make since it is assumed the wife will stay home.[32] While Erik first focused on work reasons, he also admitted that he could rely on the fact that his wife could take maternity leave at her job for six months. His views on his wife's responsibility appear when he talks about daycare. Notice that *she* put their son in daycare. While these more traditional fathers are happy to become fathers and want to spend time with their children, they still view most childcare tasks as their wife's job, and this extends to decisions about family leave.

More commonly, men wanted to take as much leave as possible, and this generally worked out to be one or two weeks. Taking two or more weeks, however, was not uncommon, and for these fathers there was a sense that the time was needed:

I got two weeks when Aiden was born, and that was good; we needed every bit of it. (Brent, regional planner)

I think it would have been worse if I was trying to work, and it would have been worse for her, because I wouldn't have been either not able to function or work or I would have not been able to do anything at night and just let her do it. (Joel, government worker)

I took two weeks, you know, for one because when she came home, you know, just to, you know, take care of her. You know, and so I could take care of Alexis while she was, you know, still, you know, healing. Because when she first got home, for a day or two, she had fevers and stuff like that, so I was taking care of them, of everybody (Vernon, bank supervisor)

Taking a longer leave was particularly common among first-time fathers, who saw their leave as an opportunity to learn the basics of parenting, including changing diapers, feeding, and sleeping patterns. There was some sense that the excitement of becoming a father meant that it would be more difficult to focus at work (e.g., Joel). In addition, many fathers acknowledged their wife's need for help. In Vernon's case, it was a clearer need in that his wife was sick and needed to be cared for along with their newborn. In other cases, it was more indirect, as with Joel's suggestion that his wife would have more to do on her own if he were not home during that period.

While not common, there was a sizeable minority of men who took extended leave (more than two weeks and usually four to six weeks). The fathers who were able to take off the most time with the least difficulty tended to be teachers or other school employees. Russell, who was a teacher at the time of his first son's birth, was able to spend an extensive amount of time with his firstborn: "I basically spent the summer, that first summer with him, just being a stay-at-home dad." Because his son was born during the summer, he had about two months when he could stay at home with his son. Following that, he became a college coach, which meant he had less time, though still more than average. His second child was born in April, a slow time for his sport, and so he was able to take about five weeks off. His third (and last) child was born in late fall, and so he had time over winter break, though less than with his other two sons. Similar to Russell, Ross, the school psychologist, had a full month with his newborn son, who was born in July.

While most fathers took off as much time as they could, some fathers admitted they did not take off the full amount of time available to them. For example, Harvey, an operations supervisor, admitted that he had saved up several weeks of vacation time but took two weeks off when his baby was born. These fathers provide mixed evidence of changes in fathers and ideas about family leave. They are certainly taking off more time than fathers did in the past, but there is still room for them to do more.

The fathers I interviewed generally fell into three categories: those who took no time off or only limited time (no more than two or three days), those who took off a week or two, and those who took more extended periods of time off. The first group was the most financially limited or constrained by employers. The second group had jobs that allowed them vacation or sick leave. The third group often had built-in flexibility or benefited from recent state policies (see the section on California later in this chapter). Consistent with previous research, the better-educated men and those occupying higher-prestige jobs were able to take longer leaves.[33]

Unpaid Leave

The most common reason for not taking time off or taking only limited time off was financial. Most of these fathers wanted to take time off but could not afford it because any leave was unpaid. Economic costs are often the primary reason fathers do not take leave.[34] While relatively financially secure, Cliff, a pilot, remarked how unpaid family leave affected his decision about taking time off:

> They offer family leave, but it's unpaid. So you can take time away from work, but the downside is you don't get paid for it. . . . So the long and short of it is I didn't take any time; I mean, I took time off right when the baby was born so I could be there, but not an extended period of time after the baby was born.

For him, and many other fathers, access to family leave is useless when it is unpaid. Cliff also weighed the fact that his wife had several months of maternity leave, and he was working three four-day shifts a month for a total of only 12 work days a month. Even given the relatively small number of work days, Cliff changed schedules after their first child so that he could be at home more (see chapter 6). Gary, the service manager, echoed Cliff's concern about unpaid leave:

> He was born at the end of the summer, and we had already taken a summer vacation. And I saved up a week, so we—so I had a week left, and I took that, I took that week. But I could—I think it was two weeks that I could have off—it might have even been three—but unpaid. I mean, unpaid is worse than going back to work, so we just opted for what, you know, what I could take paid and go with that.

By emphasizing that "unpaid is worse" than working, Gary illustrates the notion that fathers are still expected to provide financially for their families. The fathers who took less time off were generally limited by their ability to take time off without pay. While many of these fathers would be classified as middle class, the working-class fathers I talked with were even more likely to take less than a week of leave because they did not get any paid days off. A day off, regardless of the reason, meant no pay. Many fathers, especially low-income fathers, feel they cannot afford unpaid leave.[35] Immediate costs obviously include lack of pay, but there are also longer-term costs of missing time at work, such as diminished chances at promotion and lower or nonexistent raises, possibly due to a perceived lack of commitment.

Using Vacation Days

Related to the issue of unpaid leave is the fact that most fathers used vacation days to take leave. Even when parental leave is guaranteed, the fact that it is unpaid means that most fathers do not use formal unpaid parental leave but opt instead to use paid days such as vacation, sick, or personal days.[36] Several previous studies have found that most leave taken by fathers is classified as vacation or sick days.[37] This finding was also clear in my study, particularly among fathers who took one or two weeks off for the birth of their child. When I asked Kyle, an operations manager, how he was able to take time off, he responded, "I had to take five days of my earned vacation. Yes, ma'am." There was a sense that his employer did not see what he considered a special event as deserving of special consideration. Instead, he was forced to take days from his "earned vacation." Leo, the technician, also expressed concern over getting paid: "I would get FMLA, but I wouldn't get paid for it. So this way, if I take vacation days, I get paid for it." It was common for fathers to "choose" to take vacation time over unpaid leave.

Taking vacation days was also a strategy for professional men. For example, Sean, a lawyer with three children, took five weeks off when each was born: "I did take five weeks off vacation when each kid was born. So I have no vacation. I use five weeks, and then I'm accruing it the next two years until we have another kid. We're not having any more." His example shows that those who have good vacation benefits and save up all their vacation can have several weeks to spend with their new baby. But it also shows that the decision to use vacation time for children requires saving up vacation days and not using them for vacation. Sean has spent the last six or seven years stocking up on vacation days and using them for the births of his children. This would not be viable for fathers who get limited or no vacation time.

Informal Practices

Perhaps because of the lack of formal policies providing paid leave, a number of fathers took time off through more informal channels. This was the only way new employees could take leave. Frank, a design manager, had recently started working at a large company when his second son was born. Officially he had no time off, but his supervisor told him he would look the other way and let him take two days off:

> They kind of let me miss a couple days just, ya know, without anybody noticing that I was gone, which I appreciated. It was a nice gesture. . . . It's just kind of weird, like, "okay, we won't say anything if you don't show up for a couple of days." So should I say thank you? Should I say okay? Or should I have been brave and then say, "no, no, no, I won't take them off." Would that have helped me in my career?

Frank was more fortunate than some new fathers who find themselves with no time off, but he did not feel very fortunate. Because he was so new at his job, he was not sure what to do. He took the two days but felt guilty about getting special treatment. Furthermore, he still questions whether his decision to take those "free" days hurt his career.

While getting such special consideration was less common in blue-collar work, there were some exceptions. Dustin was working a forklift in a warehouse when his son was born. He was at the warehouse when his wife went into labor and relays this experience:

> They gave me three days, paid days, off, and they were pretty good about it. I left in the middle of my shift. My wife called me: "my water broke." And so they let me just leave right on the spot. So I went straight home, and we went to the hospital. They were pretty cool about it. They said, "three days we'll just cover the rest of your shift," and I had three days from that point on.

In Dustin's case, he had not planned exactly what he would do once his wife had the baby but was pleasantly surprised by the ease with which he could leave his shift and be given three days off. Still, he did not rely completely on his employer's goodwill and saved up vacation days so that he could work half days for a week (from 2 to 6 p.m.) following the three days off. Walter, a supervisor who had a bit more autonomy regarding his schedule, only took a few "official" days but used his flexibility to shorten his days, go home for lunch, and take half days on Fridays for several weeks:

> I don't think I took off more than a few days. . . . I don't know how real religious I was about it, but I was taking a half day every Friday or something. I did work out something for several weeks that was really not even on the books. I think now things are a little more formal as far as keeping up with leave and all that.

Walter's strategy for spending more time at home with his wife and newborn was unofficial, something he could manage because of his position and experience at his place of employment. In cases such as these, men are on the record as taking a short leave but in fact are able to spend significantly more time at home because of other ways of cutting back at work.

Some fathers pieced together a week through negotiation or other informal channels. In some cases, arrangements were quite vague. Ian was in the music industry at the time of his first child's birth. Although he was working for a large company, he worked in a small division and found himself squeezing a week out:

> I took a week off. And yeah, I just kinda—I think I negotiated for like a couple of days. But I had pretty relaxed people that I worked for, so I just didn't show up for a few days extra. And it was fine. You know, I called and checked in and stuff, but it was, you know, it was kind of—I worked for a big multinational company with very distinct rules about time off, time for babies, vacation time. But I worked in a little, tiny division that nobody really paid much attention to. So and I had a boss who was like, "If you need to go, go. Do what you need to do.

You're having a baby, so at least take, you know, a few days off." And I extended it to a week, and it was a nonissue at work.

He is still not clear how the week was counted at work. He says he took two days of sick leave but does not know how his boss coded the rest of the time. Even within a company that is supposed to have "very distinct rules," he wound up working out a week off work. This may or may not have worked to his benefit. He thinks he got away with something by taking a week off when he only knows two days were counted, but a company such as the one he describes would most likely have policies concerning family leave. However, it is likely these policies do not include paid paternity leave, and he might have wound up with a better deal than he would have gotten officially. Two years later, his wife got pregnant with their second child, and they decided to move closer to family. In the process, he left the music industry and became an insurance agent. Even so, he found himself in a similarly vague position the second time around:

The position that I have, there is no such thing as vacation time. I mean, it doesn't exist. I don't have to take sick days. It's just I am kind of my own person as far as that stuff goes. So I just took off for a week, and I checked email just about every day and called in and checked my voice mail. So I was kind of still like trying to maintain some loose presence. But if I had—I had let everybody know, like all my clients and anybody that I was working with, and then people in my office too, like, "Hey, I'm gonna, when the baby comes"—and she wasn't induced or no c-section or anything, so we didn't have an exact due date—"when the baby comes, I'm going to be not scheduling appointments around this like two-week, three-week period, just in case it comes anytime in here." So I had tried to make things as light as possible for myself and then left a laundry list for our account—my account manager back at my office.

In this case, he is paid a flat salary and then a commission based on sales. Therefore, he can theoretically take off as many days as he wants, but any time he takes off means he is not making sales and not earning money.

He did "maintain some loose presence" in order to keep track of clients and make sure nothing big came up.

Others were more successful in negotiating nonvacation time. Brent, the regional planner, was able to take two weeks using sick time: "It was negotiated, verbal negotiation, not a policy." But his arrangement relied on one person, his boss, rather than a policy that would apply to everyone in his workplace. Not everyone found their workplace so supportive.

Resistant Workplaces

Some men feel discouraged by employers and co-workers from taking leave.[38] Employers may resist the notion that fathers want to be actively engaged in family life.[39] And fathers may be aware of this attitude, as they often think employers and supervisors, as well as co-workers, look down on those workers who take parental leave.[40] Therefore, some fathers limit their time off on the basis of career opportunities or fear of repercussions for one's career. Erik, the landscape architect, decided not to take time off because of expectations in his workplace:

> You know, I wasn't able to [take time off] because my work, even though it's flexible and everything, yeah, there's like an expectation that you're kind of to be there, and you're given a hard time. Like, if I were to just take a whole week off, you know, it was—it's just—it's implied that it's probably not a good idea.

Erik talks about "a whole week off" as if that would be an exorbitant amount of time. He indicates some amount of flexibility with his job, but he does not seem to think it is a good idea to actually use this flexibility, in part because of his fear that he would be "given a hard time" and in part because of his own work ethic.

Occasionally, fathers actively fight their resistant employers. Garrett, a restaurant manager, found his boss to be very resistant to his requests for time off:

> I tried to explain to her that the reasoning behind it was, you know, I didn't know what we were doing. I mean, we were having a baby. You

don't know what that's gonna entail. I mean, I just didn't know, 'cause I know the baby's up and down all night, and mom can't stay up for days and days while I go to work. I just made a decision early. I mean, I didn't spring it on her and say, "Oh, by the way, I'm not gonna be here for a month and a half." I gave her plenty of notice, you know, that that's what we were gonna do.

Garrett felt strongly about taking an extended leave and planned well ahead. Like other fathers, he saved up vacation time and some money to provide a cushion for when neither he nor his wife would be working. He wound up taking six weeks off, two weeks of vacation days and four weeks unpaid. He wanted to have enough time to bond with his new baby and to figure out parenthood with his wife. He remembers taking shifts with his wife to watch the baby—feeding, changing diapers, and drinking lots of coffee to stay awake and watch his baby sleep. It was a real struggle with his boss, but he had made up his mind that he was going to take off these six weeks. For him, it was an important choice in starting his new role as a father. An important side note is that Garrett's wife had paid maternity leave. The fact that he struggled to take time off (with several weeks unpaid) while his wife took paid leave as a matter of course highlights the persistent gender differences in workplace policy. Paternity leave is less common than maternity leave in American workplaces. A considerable number of employers are unaware of FMLA's coverage of men, and some explicitly disapprove men's use of paternity leave, often based on the assumption that fathers are not primary caregivers.[41]

Where's Paternity Leave?

After FMLA, there was a large increase in men with access to family leave. However, access did not translate directly into leave time. According to the Commission on FMLA, in 1995 only 3.6 percent of private-sector employees took leave under the new policy. This increased to 6.5 percent in 2000.[42] While earlier studies showed little effect of FMLA, expansion of leave policies at the state level has been associated with increases in fathers' leave-taking.[43] Still, most fathers do not view time they take off around the birth of a child as parental leave, and few fathers specifically take leave as part of

FMLA. Instead, most fathers only take leave if they can get paid days, usually by using vacation time, as noted earlier.[44]

Several fathers told me that they were unaware of FMLA or that they could take paternity leave at all.

> It was pretty modest. It was not—I didn't take six weeks off. I didn't take paternity leave or whatever. I'm not even sure if we can do that here. (Walter, supervisor)

> Vanessa took her six weeks of FMLA. I just didn't know that—I didn't know that a father had the FMLA thing either. At that time I didn't. So I didn't take six weeks, but she took six weeks. (Vernon, bank supervisor)

The fact that many fathers do not know what their rights are is troublesome. This ignorance may be sustained by working in largely male work settings, whereas men who work for larger companies with a substantial female labor force have a greater awareness of their access to family leave.[45] While most men were happy for their wives to take time with their newborn, some questioned the difference between the amount of leave women and men are offered:

> My wife is a professional also, so she took off eight weeks maternity leave, and I took off two weeks on the heels of that. So Savannah didn't go into daycare until she was ten weeks old. We just wanted to prolong that time as long as we could. I burned all my vacation time. We also burned all her maternity leave. . . . Where's paternity leave? Where was that? How come I had to take two weeks vacation, my ex-wife got eight weeks maternity leave? I would have taken paternity leave if it had existed. (Bruce, independent producer)

Bruce is one of the few fathers who pointed out the perceived injustice of most employers' policies regarding family leave. He sees as unfair the ability of his ex-wife, and women generally, to take maternity leave while he does not have the option of paternity leave. At the time, he and his wife wanted to keep their daughter at home as long as they could. Even using up all his wife's maternity leave and all his vacation, it only worked out to ten weeks.

Curtis, a firefighter, who was able to take one month of paternity leave, expressed some displeasure with the gender inequality in leave time: "It would be nice if you could take as much time as your wife off, you know, to start the process of raising your child. But you know, in all reality it doesn't happen that way." While he took more leave than most fathers, he wishes he could have taken even more time, citing a nearby city that offers all employees three months paid leave. Because he recognizes the unfairness in how companies treat new parents, providing more leave time for new mothers than new fathers, he and fathers like him signal some possibility of men taking advantage of more generous leave policies. A recent survey found that over 80 percent of people think employers should support family leave for fathers.[46]

While some fathers are unaware of federal family leave policy, and most of those who are aware feel unable to use it because it only provides unpaid leave, there is some evidence that family leave may be more effective at the state level. A study of fathers of newborns in states with job-guaranteed parental leave found an increase in both the number of fathers taking leave and their length of leave following state legislation.[47] While I am not directly testing state policies, it is clear that fathers in California, where paid leave became available in the early 2000s, took longer leaves than fathers in North Carolina, where there is no such policy.

Signs of Change—California's Paid Family Leave

In July 2004, the state of California enacted paid family leave (PFL), in which any worker who pays into the state disability insurance program can take up to six weeks off work to bond with a newborn or care for a sick family member. This policy is different from FMLA in two very important ways. First, the leave is paid, with up to 55 percent of weekly wage compensation over the six-week time period. This works through an employee-paid payroll tax and is built on the state disability insurance system. Second, coverage is near universal because there is no minimum company size and no minimum period of time with one's current employer.[48]

While women are more likely to use the PFL program than men, there has been steady growth in men's proportion of leave. In 2004–2005, men filed

17 percent of bonding claims, while this increased to 26 percent of bonding claims in 2009–2010. Wage replacement and the legitimacy of a state-sponsored program likely contributed to this increase. Based on a 2010 survey, California employers have noticed this trend. One-third of employers said the number of male employees who took paid parental leave was greater than it was five years ago (compared to only 5 percent who said this number was less). At the same time, employers noted little change in women's leave-taking over the same five-year period. While men still lag behind women in length of leave, the median time for men taking bonding leave is three weeks.[49]

Apart from school employees, there was a marked difference in the number of fathers who took extended leave in North Carolina and California. In North Carolina, only a few (3 out of 44) took extended leave. In California, on the other hand, almost one-quarter of new fathers (6 of 26) took extended leave. Certainly the fathers in California were more fortunate in living in a state with a work-family policy, one that first applied to state workers and later to all employees. Eugene worked for the state and was able to get paid time off: "I don't know whether I took sick leave or vacation time. We mighta had—what do you call it?—it wasn't called paternity leave, but it was fathers taking time off like mothers taking time off. You can take a little time off to be a father. But yeah, there was no financial sacrifice to do that." This was before the current policies, and so it was not labeled paternity leave but considered family leave. With the current policy, most California fathers found making these arrangements easier than their East Coast counterparts did. Ralph, a systems administrator, took a month of leave and transitioned by working from home:

> I took off a month when the twins were born. But then again, with the twins it didn't count because I was working at home, so I took off a month completely. But then even for the next two years I was just on the other side of the door if an issue came up. I stepped out frequently and helped change diapers or something like that. And I dealt with them at night—one of the twins at night—for the first solid year.

He took two weeks of sick leave and then two weeks of paid leave, though he is not sure how the paid leave was coded. Because he was working from home, he felt a relatively smooth transition from his time off to going back to work. He admits that he would interrupt his work to help take care of his twins. Joel, the government worker, also took family leave for about a month. As with Ralph, two weeks were coded as sick leave: "We have sick leave. They let you take part of your sick leave to bond with the kid or any-thing—they call it family leave—like, if I have to take them to a doctor. So I took that time and then I think an extra couple more weeks. I kept getting different answers, so I just took it and let them figure it out." Yet another father, Curtis, the firefighter, also took paternity leave for about a month. He tried to explain how it was counted: "It comes—it basically comes out of my sick leave. So it's just coded different. You know, it's coded as paternity leave, but it comes out of my sick-leave bank." His son was premature and in the hospital for two weeks. His wife stayed with his son most of the time he was in the hospital, but then he took a month, starting when his son got out of the hospital. Curtis also wound up taking three more weeks off when his wife had surgery. His son was just under one year at that point, and he took the time to take care of both his wife and child.

A good example of how fathers have benefited from changes in the California family leave laws can be seen when looking at the case of Brad. A physical therapist, Brad's amount of parental leave increased with each child:

The first time, for the oldest kid, I took off a week, I think. And really, it was our firstborn, and we had my in-laws, and my mother-in-law was helping, my mother was helping. And I was really just in the way. . . . And then so I said, you know, "I'm not gonna do that again." So when my daughter was born, I waited 'til my wife had to go back to work. . . . She went back I think after eight weeks, and that's when I took off work. . . . I stayed home for four weeks, and then my wife kinda returned to full-time work. She didn't like just go back part-time, so I was with them by myself. But you know, I think it was a really good experience. . . . The third one was born—he was born in February two years ago, and the state had just passed this new family leave program where you can kind of get paid while you're off. So it didn't go into effect 'til July, so I waited until October to take it. And he was close to eight months I think at the time. That was much better, you know: he was a little older, there was much more he could do. It was much more interactive. So that was a lot, a better experience I think, even more so for me. I took off six weeks that time and just hung out with them.

Brad took one week with his first child (vacation), four weeks with his second child (vacation), and six weeks with his third child (paid family leave). A combination of factors contributed to this increase in time off. Most obviously the availability of paid family leave made this not only a possibility but an attractive option. Still, Brad took into account the needs of his family and what would work best given his wife's work schedule and time off. His wife worked full-time until their third child, so they combined his leave and her leave and also called on their parents to watch the kids when they both worked. Once their third child was born, his wife went half-time after her leave and then full-time when Brad was home for six weeks and then back to half-time. At this point, their offset schedules were not enough to coordinate childcare, since her parents were no longer able to watch their kids and his parents could only watch them once a week.

Conclusion

Having a child made the fathers in this study reevaluate their priorities. It is clear that most new fathers see their child as their most important priority, and this means that work loses at least some of its importance. Many expressed the idea that they had to make choices that reflected these new priorities. One of the very first decisions they had to make was how much time to take off work after the birth of a child. Here, however, the fathers found their choices constrained. Fathers' decisions about leave took into consideration finances, employer views and career concerns, gender-role attitudes, job flexibility, and leave policies. This study found that, first, as with previous studies, fathers with middle and high occupational prestige were more likely to take leave than were fathers with low occupational prestige.[50] The implication is that, "in the absence of paid job-protected leave, poorer and less economically secure fathers may be less able to spend time with their infants and partners during the transition to parenthood."[51] Money was particularly important for fathers taking short or medium leave. Those taking short leave had little choice, given that they could not afford to take any more time off. Those who took medium-length leaves also considered finances but were able to take more time off primarily because they used vacation days.

Second, employers' support of new fathers' changing roles at home was an important factor in determining how much time new fathers took off. Some employers are not supportive of new fathers' changing roles at home.[52] Fathers who worried about employers' reactions and the potential effect on their career took shorter leaves. On the other hand, a number of fathers in the medium leave group found supportive bosses or supervisors who often worked around formal policies to allow these new fathers additional time off. Third, men's views of what the appropriate roles are for them and their wives influence decisions regarding family leave. It may be that "fathers privilege mothers' desires and choices" concerning parental leave.[53] This was most notable among fathers who took limited time off and were less concerned, knowing their wives would be there to take care of their newborns. Yet fathers with egalitarian gender beliefs are more likely to take leave and longer leave.[54] This was evident more often with the fathers who took long leaves. These fathers sometimes even noted the gender inequality in leave, wishing to have even more time with their children.

Fourth, job flexibility and employment policies were particularly important for fathers who took extended leave. Fathers who work in school settings realized the advantage they had in acquiring longer-than-usual leaves with their new children. Finally, California's family leave policy seems to have already had some impact on new fathers, as the California fathers were disproportionately represented among the fathers taking extended leave. As a result, California fathers have more choices than North Carolina fathers do when it comes to this first critical decision regarding work and family. These fathers were at the forefront of the impact of changing policy as they took advantage of the longer leave while acknowledging their fortune compared to earlier fathers. In the next chapter, I present fathers' ongoing work-family dilemmas beyond paternity leave.

THREE

Work-Family Dilemmas

What do you think is the hardest part about being a father and working?

Time. I mean, it's just, you know, it's just hard to have time to do both, to do both jobs because they're both full-time jobs, I mean, if you really work full-time. (Brett, carpenter)

A recurring theme when I talked to fathers was that they think of themselves as having two full-time jobs. It is obvious that being employed full-time would count as a full-time job, but it is more unexpected that these fathers think of their role as father as being a full-time job. This harks back to Arlie Hochschild's notion of the second shift,[1] only this time it is men who think they are coming home to a second job. In contrast to the second shift that women face, men spend more of their home time engaged with children, with housework a distant second. This also means that their second shift is more rewarding because they want to spend time with their children. However, it is not without its costs, as fathers increasingly experience stress as they attempt to be good workers and good fathers.

A recent report by the Families and Work Institute concludes that men are now going through what women went through when large numbers first entered the labor force. However, men's big change is at home, being more involved in the daily tasks of raising their children. And while women felt they still needed to take care of the home even after adding their new work role, men today still feel as though they are more responsible than their partners for earning a living even after becoming more involved at home (and having partners who earn money too). This pressure to "do it all in order to have it all," as women once did, has been called the "new male mystique."[2]

In this chapter, I describe some of these pressures and men's feelings of imbalance. As the preceding chapter noted, men's priorities shift once they become fathers. With a new focus on families and the continued importance of breadwinning, fathers often find themselves in a situation where they need to juggle multiple roles. It is not as though they did not have these roles before, but the greater demands of some roles without a diminished demand from other roles means that there are greater overall responsibilities and a resulting strain from these multiple responsibilities. It also creates a situation in which there never seems to be enough time. The resulting work-family conflict comes from both directions. First, there is a sense that work creates conflict and restricts time with one's family. Within work-to-family conflict, work produces stress, both in terms of the absolute time it takes and also in terms of the tasks that need to be accomplished within a certain period of time. Certain types of work, such as overtime and being on call, create added stress for fathers. The most obvious and emphasized outcome of too many work hours is limited time with children. However, many fathers shift their nonwork time to their children and therefore feel they do not have enough time with their partners or alone. Second, while less common, there is also a sense among some fathers that family creates conflict. This most often is expressed by men feeling they are not putting enough time into work because of the demands of family life. Finally, the blame does not always simply lie with work or family exclusively, as some fathers experience shifting priorities, focusing more on work (and less on family) at certain times and more on family (and less on work) at other times.

The Balancing Act

As noted in chapter 2, being there is crucial to being a good dad. But being there does not always come easy. For some it is an occasional conflict, while for others it is an ongoing battle. But for most, it is part of a quest to be a better dad, better than fathers of the past, who were notoriously absent.

There's no perfect dad, I guess. If there is a perfect dad, I want to try to be that person because I know . . . I just hear all the time that people wish they had a better mom and dad. (Kyle, operations manager)

I got two teenage kids, and they're into recitals and sports and a whole bunch of things. And I've got to be real careful for that because I don't want the kids to grow up and say, "Well daddy earned a good living and provided all these things, but he wasn't there." So I hear that story all the time, and I was hoping that I would not be in that situation. (Darius, housing program manager)

Darius explains that he tries to make arrangements when his kids have an important event, but he also admits, "some things just can't be avoided" at work. No matter how much he wants to be there, Darius realizes that being there can be a challenge. This is quite simply due to the fact that these fathers have to make sure they get their work done and, beyond that, to make sure they do not have any scheduling conflicts for events that occur during the day. Fathers today know that fathers in the past, and some of today's fathers, were not there for a lot of their children's important accomplishments, let alone everyday life. These fathers are aware that their presence (or lack of presence) will affect their children, and their children's future view of them as fathers, so they try to navigate their work schedules to allow them to be present for these events. But it does not always work. In the end, the imbalance is often caused by the simple fact that these men are occupying multiple roles.

Too Many Roles

While an increasing number of studies focus on work and family issues, there are still few conceptualizations of the dynamics involved in connecting work and family characteristics to work and family outcomes. Sociologist Patricia Voydanoff argues that multiple work and family roles may lead to either negative or positive consequences. Under role strain theory, more roles mean more demands and role incompatibility, which lead to more role conflict. This may be produced by overload, which is created when an individual does not have the time to execute all of his or her roles, or interference, which exists when "conflicting demands make it difficult to fulfill the requirements of multiple roles."[3] Throughout my study, several fathers mentioned their struggles in balancing multiple roles. Kyle, an operations manager, tried to express how hard it is for him: "You're kinda balancing three things at one time. Workplace, being a husband, and being a dad. It's hard. It's one of the hardest things I've had to do." As Kyle suggests, being a dad is its own role, something that he needs to find time to do apart from being a worker or even a husband. Jacob, a writer who quit his teaching job, also describes the difficulty in occupying multiple roles:

> My theory is I can do two things at once. I can't do three. I can kinda do three, but I definitely can't do four, and the fourth would be teaching full-time. I was teaching full-time, being a dad, being a husband, or I can write full-time and be a dad, be a husband. But I can't write, teach, be a dad, be a husband.

For Jacob, he was pushed to the edge by taking on four roles, which resulted in him quitting his teaching job (see chapter 6). He also told me that being a good dad is more important to him than being a good husband, and so for now his focus is on how he can write and meet his deadlines and still be a good dad. In both these cases, and in others, the point is that now that men see their role as father as an important one, there is more potential for conflict with other competing roles. Furthermore, since breadwinning is no longer the only or main responsibility of good fathers, time at work is more likely to be seen as a competitor for time with children.

Devin, an assistant professor at a state university, feels a direct conflict between his work responsibilities and his family responsibilities. He likes teaching and is generally happy with the students, the variety of courses he gets to teach, the flexibility of his schedule, and his colleagues. However, he has a heavy teaching load and several committee assignments that keep him busy, as well as the looming fact that he does not have tenure yet. Devin's wife was in career transition attending the local university when they had their daughter. She has stayed home for the past four years and is starting to feel "a little bit stir crazy." Devin was very cautious in talking about his wife's role, claiming that her staying home has been good for their daughter but also suggesting that it has been a financial strain and potentially unnecessary. The whole situation has created a bit of tension between Devin and his wife:

> It's hard because I feel like I'm trying to do a lot of different things with work and with being at home. . . . She feels like I get time away where I'm not responsible for somebody when I go to work, which is true: I don't have to be responsible for Ava when I go to work. And she would like that time away where she doesn't feel like she's responsible for somebody. It's just hard because I feel like *I have responsibilities at home and I have responsibilities at work*, and so the free time that I get is to go to work, and that's not really fun time for me. So that ends up being a real sticking point between us. (emphasis added)

Devin's case highlights the struggles that working mothers and increasingly working fathers have to deal with. He is taking on a second shift of sorts. And while his wife thinks he gets a break from caretaking responsibilities, a break she does not get in her 24/7 role of stay-at-home mother, he does not agree that work is much of a break. It also highlights the point Kyle and Jacob were trying to make when they talked about balancing multiple roles. When fathers see home as a responsibility, their work and family roles compete more directly. And then it becomes an issue of time.

Time Crunch

> There's not enough time. Period. To do the good job at work, to be with the family, and then actually to have some time to do things I might want to do. (Brent, regional planner)

In a study of fathers' employment and childcare, April Brayfield concludes, "time, as a finite, scarce, and valuable resource, is an instrumental facet of the parent role."[4] Many fathers feel like they are rushing through the day. Gary, a service manager, expresses his displeasure at being the one who not only has to rush but also has to rush his son: "I don't like having to be the, you know, the one that's telling him to hurry up and let's go, and that seems to be so much of what—what I end up doing all the time: 'Look, gotta go to school, gotta go to work, gotta gotta gotta go.'" He does not want to be the "gotta go" dad, but he feels that there is always a time squeeze that requires them to be in a constant rush. Sean, a lawyer, goes to work early and eats lunch while working so that he can leave at 2 to pick up his son: "This morning I actually got in at quarter to 6, and that way I could leave at 2. I work through no lunch. I just eat at my desk, because we only pay for daycare until 2:30 with my middle son, so I swing by and pick him up. So our schedule right now is incredibly tight because of the kids." Sean has no time to spare in this tight schedule. He and his wife also arrange their work schedules so that they are constantly trading off children. It adds some pressure, but it also allows him to spend more time with his children. Another example of tight squeezes is Kane, a father who works three jobs (all part-time) but still manages to drop off and pick up his son from school: "I usually work early in the mornings. I drop my son off at school first, and then I go work for about three hours, and then I pick him up during my lunch break. And then based on the day, that determines if I go to another job or I go back and work the rest of the day." Kane admits that he is often rushing back and forth but feels this is the best way to be there for his children.

Bruce, a divorced producer, works mainly weekends and, in an effort to make the most of his time with his daughter, tries to squeeze all his errands in before his time with her: "If I gotta go to the grocery store or pick up some dry cleaning, I'm really trying to get all my human errands done before I pick her up on Mondays. . . . She don't need that. I have limited time with her. I don't want any minutes to be gobbled up by that crap." Many parents who work nonstandard hours may have their children around more during the day, including while performing errands, but quality time with children becomes even more crucial for single fathers (see chapter 7).[5] Some of this time squeeze cannot be helped, but a lot of it is done in an effort to be as involved as a father as possible.

Work-Family Conflict

Business professors Jeffrey Greenhaus and Nicholas Beutell define work-family conflict as "a form of interrole conflict in which the role pressures from the work and family domains are mutually incompatible in some respect. That is, participation in the work (family) role is made more difficult by virtue of the participation in the family (work) role."[6] According to the 2008 National Study of the Changing Workforce, a nationally representative survey of American workers conducted by the Families and Work Institute, men are now more likely than women to report work-family conflict, a reversal of the pattern in the late 1970s. A majority (55 percent) of fathers now experience work-family conflict, and conflict is more prevalent for fathers in dual-earner couples than for those in single-earner couples.[7]

Most of the fathers in my study felt some type of conflict between their work and family roles. Often there was some sense of feeling overwhelmed by the sheer number of things that needed to be accomplished at both the workplace and home. Jacob, the writer, feels as though he is being pulled in both directions. He has attempted to combine work and family by working around his children's schedule. Therefore, he gets his kids off to school and then starts working, but since his youngest only goes to school for a half day, he stops working when it is time to pick him up. He then devotes his afternoon and early evening to his children and goes back to work (at home) once they have gone to bed. Occasionally, he tries to squeeze in some writing while his children are engaged in some other activity. As a result, he says this schedule is wearing on him:

> I really would like a time where I would just work for a section of the day and then I don't work for the rest; I'd like to try that out, because I'm getting fatigued with the whole things of work and family. It's so draining. Being with the kids, and really being with them, takes a lot of energy, and I'm having less energy at night than I used to have, and I kinda just like the idea of getting up, going to an office.

Jacob is tired because he is constantly either working or "being with the kids" and constantly going back and forth between the two. For him, being a father is a very active role, so he puts quite a bit of energy into his time with his children. Jacob's goal is to separate work and family more, which he thinks will be possible once his youngest starts school full-time. Of course, in this study, the amount of conflict and whether this conflict was more a result of work or more a result of family varied quite a bit. The next sections focus on work conflict and home conflict.

Work Creates Conflict

According to a newly released study, 64 percent of workers blame work for work-family conflict.[8] This is not surprising given that a vast majority of men and women would prefer to work fewer hours, and other studies have shown that work creating conflict in the family is more common than family creating conflict in work.[9] In talking with fathers for my study, these issues arise as fathers commonly refer to work as a source of stress. Some of it has to do with the tasks that need to be accomplished, but most has to do with the limited amount of time they have to accomplish these work tasks. This leads to a feeling that fathers are constantly working. Brent, the regional planner, expresses how this intensity at work is ongoing: "Right now it's a bit stressful. It's just—and I say now—I look back—like at first it was, you know, "Oh, boy, the last three months have just been intense," and now I'm looking back, it's like the last five years, it just hasn't stopped, you know. You just get to a point where that becomes the norm." This is a perfect example of how men can get carried away with their jobs and realize that in working so intensely for years (which may go by quickly, seeming to be only months), they have missed out on family life. Brent feels conflict regarding "this inner need to be dedicated or committed" to his work: "I'm just very conscientious about it and have a problem, I guess, either drawing a line, saying no, putting limits, something in there." Brent commonly misses his pregnant wife's appointments (see chapter 4). For fathers like Brent, commitment to work puts them in a position where it is difficult to choose family over work.

Although conflict between work and family can go in either direction, there is evidence that work creates greater problems for family life than vice versa.[10] Much of this may be due to what social scientists call hour mismatches, or the idea that people's ideal work hours differ from their actual work hours. Jeremy Reynolds and Lydia Aletraris, two sociologists at the University of Georgia who have been studying hour mismatches for the past several years, find that while men's actual hours increased between the late 1980s and early 1990s, their preferred hours decreased.[11] Hour mismatches are common, with some scholars estimating that at least 60 percent of American workers experience hour mismatches, and of these mismatches, the majority want to work fewer hours rather than more hours.[12] Furthermore, these hour mismatches can be considerable, with a desired reduction (or increase) of at least five hours per week, and this mismatch is greater for those who want to work fewer hours, with an average desired decrease of 20 hours.[13] To add to matters, hour mismatches tend to be long lasting. For example, in Reynolds and Aletraris's study, only 16 percent of men with a mismatch at the first time period resolved that mismatch by the later time period.[14] Furthermore, it is quite common for workers who are initially satisfied with their work hours to become dissatisfied. More than one-half of workers who said they wanted the same hours at the first time period wanted to work fewer hours at the second time period. Although some studies find that men and women are equally likely to experience hour mismatches, others show hour mismatches are more prevalent among men.[15]

Too Much Time at Work

Several fathers in my study said they feel some conflict with their work role. Often this has to do with the number of hours required or expected at work. This is the most basic infringement of work on family time as it is a zero-sum game. More time at work means less time at home. Fathers often feel as though work takes up more time than it should, leaving them limited time for family. This is a source of tension for many fathers who feel that they cannot easily reduce their time at work. For example, Corey, a park planner, talks about work and family as requiring separate "bundles of energy." Most of his stress comes from trying to figure out when he can devote energy to each and how this will impact his family:

> For me the regular tension is I need to be at work; it takes oftentimes more than the allocated, the exclusively allocated time between 9 and 6. . . . So the tension is that whenever my work requires more time, whenever I get stuck in a meeting that goes over time or whenever there's another requirement for a nighttime meeting that takes me away, there's tension there, and there's a need to resolve it somehow.

For Corey, his son, wife, friends, housework, and paid work each require "a bundle of energy," and often he feels there is not enough energy (or time) to fulfill all requirements, particularly with regard to his time with family. While he seems to put work and family on an even playing field ("they demand the same hours of the day"), he more often thinks that he spends more time than he should at work. This results in tension when work requires him to go beyond the allotted time, since his family never seems to get the full amount of time. Corey is similar to other fathers who work more hours than they would prefer because of a combination of their family's economic need and job demands or employers' needs.[16]

Even those who reduce their work hours find themselves trying to put it all together. Claude, a barber and single dad, has consciously reduced his work hours since adopting his son but finds that it is difficult to please his customers without scheduling appointments close to the time he is supposed to pick his son up from school.

> I used to work longer hours here at the salon. I used to take, you know, 5:30 appointments. . . . You have to allow a half hour to get into town, and that's generous—I mean, that's not generous, that's on the lean side to allow a half hour to get to his school during traffic. And so there's been many times I'm ripping my hair out, what's left of it, to get to pick him up and 'cause I will take—sneak that last customer in that has to get it done because they're going to an important meeting—tell me—let me tell you, the stress is there. . . . You just do your best to hold everything together.

Claude feels both a sense of responsibility to his son (and to picking him up on time) and to his clients, whom he finds difficult to turn down even when it pushes him to stay a little later and leaves him with a smaller window to get to his son. Wanting to do it all for his son and his clients causes a time crunch that results in stress. His time squeeze is exacerbated by the fact that his salon is at least 30 minutes away from his son's school. The other issue is that Claude feels some obligation to his customers, especially those who have been with him for years, and a desire for them to look their best. Still, this means that he finds himself all too often rushing to finish work, rushing to get through traffic and to his son's school, and rushing to get his son home and doing homework (not to mention dinner and other nighttime routines).

Extenuating Circumstances—Overtime and Being on Call

Fathers who work unusual hours face stress over not being at home when "normal" fathers are supposed to be at home. Curtis, a firefighter, works 24-hour shifts. It generally means that he gets to stay at home many weekdays, but it can also mean being away from home for more than one day straight:

> Sometimes it can be hard because I can be gone multiple days in a row, you know, if I have an overtime shift or something. And if it's—if I work that in-between day, you know, I'll be gone for 72 hours. So sometimes, you know, ever since we've had Mason, it was not that big of a deal to be gone for 72 hours, but now it kind of tugs at me, you know, being gone that long.

Curtis feels the tension of missing time with his son when he works an extra shift, but he feels obligated (and consoled) as the family's provider to work those extra shifts (which pay very well). Therefore, his perceived role as father both perpetuates and alleviates the tension he feels in regard to balancing work and family.

Other fathers are pushed into overtime more by employers or the needs of the job. Among other potentially negative consequences, mandatory overtime has been shown to increase work-family conflict.[17] Leo, a father of seven, has had a colorful work and family history. He has held many different types of jobs including his position as a sub/temp in a school kitchen immediately before his current job. When school funding was cut, his hours got cut from 40 to about 10 to 15 hours per week. In searching for another job, Leo's focus was on his ability to provide for his growing family. With seven children from four different relationships and a pregnant wife, he has many expenses. Unfortunately, his new job as a warp technician at a fiber optics plant involves many more hours than his old job did: "I've always had hours where I could be there, and then all of a sudden I'm working this job with these hours, these long hours. It's like a 35-minute ride, so I'm actually gone 14 hours out of the day." Leo recently started this job, so he does not want to make trouble for himself. He estimates that he is working at least 70 hours a week, usually noon to midnight Monday through Saturday and some Sundays. Our interview was conducted on the first weekend he had off in a month and a half. He expects his hours will go down to a more manageable 40 to 50 hours per week since his shift is supposed to start at 4 in the afternoon and go until midnight. Leo feels a sense of pride from being asked to work so many hours because almost all the others who are working long hours have been there for many years, so it seems an indication that his employers like him and think he can handle it. Still, Leo feels his hours will need to change to accommodate his family more:

> I feel like right now the work is overshadowing my family, and the family's more important to me. So I'll get the work to where it needs to be, to the monetary level I want to be at and to where I feel comfortable. First of all, I've only been there 90 days, so I'm still probationary until six months. . . . I just make sure it's a secure—it's going to tone back so I'm using it for what I need to use it for right now, but my family is really important to me and my children are really important to me. . . . All I can do is deal with it right now.

Leo finds himself in unchartered territory, working so many hours. Throughout his relationship with his wife, about two years, he has had work that allows him to be at home a lot. He wants to spend more time with his family, but he feels like he fits in at his current job, something he has not always felt, and wants to make sure he makes it through his probationary period. Although he suggests he is dealing with it, the extra hours create tension for him.

Other fathers feel a strain when they get called into work at off hours. This can work through getting called for extra shifts or extra hours when on call. Kyle is an operations manager for a cleaning company. He characterizes his office as a negative environment and has a tenuous relationship with his boss. When we started talking, he immediately indicated that his job is really stressful because it interferes with time with his family—his wife and infant son. He does not have a standard schedule but rather is on call all the time—"24 hours a day, 7 days a week." This means that he might put in a full day of work and then be called back to work at any time. While this does allow for him to start work late or leave early on occasion, Kyle seems more focused on the times when he has to work at night or early morning. He feels particularly frustrated when he needs to go back to work at night when everybody is in bed:

> If you work a full day—that would mean eight to nine hours a day— you come home, have dinner with your wife and the little one, and you feed him his bottle, give him his bath, feed him his bottle, put him to bed, and then you have to go out and do field visits with the franchise owners. So you're out working, it could be 9 o'clock at night, could be 2 o'clock in the morning. I hate leaving the house after I've already, ya know, put everybody to bed. . . . I just hate leaving the house after I've been home, ya know, for the day after you work all day. I hate going back out, because after you're done working, you need to be at home.

For Kyle, the issue is being on call all the time, "24 hours a day, 7 days a week," as he would say. Since he is on salary, his hours are not really set during the week, so he feels some freedom in the fact that there are no particular requirements Monday through Friday. However, he still feels as if he has to "deal with work all the time" and wishes he could stay at home once the day is done. Being on call makes it difficult for Kyle to balance work and family:

> Last night I got a phone call at 9:30, I got one at 10 o'clock, I got one at 10:30. I got three right in a row, 30 minutes from each other. I'm trying to go to sleep, let it wait until tomorrow. It bothers me a lot. . . . Anyone would figure, if you get a phone call at 10:30 at night, you don't want to think about it. I guess just close your—at 5 o'clock, and if I don't take care of it on Monday, it'll be there Tuesday when I get there. I'll take care of it then. It's just that when I'm at home, let me be at home, because it's kind of a—and I really don't know the work life to personal life, family life, I guess you would say—I don't know the balance. But I do know that you have to have a personal life.

Kent, a divorced gas company serviceman, also struggles with being on call. For him, it directly interferes with his time with his children. Kent has joint custody, split equally with his ex-wife over two-week periods. They have a 2-2-3 arrangement in which he gets the children Monday and Tuesday, she gets them Wednesday and Thursday, and he gets them Friday, Saturday, and Sunday one week and then they reverse days for the following week. Because his children are young and because there is no other adult in his household, he cannot have them over when he is on call. He is only on call every six weeks, but this can create problems depending on the timing. Kent notes with sadness that he misses having his children when he is on call:

> I would love to come off call at work, but that's not gonna happen; there's no chance in that. Because if they came off call at work, I wouldn't—the days, the weekends, or weeks that I have the kids, I wouldn't have to let her have them. And there for a while I been on call for seven days straight, and if it's still on the weekend I was supposed to have the kids, I wouldn't have them for like two weekends in a row in a week.

His ex-wife takes the children when he is on call, but he would like to avoid this. Unfortunately, he knows that he cannot come off call because all servicemen are required to be on call as part of their position.

Impact on Time with Children

I probably feel a little guilty about the child time. . . . When I come home, I think I've got this sense that I'm already kind of behind in terms of my share of the time. (Walter, manager)

Many fathers express the desire to spend more time with their children. This finding is comparable to national data showing that a majority of fathers feel they do not spend enough time with their children.[18] While previous studies show that fathers are more likely than mothers to feel this lack of time with their children, these differences are due to gender differences in time away from home at work.[19] For fathers who yearn to spend more time with kids, work and family are not balanced. Rather, work interferes with family because the more time they spend at work, the less time they have with family. Past research has found a negative relationship between work hours and work-family balance.[20] According to the recent Families and Work Institute report, three-fifths of men who work 50 or more hours per week report some or a lot of work-family conflict, compared to 29 percent of men who work less than 40 hours per week.[21] Joel, a government agent, describes how long hours bother him even more since having his son: "I'd like to spend more time with him. I mean, 10-hour days on average have always kinda bothered me with this job, but now that I have the kid, it more than bothers me." Even though Joel never liked working long hours, he feels the lost time more since having a child. And the fact that much of this extra time at work is not particularly meaningful—as he says, "just going through paper work"—adds to the dissatisfaction with his sense of imbalance. As mentioned earlier, it is rather common for workers to prefer to work fewer hours, and these hour mismatches, while not necessarily constant, tend to be long lasting.[22] But like other fathers, Joel rationalizes that "it's not bad" since he is generally home at night and almost every weekend. He can feel better because there are other fathers spending less time with their children. In addition, having a wife who can stay at home means he does not have to worry about his son.

Some fathers realize that they cannot do everything and just try to be there for the "important" events. Jerry, an independent video producer, explains that he does the best he can to be there for the actual events: "It's very difficult to schedule everything so that I can make sure I can be there for them. But most of the time, I was just there for the events. A lot of the times, I had to work up until the event, and I would get there, but Sandra was going to make it happen." As with men who work longer hours, men who have more demanding jobs also experience more work-family conflict than those with less demanding jobs.[23] Jerry felt "torn" over a particular event in which he almost let his son down. On the day of his son's prom, he had to work throughout the day, when he had promised his son he would be home helping him get ready. He called home numerous times but still felt a tension because he was not physically available to help his son run last-minute errands (flowers) and prepare (get dressed). But his stress comes from not wanting to choose between his work and his family and not wanting either to suffer. He does not want to miss these significant moments. In the end, he made it home for his son, helping him with that last bow-tie adjustment and seeing him off to the prom. Jerry's behavior is consistent with several studies that have highlighted ways in which fathers navigate their work-family conflict. In this sense, Jerry adapts by working ahead of time and extra hard so that he can be present at all the important events in his children's lives.

Art, an operations manager, foresees the potential conflicts he may have as his daughter gets older and gets more involved in activities that would benefit from his attendance:

> As she gets older and is doing more things, then the question will be, is there a problem attending certain events or being around for certain activities that, you know, as she's doing more things during the weekday and things like that and—I think those are the main things right now, just the—just having the days when we don't interact at all and then being on call. So that's mostly it.

Art worries about missing upcoming activities but also hints at a larger issue, that he has days now when he misses his daughter altogether. Since his job requirements come first and he cannot adjust his schedule, he knows his responsibility to work will interfere with seeing his family. Art's experiences are consistent with a study that found that men and women make an equal number of sacrifices at work for family life, but men's sacrifice is most likely to come in the form of working additional hours rather than cutting back. Men tend to make more sacrifices at home than women do, most often by missing a family occasion.[24] Furthermore, Art's source of stress comes from his understanding that work does not give him room for adjustment, which means that he misses out now on everyday life and possibly later on special events.

Another point of agreement is that fathers often feel they cannot do much about their situation even if they are unhappy. Corey, a park planner, wishes he could work less and spend more time with his son but feels helpless to change things: "I would like to have more time with him. I don't know how to make that happen, because the job I have is the job I have. It'd be neat if it didn't take quite as much time." Corey mentions the financial needs of his family but also feels as though his wife could help out by getting a part-time job. This would result in a more stable financial situation for their family and also would create a more equal split of time with their son. In the past when they both worked, they had offset schedules in which one of them was at home in the morning before school and one was at home in the afternoon after school. Corey preferred this arrangement and would like to establish a similar routine again.

Time with Partner

Some fathers feel that they have reached a pretty good balance with time at work and time with children but that they do not have enough time with their wives. Researchers have speculated how parents have been able to increase their time in the labor force while spending a sufficient amount of time with their children. In *Changing Rhythms of American Family Life*, distinguished UCLA professor Suzanne Bianchi and her colleagues suggest that one strategy is for married parents to reduce the amount of time they spend with their spouses.[25] Indeed, studies show that married people with children at home spend about 90 minutes less on weekdays and three hours less on weekends alone with their spouse.[26] When both spouses work, spending quality time as a couple becomes even more difficult.[27] This distinction becomes important in considering work-family balance as having distinct components in which wives and romantic relationships are sometimes considered separately from children (although often they are lumped together). As with time with children, fathers are more likely than mothers to feel as though they do not spend enough time with their partner.[28] Darryl, an administrative assistant, expresses his satisfaction with the amount of time he has for his children but dissatisfaction with the amount of time he has for his wife:

> I don't feel like there's a strain in regards with what I have to do for my kids, but I do feel like there is not enough time for my wife and myself, for us to do things, and partly as a result of working every day with my kids' activities. But like I said, it's not like I want to put it on the kids, like they're taking up too much time. It's like there's never enough free time, not enough vacation time, not enough hours in the day to try and relax and have some sort of activity on your own. So

it's just enough to try and rest and recuperate and get ready for the next day. The day seems too short.

Fathers like Darryl feel the main source of conflict is from the lack of couple time. These fathers spend their time and energy fulfilling their roles as workers and fathers but wind up with less time for their role as husband. Some fathers acknowledge this discrepancy in time for children versus time for partners but do not have a problem with it. Others feel it will eventually balance out when the children leave, and yet others wish they could spend more time with their wives now. Duane, a school security officer, also notes his busy schedule and how it is usually couple time that comes in last place:

It's hectic, trying to find that balance. . . . We're always on the go. We're always doing something. And our day is just shot during the week, during the school year. We're just busy, busy. . . . You want to try to get the kids in, make sure they're doing what they need to do and have some time for this. It's busy. And I, the wife and I, we really don't have time for each other until a few hours on the weekend, and during breaks. If it wasn't for the breaks during school, I don't know what.

This is a common theme. Work is a given and takes up a good part of the day. Then fathers want to make sure they get time with their children and that their children are fitting everything in on their schedules they need to fit in (homework, extracurricular activities, etc.). This means there is not much time, if any, at the end of the day for parents to have their own time. It is generally assumed that a relationship "will hold," while work and children require immediate attention.

But putting marital relationships on hold can cause some strain. Sometimes the stress of work affects men's relationships. Harriet Presser, author of *Working in a 24/7 Economy*, argues that today's work schedules, particularly nonstandard hours, have the potential to change the nature of family life and that this is a critical issue in looking at marital instability.[29] Kyle, the operations manager who has no set hours during the week but is on call 24 hours a day, 7 days a week, feels his situation is very stressful because he can get called at night after his baby is in bed. It also disrupts his wife's sleep:

My wife didn't want to deal with me coming in so late in the morning, at 3 or 4 o'clock in the morning. So she went down to the beach house, . . . took him down to the beach and her parents and stayed from Wednesday night and came home Sunday afternoon so she wouldn't have to deal with me coming in and out, waking her up, leaving. . . . It puts a lot of strain on me, which then puts a strain on my wife.

Being constantly available for work creates a lot of stress for him, as it forces him to put work before family when he is called in. His wife's reaction to his "on-call status" is to leave and avoid the inconvenience of him waking up her and the baby. This means that not only is he forced to work at difficult hours, but these odd hours may in turn result in him "losing" his family for the week. This situation puts stress on him, his wife, and his relationship with his wife.

Other fathers feel as though their lack of time with their partner could affect their relationship, as well. Erik, a landscape architect, talks about the consequences of having a lack of couple time: "Every time, just with my wife, it's tough. So there's a lot of—you know, like, not having just one-on-one time between us makes it hard and makes it so that we're not intimately connected as much anymore, so it's—you know, arguments are harder to resolve." The stress of combining work and family puts a strain on his relationship with his wife. It is another case in which he fulfills his work duties and spends time with his children, but his marital relationship falls through the cracks. In other words, trying to balance time for work and time for children has left his wife out of the picture. He feels as though missing out on that alone time makes it more difficult for them to relate to each other, which then makes arguments a little more prolonged.

Lack of Personal Time

Some fathers put so much effort into their work and family that they find themselves with little personal time. Vernon, a bank supervisor, feels that his lack of time for himself has contributed to a substantial weight gain:

I feel that because of my work schedule, that the time that I'm not working, my family is owed that time. So then I end up losing my time. . . . Since I've been working at the bank for 12 years, which may not sound like a lot, but I've gained 30, 35 pounds in 12 years. That may not be a lot, but to me it is because I never gained weight like that before. And I think it was probably because I don't really separate any time for me to do anything because, like I said, I do work and family [laughs]. So there's very little time in there for me. And so I—I see my time as the time with the family, so that's what I do.

Vernon feels like he has no time to spare for himself because when he is done with work, he feels an obligation (and desire) to be with his family. Therefore, his time is completely divided into work time and family time ("I do work and family"). Any time away from work is spent with his family rather than by himself, which severely limits his personal time. Brent, the planner, mentions his desire to add health to the list of things that need to be balanced:

I realize that I need to try to do a better job of balancing home life/ work life but also my health, you know, with all of this. When you have night meetings a lot, that regular appointment at the gym becomes not so regular, because when you do get a free night, you're gonna go home, because you want to see your kid and family and you're tired, you know. And people can talk all they want about getting energy from working out, but I get no energy leaving here at 6 or 6:30 and still not getting home until 7:30 or 8, you know, just in time to bathe my kid and put him to bed. That doesn't give me energy thinking all the time while I'm on a treadmill or doing a Nautilus machine that I could be home with my kid right now.

Time spent exercising is time away from his family. If Brent goes to the gym after work, he will only get to see his son for a little bit. In the end, he chooses to go home. Corey, on the other hand, attempts to combine work and personal time when possible. He does this by biking to work since he feels he could not possibly fit in exercise any other way. This still results in some tension since it means leaving a little earlier in the morning and returning a little later at night, which leaves his wife to take up the extra tasks during these times. Again, the issue comes back to having limited time and having to split that time between work and family. Nevertheless, time for oneself is not a big source of stress for most fathers, consistent with previous studies that find that fathers are less likely than mothers to express time strain regarding their own free time.[30] Fathers in my study tend to make sure they have time for their children, and secondarily their wives, before themselves.

Family Creates Conflict

I'm painting my daughter's room right now, you know, and it's like I come home, I paint the room. It doesn't matter that I've been working all day (Hector, manager)

While less common, a significant minority of fathers in my study feel as though family interferes with work tasks. According to a recent study of work-family conflict, about one-fifth of workers blame their family role for their feelings of conflict.[31] Fathers, like mothers, often feel caught in the middle of their work and family. They feel the demands from their work and think they should be doing more, but at the same time, they feel they should be at home more. Ralph has a 7-to-4 schedule and makes sure he is out the door at 4, but then feels as though he would like more time to finish work tasks. However, he knows how important it is to be home as soon as possible since his wife stays home all day with their three children:

Despite my being strict about my hours, working 7 to 4, there are frequently times in which I wish I had more time to do stuff at work. But, and that's—in a way I feel guilty about if I spend any more time at work; I feel like I have to leave at 4 and get home also because by the end of the day, she's going crazy with these kids, and they're fighting and making a mess or whatever, and she wants a break. And so frequently I will get home, and the moment I walk in the door, she'll go off and go into the office and close the door and expect me to handle them. And they're—maybe they haven't napped, and they're all crabby and tired and fighting or something like that. And that's always, that has always bothered me, and I've complained about that because I say *I'm going from one job to another*, and I want like ten minutes to decompress after I get home. . . . In some ways, I feel guilty about it; that's one of the reasons I feel guilty about staying longer than 4, because I know that it's not that easy at home, and Lisa is exhausted. So I feel like it's my responsibility to get home and help her out. (emphasis added)

Because Ralph has worked from home before and has been very involved in raising his children, he knows how stressful it is for his wife to be home all day. This is what drives him to rush out of work at 4. Yet he also feels as though he is taking on a "second shift" when his wife dumps their children on him as soon as he walks in the door. Ralph just does not feel as though he gets a break from work or family. Based on the National Study of the Changing Workforce, working fathers' claim of working a second shift is valid, as the combined hours spent in childcare and housework adds up to 46 hours per week.[32] This second shift can also develop into a "time bind" as home becomes more like work.[33] The pressure to be with family can put a strain on men's ability to accomplish all their work tasks.

Even when men do not feel any internal conflict, putting pressure on themselves to be home more, sometimes they face pressures from their wives. Adam, a divorced father, shows how such tension can be created by external forces: "I was made to feel guilty when I had to work or when I wasn't home on time because of work." In this case, his guilt was based on an expectation held by his wife. Devin, the assistant professor, talked about his responsibilities at home as well as his responsibilities at work. Since his routine involves getting his daughter ready in the morning and having breakfast with her, it becomes a problem when he is busy at work:

It's problematic in the sense that I feel that I—the way my schedule's set up and the expectations that Ava has, or what—who's going to be doing what in her schedule, that there are times when, I mean, I can't get started on work until after 9 o'clock. And then I'm staying up really late, and I end up losing sleep. And so that makes it really hard.

Devin's daughter, Ava, has come to expect that her dad will have break-fast with her every morning, and he specifically refers to "her schedule" as something that affects him. While he views this as an important ritual, he also feels some stress when he gets to work late or needs to make up for it on the other end by staying up late. This may result in bringing home stress into the workplace, a pattern that is more common among husbands than wives.[34]

At times, some fathers feel as though they are not doing enough at work. Walter, a college administrator, has some flexibility in his schedule that he uses to spend more time with his family in the mornings and afternoons. However, he feels a little guilty about shortchanging his work: "So the tension I think is, I do feel like I spend too much time getting to work a little later than what seems like the right time to be there and leaving a little bit early and taking more time at lunch to help out." His source of tension is his conscience about his work commitment and whether he is forsaking his work responsibility by choosing to spend a little extra time with his family.

Roy, a manager, talks about his decision to cut back at work but still feels a lingering sense that he should be doing more:

I think there's constant conflict because there's so much more I should and could be doing with work. . . . It is what it is. I've got flex-ibility, my boss isn't but eight hours from me. He has no idea what I do every day as long as I get my numbers. So it's a lot of stress be-cause I own my number, but I have flexibility. So I think that's where I fight with it.

Even though Roy says he is happy about his decision, he seems to still feel some tension about what he has sacrificed occupationally, his chances for advancement in the company. It is almost as if he is trying to justify his decision to himself. Another source of tension comes in the form of his flexible schedule. While this allows him to take his children to appoint-ments and generally spend more time at home, he still knows he will have to get the work done and is not completely sure about when to fit it all in.

Russell, a school administrator, talks about the struggle between work and family and having to make choices, but those choices seem to be driven by the work end: "Every day is a struggle. I mean, I don't think that there's a day that goes by that I don't at some point have to make some choices. . . . In the kind of job that I have right now, there's always more that can be done. There's always more time that I can be there." Russell wants to make the right choices and does not want to put work above family, but there is a pull that he feels toward work. The idea that he can always do more at work and can always spend more time at work seems to weigh on him. But the phrasing is in terms of work rather than in terms of family, as he does not say that he could always be at home more. In other words, time spent with family is time taken from work.

Even those fathers who are very involved in raising their children can feel some pressure due to commitments to work. Sean, a lawyer who works three-quarters time, explains, "I always put family first, but then I always get stressed out about am I taking too much vacation: 'Do I have this due?' That's just how it is." Even though he has made the choice to prioritize family, he still thinks about whether he is doing everything he should at work. So while he feels tension over his choices concerning work and family, he ultimately feels good about the choice to put family first. It probably helps that he has a secure job, one from which he feels he cannot get fired, but he has made some sacrifices in terms of advancement. He could have the potential to move up if he put more time in, but he is not interested in getting to the highest levels at this point. Jacob, a writer who works at home and schedules his writing around his children's schedule, still thinks about work a lot:

At times there's quite a lot [of tension], yeah. Depends—it depends on how much a deadline is looming. . . . For me it's particularly hard because my work time's consuming to me; it'd be easy for me to think about nothing else but my work because it's not work in any kind of normal way of thinking about it. I'm sitting there imagining scenes. It's like being a kid in a sense.

The nature of his work means that he can think about it all the time. Even though he limits his time to sit alone and think or write, he finds himself thinking about his stories throughout the day, including when he is with his kids. However, while these fathers feel stress over their greater time with family, they still feel like they have made the right choice.

Shifts in Balance

Balance (or imbalance) is not necessarily a static state. Ian, an insurance agent, experiences a weekly shift in balance. He feels balanced at the beginning of the week, after having spent the weekend with his family, but through the week feels more pressure to be at work and thus less balanced:

> I always feel like really balanced, and I feel like really connected to my family and stuff. I just spent the whole weekend with them, and that was where my focus was. As I get into my week and I get really busy, and I get like really like focused and busy at work, and I don't, you know, like—I don't like to take calls from family or friends. I mean, I take 'em, but I'd rather not 'cause I like to just like dig in and like be in work mode. . . . And I'll start to feel like this maybe kind of crunch, where like I don't know how I can balance it all because I really need to like focus at work. I need to be staying 'til 7, 8 at night if I have to, which I haven't done. But I get this like kinda this pit in my stomach like I am not going to get it done, like I gotta start going in earlier and I gotta stay later. . . . But then literally I'll get to like Friday, Saturday, and I'll be like, "Work," like, "I don't care," you know—like, you know, "I'll go in late on Monday."

This extreme shift in emphasis on family versus emphasis on work occurs each week for Ian and results in frequent fluctuations in his sense of obligation. As the week progresses, he feels more and more obligated to focus on work and to exclude communication with family during work hours. Yet he continues to go home for lunch most days during the week. And when the weekend comes, he is able to put aside work and focus on his family, to such an extent that he will go in late on Monday.

Other fathers feel shifts in guilt over work and guilt over children. If a father focuses a lot on his job, he may feel guilty about not spending enough time with his family. On the other hand, when these same fathers shift their attention to family life, they sometimes feel they are not giving as much as they should at work. Todd, a single father, expresses these pendulum swings:

> I've felt guilty that I'm not doing as much for work, for my job, so the pendulum sort of swings now and then that, you know, I'll travel a lot more and put a lot more emphasis on work. And then I realize that I'm short-changing the children, so then it swings back to "I've gotta take care of my kids." And then the work starts to suffer. So I do swing back and forth between, you know, feeling guilt over work and feeling guilt over the kids. But I always seem to make it work.

This single father feels a constant squeeze on his time as he drops his children off at school before work and rushes to pick them up after work. This leaves no room for extra time at work or at home (in the morning). He was able to cut back on travel while going through his divorce and has tried to combine his work and family roles by taking each child on a business trip with him.

Conclusion

In this chapter, I have demonstrated that fathers experience a great deal of conflict between their work and family roles. Recent national surveys show that men now experience more work-family conflict than women do. My interviews with fathers develop a fuller picture of fathers' work-family conflict, bringing to light the deep feelings and turmoil that men experience in trying to continue their role as provider while being a good father. A common theme is the difficulty of juggling multiple roles, something women have experienced for years. Most of the stress originates from work, often due to long hours, and this is exacerbated by the need to work overtime or to be on call. The result is that many fathers feel they do not spend enough time with their children. Also, those who have managed to spend "enough" time with children often find that their time alone with their partner suffers, and others note a lack of time for themselves, which can have detrimental effects on one's health. While conflict more often goes in the direction of work to family, with work pressures affecting family time, it can also go in the opposite direction, with family obligations infringing on work time and some fathers feeling pressures to participate at home, meaning they feel guilty about not getting work done.

While all of these fathers talk about the stress and difficulty that come along with trying to balance work and family, it is important to note that a new emphasis on involved fatherhood is not without its advantages. The role-enhancement approach, or "expansion hypothesis," suggests that having more roles means earning more rewards and handling roles better, which limits negative consequences and instead results in greater well-being.[35] Rewards may include more income, better self-esteem, and greater chances for social relationships.[36] While there was initial concern about women's multiple roles as wife, mother, and worker, research shows that women with multiple roles have higher levels of emotional well-being than those with fewer roles, and this may be the case for men as well.[37] Other evidence suggests that involved fathers develop closer bonds with their children and better marital relationships.[38] Some researchers argue that the literature on multiple roles too often considers individual roles separately rather than as part of a system. Under role theory, researchers need to take into account a total role system in which role balance may be most beneficial for those who occupy multiple roles.[39] This book seeks to examine working fathers' role systems in order to understand how men can best balance their multiple roles. The next four chapters examine men's strategies for combining work and family.

FOUR

"Old" Dads

Matt's Story

Matt, a 46-year-old high school graduate, works as a delivery driver for a large company. He has been with the company for almost 30 years, delivering packages for about 20 years. He considers it to be a physically demanding job, but one that he enjoys as it allows him to meet and develop relationships with a lot of different people. But he works long hours and is away from home about 12 hours each day once travel and lunch are factored in, leaving home around 7:30 in the morning and returning around 7:30 at night. A typical workday begins with a morning meeting and departure sometime before 9 a.m. It generally takes him all day to empty his truck (i.e., deliver all the packages), at which point he has to do "a pickup run" in which he picks up packages from daily customers. He often does not arrive back at the distribution center until 7 p.m. Matt is married with three sons, two teenagers and one preteen. His long work days mean he is not home with his children when other fathers are:

I spend more time away from home because of work than anybody else I know of. I will be working, delivering packages, and dads who are home from work eating supper with their families will come to the front door, and I'll give them the packages. They're at home, you know, for 10, 12, 15 hours a week more than I am, so they, the way I see it, they have a lot more time to, you know, to take care of, to interact with the kids and to play the games and to, you know, take them to ball games and stuff like that. With me, I work so many hours that, by the time I get home from work—and it's always been like this— by the time I get home from work, supper's over with, everybody's eaten, the food is either—my plate's in the microwave waiting on me, or I get it out of the refrigerator, everybody's in their different rooms, you know, *anything that has happened during the day has already happened*. (emphasis added)

Here Matt expresses a sense of loss, counting the hours that he is *not* there and knowing that he has missed "anything that has happened" at home. Matt was one of the few fathers that made a negative comparison of themselves to other fathers. By highlighting other fathers "eating supper with their families" and calculating how many more hours they are at home, Matt admits that he is not fulfilling the more active role of father. Rather, restrictions on time at home mean that he cannot be a part of his sons' daily activities. Instead he takes on a more limited role of disciplinarian: "I end up, you know, just being more of a punisher, or I'm the one that says, 'Okay, you're grounded,' or you know, 'Okay, you go to your room,' you know, or 'Your mother called me on the phone,' you know, that kind of person. I just don't have the time at home to, you know, to be there." His absence means his role as disciplinarian is a very specific one, the type that comes in *after* everything has already happened and decides who is in trouble. Again, Matt emphasizes not being there and how it pervades every aspect of fatherhood for him. When I asked Matt why he works so many hours, he responded,

It's demanded, it's part of the job. You work until the work's done. It's basically forced overtime. . . . I've asked them many times about a reduction in overtime, and they just—they can't accommodate it on a day-to-day, week-to-week—they just can't do it; they don't have the power. There's not enough people there to pull work off of me.

Matt further explains that his most recent contract addresses overtime but offers only minimal protection and little enforcement. Specifically, the contract states that if an employee works more than 9 hours and 45 minutes three days out of five, he can ask to reduce his hours. However, Matt thinks it is too easy for the employer to get around the limits: "If you think about it, 9 hours and 45 minutes for me, if I start at 8:40, that means they can work me until 7:09 at night, every night of the week, and not violate the overtime clause. If I get off at 7:09, I get home at 8:00" (This calculation assumes 45 minutes for lunch). While workplace duties and policies create long work days for Matt, his family decisions can be seen to play a role in his acceptance of these hours. First, Matt's wife stayed home for most of their marriage, putting all the pressure to earn on Matt. Second, their family expenses have grown over time, as his three boys produce a $1,000 monthly grocery bill and his oldest son required some unexpected medical treatment. Because of these costs, Matt actually added an extra shift on Saturdays.

Conceptualizing "Old" Dads—Masculinity and the Provider Role

Early sociologists such as Talcott Parsons emphasized the importance of separate roles for men and women—the instrumental role for men and the expressive role for women. Men's primary roles as worker and provider were seen as key to the functioning of family life and the larger society. It was argued that a woman could not love a man who did not take (financial) responsibility for his family.[1] Noted economist Gary Becker elaborated on this model, claiming that specialized roles create mutual dependence among spouses and in turn increase marital stability.[2] Harvard business professor Rosabeth Moss Kanter, in her classic book *Men and Women of the Corporation*, identified a "masculine ethic" that underscored traditionally defined masculine skills, such as "a capacity to set aside personal, emotional considerations in the interests of task accomplishment," as key to success in management.[3] This "masculine ethic" is also closely tied to images of the ideal worker, one who is able to focus completely on work while setting aside family.[4] Later, as women's roles changed dramatically and men increasingly faced pressure to become more involved at home, Shawn

Christiansen and Rob Palkovitz argued that we should not lose sight of the continuing significance of men's provider role. They contend that providing is a form of paternal involvement but that this form of involvement has not been widely recognized as such for three reasons.[5] First, it has long been *assumed* that fathers will provide for their families. Second, providing is largely *invisible* because it takes place outside the home and the resulting income is not always obvious. Third, there are many *negative connotations* applied to the provider role. Among other positive outcomes, they argue that providing helps children's development and makes it possible for fathers to be involved with their children in other ways. Furthermore, providing is important to men's self-identity. Fathers who see providing as an act of involvement may not feel that their work and family lives are in conflict.[6]

Men identify themselves, and are identified by others, based on their work and occupation. Work is a source of both self-esteem and prestige, and this emphasis on work crosses race and class status.[7] Nicholas Townsend, an anthropologist, asserts that while fathers experience competing ideals and responsibilities, there is a general sense that work, home, marriage, and children are part of a package deal, all necessary elements in making a good father.[8] As he highlights the element of work, Townsend contends, "Work and employment were essential to their sense of accomplishment and worth: Work was what they did and work defined who they were."[9] Therefore, employment is not only central to masculine identity but also to fathers' paternal identity. The men in Townsend's study could generally be classified as providers, and they were convinced that working long hours was good for their children, mainly because it allowed their wives to make parenting their primary role.[10] Furthermore, public perceptions of father involvement, while increasingly including nonfinancial support and activities, still place a good deal of importance on financial support.[11]

In this chapter, I focus on the experiences of "old" dads, or fathers who see their main role as provider. As mentioned in the introduction, I define the three types of fathers in my study in relation to the changes they make in the workplace in order to be more involved at home. In the case of old dads, these fathers make little or no change to their work lives when they become fathers. These fathers fall into the more traditional notion of fathers as breadwinners. They see their primary role as one of provider. Some old dads make changes, such as increasing their time or commitment to work, that are in opposition to family involvement. These fathers in particular may fit the dictionary definition of a workaholic, "one who has a compulsive and unrelenting need to work."[12] In thinking about how this concept fits into the issue of men's work and family decisions, I emphasize that old dads make decisions about work that focus on financial obligations and do not necessarily take into account time with children. These fathers fit the "old" image of the good provider, one that dominated American society for a good part of the 20th century but whose heyday is in the past.

I'm the Provider

The focus of most of these dads is to provide for their family. In my interviews, the importance of providing came up early in our discussions of their role as father:

> First is, obviously, I am provider. I do this so we can have a house, food, and do stuff. So that's sort of the first thing that I have to obviously guard against. (Howard, bank executive)

> My main role is I guess providing financially for the family, and making sure that he's got enough. Especially since I'm the only one working, I guess I feel that way more. (Joel, government worker)

As Joel suggests, this sense of obligation is particularly strong for those men who are the sole providers for their family. It also weighs heavily on men with unstable employment:

> The most important thing is earn a living. . . . I have to have that for a family and it has to be reliable, so there's a little bit of conflict there because my work is not necessarily going to be there all the time because my job is a political job. . . . So the potential loss of employment is real. And that's—if I was to not be able to bring home the money, then I would have failed in the biggest role I have. (Eugene, political consultant)

The possibility of not being able to provide for one's family makes some fathers question themselves. The desire to provide is so strong and the consequences of failing are so dire that many men evaluate their success as a father and family man in terms of financial success. While failure to provide is more hypothetical for upper-middle-class fathers such as Eugene, some fathers find themselves on the other end of the spectrum, scraping together enough hours to provide for their families. Brett, a carpenter, often works less than 40 hours a week, and while he enjoys spending that extra time with his family, he says that they need more money: "It's good when I work 40 hours because, you know, the money's good. I need the money. . . . I feel like I need to work more, even though it's nice having time with the family, just because of the money. . . . Ever since we've had kids, I opted—if I miss two hours of work, it's noticeable." For Brett and other hourly employees, every hour means more money for their family. These blue-collar fathers often feel a more constant pressure to provide.

Other fathers acknowledge that they would not be as driven to work if they did not need the money. Matt, the delivery driver, talks about what he might do if not for economics: "If it weren't for economics, you know, I would be living in a hermit shack next to the French Broad River somewhere. Everything's driven by economics, you know—done a couple of Outward Bounds school courses, so, you know, I could lead the life or live the life of leisure, but economics drives everything." Corey, a 45-year-old park planner with a stay-at-home wife and an adolescent son, is not particularly thrilled about working long hours but feels it is necessary for his family and uses that perceived responsibility to keep himself going:

> You know, the reason I work is because I have this bill habit, and for some reason no one has given me a trust fund. If I didn't have to work, I'd be hanging out at home; that's my preference. . . . But work is a necessary behavior, because it has to be done. There have been periods in my life where I've had to work a lot. And I've been fortunate that some of those periods that work was really fine and interesting and attractive all by itself. And I didn't have to resort to mental and emotional manipulation to stay with it. Other times and unfortunately probably more times than not, I had to really remind myself

that the reason I do this 80-hour work week and I'm running all over the state serving clients who frankly I don't care for their haircuts and their language and whatever they're doing and completely unattractive to me, it's because I have an obligation to keep the roof over my family's head; that's my job, and that's my function as a spouse and father in that moment. It's been an expression of my commitment to them.

Framing work and providing as an expression of commitment is common among fathers who see their main role as provider.[13] Corey is a reluctant provider. In fact, he and his wife have switched breadwinner/homemaker roles on and off throughout their son's childhood. When Corey's son was born, his wife stayed home while he went out to work. However, when he lost his job, his wife went out to work while he stayed home. He was the primary caregiver for a few years as he tried, often unsuccessfully, to do consulting work from home. At one point, Corey told me that he had "ambitions to be as maternal as [his] wife." Yet his current arrangement involves long hours at work while his wife stays home. As a result, he must convince himself that working long hours is not only necessary but an expression of commitment. So while he would prefer to hang out at home, he knows his hectic work schedule means he can pay the bills:

Because we need to pay our bills and because I don't necessarily have discretion over the activities that are required in my work, it typically dominates the decision-making process. I have to do some of the work, family job; that's where the time goes, even if it means some form of subsidy from family time.

For Corey, work and family each require "a bundle of energy and time," and often he feels there is not enough energy or time to fulfill all of his requirements, particularly with regard to his time with family. He feels as though the requirements to do whatever work assignments he has and the need to provide for his family leave him with little control over his time. The result is that work "dominates the decision-making process," and time at work often eats into his time for family. But he also sees his wife as a partner with whom he can divide tasks. Therefore, while he seems to put work and family on an even playing field ("they demand the same hours of the day"), he can put more time into work because his wife will put more time into family tasks.

Long Hours

A common theme among these fathers is the long hours they work. While the worker role is central to masculinity, working long hours further demonstrates masculinity.[14] Over one-quarter of American men work 50 hours or more per week, and the number increases to 37 percent when looking at men in professional occupations.[15] Much past research suggests long hours are more common among fathers than among men without children.[16] This obviously has repercussions for family life. Joel, a government compliance agent, is required to work 50 hours per week, on average:

> Basically it's been kinda hard: basically ten-hour days, five days a week. We have to average 50 hours a week by the end of the year; we don't have to do ten-hour days, but we have to average that by the end of year. So if you're not doing a lot of work out in the field where you're really busy, then you are in the office. And it's Monday through Friday generally, and some weeks you work after hours; it just depends on what we're doing.

American employers, in this case the federal government, often demand more work than can be accomplished in a 40-hour work week, resulting in compulsory overtime.[17] In general, long hours are common among old dads:

> Two years ago, I would probably say I worked, easy, 65 hours a week. This past year, I'd probably say I worked probably 55. And this year, I hope I don't do over 50. Shooting for 50, but it may be more (Jerry, independent video producer)

> I pretty much work 7:30 to 5:30, 6:30 sometimes—I mean normal business hours. You know, I try to get home a little early on Fridays. But yeah, I'd say kinda the normal schedule of our office is about 8 to 5. And I probably, depending on what's going on, work a little bit longer than that. (Ian, employee benefits consultant)

It's six days a week, and you have to practice after school, and the games are after school. So it's always 6, 7, 8 o'clock at night. (Chase, teacher and coach)

These long hours are often compounded by long commutes, which results in a very long time away from home.

I generally go to work, I leave the house between 6 and 6:30. I'm usually home between 6 and 6:30. (Art, operations manager)

I work nearly, I'd say, typically 50 to 60 hours a week. . . . So I leave the house about 7:30, get here about 8:15ish, generally leave here 7ish. (Howard, bank executive)

What kind of schedule do you have?

Long, long day. I'm up at about 2:15 in the morning, and I'm outta the house about 45 minutes after that. Drive to the airport, and I'm there, on average, 2:30, 3 o'clock in the afternoon typically, Tuesday through Saturday. (Harvey, operations manager)

In fact, some fathers actually increase their hours in order to reduce stress. Ian, the employee benefits consultant who works from 7:30 in the morning to 5:30 or 6:30 at night, talked about how longer hours actually reduce his level of stress:

I've started just going in an hour earlier than I used to. That's I feel like has helped me tremendously because I don't feel like, at least in the morning time, I don't feel so crunched. I was always coming in at like between 8:15 and 8:30 and I was, and I was kinda viewing it as, you know, something good because it gave me a little more time at home with Izzy in the morning. . . . But I always felt rushed getting out the door, and then I always felt crunched when I first got there like in the morning. Like people would, you know, most people would get into my office around 8, and then I'd show up at 8:15 or 8:30. And it didn't—you know, no one cared that I showed up, but I did because I'd show up 8:15 or 8:30 and things were already kind of going. So I moved and decided that I would start going in an hour earlier, so I get in a good half hour, 45 minutes before anyone's there. And I don't feel rushed leaving my house, and to me that has provided a really nice balance. And it doesn't necessarily get me home an hour earlier because I go in an hour earlier, but it provides me with like kinda this buffer zone where I was just feeling like rushed from the time I got into work 'til the time I went home pretty much.

Ian started going in earlier after his second daughter was born. He actually feels better and perceives a greater balance between work and family because of his longer hours. However, there is some acknowledgment that some work hours may not be as efficient as others. Howard, the executive manager, is bothered by employees who mess around at work but claims his work load is the reason for his long hours:

You work when you're at work, spend less time screwing around and messing around and typing emails and looking on the Internet and calling your buddies, and those types of things and actually do what you're supposed to be doing, then you can put in a full day's worth of work in 8 hours instead of having to drag it out 12, 13, 14 hours every day. Hours don't impress me; working does. I take that attitude, and right now I just have a lot of work. It takes me 10 to 11 hours to get everything done that I need to get done.

As Marianne Cooper suggests, men often talk about their own individual aspirations as a motivation to work long hours. Yet internal pressures do not come out of nowhere. Rather, they are grounded in external pressures and standards to which men compare themselves. As a result, "the force causing them to work both surrounds them and is internalized by them, creating normative patterns, understandings, and definitions about work."[18] As such, long hours are not seen as unusual but rather the norm. And this norm, one that encourages men to develop into workaholics, is more common among professional workers.[19] In law professor Joan Williams's most recent book, she also documents this pressure to work long hours stemming from beliefs about masculinity that characterize "real men" as being devoted to work. These ideas fuel competition among male workers to "out-macho each other" by working longer hours.[20]

Brent's Story

Brent is a 33-year-old married father. He has a 2-year-old son, and his wife is pregnant. Brent is also a community and regional planner. He works for the government but does not consider himself a bureaucrat. He describes his planning section as a tight-knit group but says he is sometimes frustrated with the way his director micromanages him. Brent estimates that he works 45 to 50 hours per week, stating, "a 40-hour work week is not really a norm." He explains that the section's billing system is similar to attorneys', which means he has to work well over 40 hours in order to register 40 billable hours. As a result, Brent frequently feels that he has to choose between work and family. On the day of our interview, he relayed a story about how he had an important family matter, his wife's ultrasound, and an important work matter, a press conference, both scheduled for that same morning. While he saw the clash coming, he felt he could do nothing about it and in the end chose to leave his wife at the doctor's in order to make it to the press conference:

It started out at 8:30. We were going to the hospital to the doctor. . . . By 9 we're in the doctor's room doing this ultrasound to see the baby that's on the way, which was really neat. But then I'm like, "Oh, I've got to go to this press event," which I didn't do all the math, but me being across town in time to do this without, you know, completely freaking out 'cause I'm gonna be running late and I'm the guy with the podium and microphone and all these other details: "I need to leave now." So I left halfway through that, you know, to, you know, get over to this other thing. . . . Family life right now, that's the kind of—the shortness; it's getting the short end of the stick, if that's the right phrase, right now, but that's just like—I think that little snippet told me a lot this morning, you know. I could see it all unfolding as it was happening. I could even see it unfolding earlier this week as I was looking at my calendar, but neither thing could be moved that I could figure out. You know, it's like, we're between a rock and a hard place here, and so it would be nice to stop having these sorts of choices, because I know what I'd really like to choose, but I also don't feel like I couldn't just not show up at this event.

Although Brent alludes to wanting to choose family and expresses a desire to avoid such choices in the first place, he winds up putting work before family. For him, the penalty of not showing up at a work event would be worse than not showing up at or leaving a family event. In another conversation, Brent confided that he did not feel the need to go to every doctor's visit with his pregnant wife. Part of it is that he has already been through the process before with his wife's first pregnancy, and part of it is that he questions whether going to the less important visits (ones that do not involve an ultrasound) is worth falling behind at work.

In addition, Brent's commitment to work puts him in a position where it is difficult to choose family over work. He feels "this inner need to be dedicated or committed" to his work: "I'm just very conscientious about it and have a problem, I guess, either drawing a line, saying no, putting limits, something in there." Brent's compulsive need to work classifies him as a workaholic, and his inability to draw a line results in quite a bit of stress. Nevertheless, he feels as though not getting work done would be even more stressful: "At a certain point, it's more stressful to be away from the office and not getting stuff done that you know is waiting. . . . It ultimately is my decision and responsibility, but I have allowed myself now going on years to be overextended, in my mind." Later, Brent elaborated: "Right now it's a bit stressful. It's just—and I say now—I look back like at first it was, you know, 'Oh, boy, the last three months have just been intense,' and now I'm looking back—it's like the last five years, it just hasn't stopped, you know. You just get to a point where that becomes the norm." Brent has gotten himself into a cycle that he cannot break. He is stressed because there is a lot of work to do. But he keeps working hard because he would be even more stressed if he did not. Unfortunately, he has become one of those fathers who look up and realize years have passed.

To add to matters, Brent thinks it would be unfair if he did not put his all into his work. He does not think he should be let off the hook or be allowed to miss anything that other workers would not be allowed to miss. In his eyes, every employee should be treated the same:

> I'm strong into this equity or fairness thing. It's like just because when I was single I wouldn't expect you to do me four—for me to do four night meetings a week and let the married mom go home and not have any meetings. It needs to be split up there. But now that I'm on the other side, I also I don't think that it would be fair for me just to pop on home. I think I need to carry a couple of these night meetings, and we're all gonna still share equally. And it's almost like *take the family out of it.* You're dealing with me and my job, and we all need to be able to do our jobs that we were hired for. (emphasis added)

Here it is clear that he thinks that employees should not use family as an excuse, and so the fact that someone has children should not be highlighted at all in the workplace. As with other fathers, Brent indicates that family is indeed important, but his actions, and sometimes his words, suggest that work is more important. Brent makes a great analogy between family and dessert in trying to describe the abstract importance of family in a reality that favors work:

> There's something there that, you know, you committed to the work, you're conscientious about it, you can't just drop it, but you're not exactly saying, "Well, it's so much higher on the scale than family." They're, you know, at least equal; in fact, family's probably higher, but it's almost like it gets treated like dessert, you know. It, the dessert, for a lot of people is the best part of the meal, but sometimes you fill up with all the food, you know, and then, "Wow, that dessert looks great, but I'm just—I'm gonna have a bite." You know, it's equivalent or analogous to getting home at 8:45.

Because of this, Brent winds up prioritizing work and putting more time into work, which leaves family as an extra, something that he looks forward to but that only comes after all the work's been done. And sometimes this means his family gets "the short end of the stick." Working such long hours often means less daily involvement in children's lives, which in turn can affect fathers' relationships with their children.[21]

Reliance on Wives

Since these fathers are primarily focused on work and providing for their families, they need to rely on their wives to take the main responsibility for childcare. Corey, the park planner, acknowledges the primary role his wife has taken: "It's really more of a traditional model. She's at home most of the time. She does the lion's share of running the home and the lion's share of attending to our son's various needs. . . . So she's really the primary homemaker and parent right now." Fathers like Corey describe a more traditional division of labor, one that hit its pinnacle in the 1950s. But we might ask why these fathers saw such a need for their wives to stay at home. After all, the dual-earner model is the dominant arrangement currently. To really understand their emphasis on wives as primary caretakers we need to consider their values regarding childrearing and their attitudes toward institutional daycare.

You know, I really don't want other people raising my children. (Erik, landscape architect)

Because us being young parents, you know, you don't wanna let go of your children and turn them over and their care over to people that you don't know. (Harvey, operations manager)

Especially at this age, I don't want him left alone and taken care of by a stranger. I don't care if she works, but I don't know it's hard to say. It's not I want her to stay home with the kid; I just don't trust anybody else. (Joel, government worker)

All three of these fathers do not like the idea of someone else raising their children. Joel highlights the key concepts of strangers and trust. They want someone they know and trust, and who fits this description more than their wives, the mother of their children? The desire for a parent (read: mother) to stay home drives these fathers to work long hours.[22] In fact, a large national survey of parenthood and employment found that men with nonemployed wives increased their work hours after they became fathers.[23] Joel expands on this point, even ruling out grandma as a daily caregiver: "I like to know that she's home with the girls, that they're not somewhere, you know, somewhere else, even if they're at grandma's or whatever. I'd rather them, you know, be with my wife and know that she's taking them to their doctor's appointments or that she's, you know, doing that stuff." Joel also mentions perks such as having his wife pick up dry cleaning and make dinner. And, of course, with wives staying at home, these men do less housework.

For other fathers, it was a combination of best interests of their child and best financial interests.

> It just seemed like it would be better for the kids to do it that way, for her to stay home. You know, the idea of somebody else raising your kids just doesn't seem like, you know—having them in daycare and all that stuff with somebody else is actually raising the kids more than you are. It just doesn't sound right, and with the amount of money my wife was making, it, you know, it wouldn't pay off that well. (Brett, carpenter)

> We just decided with two children, and with daycare and with everything, it would be more prudent and cost effective if she stayed home. (Harvey, operations manager)

Brett and his wife both had relatively low-paying jobs when they first had children. While it was difficult financially for the family to get by on one income, most of his wife's pay would have gone to daycare costs. Eventually Brett's wife started doing word-processing and transcribing work from home, but this was arranged around their children's schedule. Harvey's wife stayed home with their first child and was actually thinking about going back to work when she got pregnant with their second child.

Other fathers talked about the time constraints their jobs imposed. Russell, a former college coach, emphasized all the time he was away from home:

> If you're doing your job, you're here 'til late at night. You're here, nobody counts your hours. But if they did, then they'd probably have

to pay you more [*laughs*], if they counted how many hours that you actually put in—not counting getting on the phone at night talking to recruits, being on the road for three days at a time, or going on a recruiting trip and being gone for, you know, three, four days at a time. So that was—that was certainly different because there became times—I'm not sure, in fact, I know we couldn't have done, we couldn't have done—raised our kids the way we wanted to raise them—had we both been working during that time.

Russell came to the conclusion that his wife basically needed to stay home so that their kids would have a parent around. He has since moved into the "new" dad category. Other fathers also suggest a need for one parent to be home, though it always seems as though that parent is the wife. Howard, the bank executive, talks about being transformed while his wife and newborn were still in the hospital:

My daughter wasn't 18 hours old, and I was holding her in the room that night with my wife there, and I just looked at my daughter and I told my wife, I said, "There's no way I can put this child in daycare. And I just can't do it." So we decided that night that she would no longer work until the kids were of age that they could go to school. . . . I said, "I can't see you, I can't see us putting any child in a daycare, 'cause I want them to be nurtured and whatever by us." And she said, "I'm thinking exactly the same thing." So it was a mutual acknowledgment.

Howard frames it as a mutual decision but mainly talks about the issue with reference to his own thoughts and feelings. He says he does not want to put his daughter in daycare but then makes reference to a joint decision for his wife to quit work. But then he slips by saying, "I can't see you . . . ," suggesting that if his wife continued to work, it would be her putting their daughter in daycare. This is further supported by his emphasis on his role as provider and his ability to support a stay-at-home wife. He says, "I just feel very blessed and very fortunate enough that we could make this decision to have my wife stay at home and pick them up from school and work on their homework and be very socially interactive with them on all different levels."

And so even though Howard wants his daughter nurtured "by us," it is clear that the only possibility would have been for his wife to stay home.

Other couples struggle a bit more with the decision for the wife to stay at home. Harvey and his wife have disagreed about work from the start of their relationship. When they first started dating, they were both working overtime. As their relationship got more serious and they talked about starting a family, they argued about how to manage their schedules. The problem was that neither one wanted to give in: "She didn't wanna change, and I didn't wanna change either. But we knew that one of us needed to change, or we knew that both of us needed to change, but neither one of us wanted to." However, when their first child was premature, they decided that she would stay home to care for him. Given her emphasis on her career, I wondered if they had talked about the possibility of him staying home:

So in terms of staying home, was it always that she would stay home or did you ever consider you staying home?

I would never—I never considered. We never even—that was never even a possibility, I don't think. I enjoy working. And even when I worked two jobs, and I didn't have enough working. And she would if she had to, but when we—just when we talked about it, it was not even an issue that we wanted our son to be healthy and grow up the way—she had to stay home. I had no idea what I was doing. I learned everything from her. I was afraid to touch this boy all the time because he was so small. That was not even an option for me to stay home. I'd have to call her all day asking, "Honey, how do you do this? How does this thing go on him?" Ah, no, that was never even a question.

Harvey is a self-described workaholic who cannot see himself *not* working. To provide more support for his decision, he claims that he would be inept at caring for a baby. Lately, they have been talking again about the issue as his wife wants to go back to work. While he says he has never told her not to go back to work, it is not clear that he has been supportive or encouraging of his wife's career ambitions.

For those fathers whose wives are trying to return to work, there is often a feeling that their wives are the ones who need to work around the children's needs and schedules. Wives must be flexible.

> She has a very flexible schedule, so she can still do the, you know, the doctor's appointments and the dentist's appointments and the, you know, counseling sessions with teachers and stuff like that. So she's, she's very flexible. (Matt, delivery driver)

> Since I'm gone ten hours of the day, she's either got to find someone to watch the kid, which we don't know too many people, or it's gotta be when I'm home; so she only has a very small window on the weekdays, probably an hour or two. (Joel, government worker)

Matt's wife has started cleaning houses. She schedules clients while their sons are in school. Joel's wife is a massage therapist. Since they still have an infant, she schedules appointments at night or on weekends. There is an unspoken understanding that his career comes first. These fathers have already been established as the breadwinners, so even when their wives go back to work, the assumption is that they must continue their caretaker role.

Erik's Story

Erik is a 34-year-old landscape architect with a wife, a 2-year-old son, and a baby on the way. He currently works for a small firm but has recently accepted a job with a larger firm that will allow him to branch out into real estate development. Perhaps more importantly, he will earn a lot more money in his new job. As Erik put it, "there's no kind of ceiling on the money." And this higher salary will allow Erik's wife to stay at home:

> This job opportunity is the only reason we're able to do it this way. Otherwise, it'd be a huge struggle. If I didn't get this job opportunity right now—I mean, it's been a huge struggle and just constant conversation about how, you know, she just hates dropping, you know, Logan off at daycare; she struggles every day. I mean, it took her like a month or two to get over dropping him off and just seeing him crying when

she leaves, and she's—the first week, she cried all the way to work the whole time, just awful. And even though I, I feel for her, it's like, it's so stressful to hear about it every day, you know, 'cause there's nothing I can do about it. I mean, it's—we looked at the budget, we looked at the bills; there was no way she could just stop working. And I mean, even if we traded in the cars and, you know, rode our bikes to work and got rid of the cable and everything, just the bare essentials, it wouldn't work the way the economy is right now, and it's just, it's tough.

Before Erik's job offer, he and his wife both needed to work. The way Erik sees it, there was no way to cut costs so that his wife could stay at home. At the same time, his wife was constantly complaining about how awful she felt leaving their son in daycare. A couple of times his wife took the day off from work because she did not like some alteration in the routine, such as a change in daycare providers. All these stories were relayed to Erik, which in turn made him stressed, particularly because he felt he had no control over the situation. Ultimately, he felt as though he failed his family:

I like where I'm working now, but she was really, really unhappy being working and having somebody else raise our kid and having to drop him off at daycare. It was—I mean, I was getting to the point where I was just depressed and stressed, and she would, you know—I wanted so badly to provide a living for my family so that she could stay at home. I mean, it was like tearing me apart. I felt like I was a failure.

While Erik did not feel particularly guilty about having his son at day-care, pressure from his wife eventually led him to look for a new job. The acceptance of this new job has already changed dynamics in the morning. Erik now places (even) less importance on his wife's job:

She takes him and she picks him up because in the morning we're getting out the door so late that I can't be to work any later than I am, and she's able to get there and pull it off. And plus, you know, we know that she's eventually gonna be a stay-at-home mom, and so it wasn't as critical if she had a problem at work or if they, you know, had to let her go for some reason, 'cause she was late every day. . . . So she'll go and pick him up and, you know, take him home because if it were me, she'd be afraid that I would get there too late, because if you get there after 6, you pay like a dollar a minute after.

There are two factors at play here. One is that Erik sees his wife's job as expendable. He focuses on the fact that she will eventually quit her job when in fact he will also quit his job soon. The second factor is that his wife likes to be in control in matters involving their son. Erik claims that he has offered to drop off and pick up his son to and from daycare, but she insists on transporting their son because she wants to spend that time with him, and she does not have complete confidence that Erik will show up on time. This is an example of maternal gatekeeping, a situation in which mothers raise barriers to paternal involvement. Mothers who do not want their husbands to be more engaged in childcare may feel as though their husbands are incompetent or worry that their husband's involvement will reduce their own authority.[24]

Finally, Erik admits that his new higher-paying job also means longer hours and more travel. His wife is okay with these changes: "I expect to have to travel more, which my wife and I talked about, and she's fine with that. She realizes that there's gonna be some sacrifices in order for her to be a stay-at-home mom." Erik frames it as sacrifices on her part, in that she will have more work to do at home and less help from him. But he does not talk about the sacrifices he will make that involve seeing his son and new child less. Like some of the men in Townsend's study, putting more time into work is seen as a good arrangement if it means the wife/mother can stay home with the children.[25]

Consequences of Providing for "Old" Dads

Pressures of Breadwinning

While old dads willingly take on the provider role, there are some who feel that this role creates a lot of pressure for them. In response to Parsons and Becker, who highlighted the positive impact of specialization on marriage and family, Valerie Oppenheimer, a sociologist who engaged in pioneering work on women's employment, argued that specialized roles, with men as sole breadwinners and women as sole homemakers, are economically risky.[26] The most common concern among the fathers I talked with was the ability to meet their family's financial needs. Matt, the delivery driver, told me that his family's financial situation has actually become more tenuous over time:

> When we first got married, it wasn't that big of a deal, but we had— we got married in March, and our first son was born the following March, okay, and that's when she quit work. And then our second son was born 15 months later, so we quickly, you know—it fell into a, you know, pattern of, you know, just barely making ends meet. And over the years, that's kind of snowballed to the point where now it's very hard to make ends meet, very hard.

Instead of getting better, things have gotten worse as his three sons have grown and added to the household expenses, particularly grocery bills. Matt expressed a real sense of regret at the traditional arrangement he and his wife agreed on several years ago. He even suggests that his two older sons' behavioral problems come from having a mother who was always there while he was almost never there.

Whereas Matt provides a post hoc evaluation of his sole provider role, Ian, the employee benefits consultant, considers the future needs of his family:

> We can barely get by on one salary. So to provide a life, you know, for our family, we're both gonna have to, have to work. . . . We're a young, married couple with little kids right now, and we can kind of—we can get by. But you know, I don't want to just get by. I want to, you know, be able to—we live in a small condo, and the two of us want to have a backyard for my kids. And I want to be able to take vacations with the whole family and those kind of things. And those things you have to, you know—living up here you pretty much have to both be doing it.

Ian feels that his family is just getting by at this point, but he is not satisfied with their economic position. He has two young daughters, a 2-year-old and a 2-month-old. Ian points to what Townsend has labeled the protection and endowment facets of fatherhood.[27] He wants good housing and opportunities for his children as they grow up. There is also some sense that Ian wants more material items himself.

As much pressure as Matt and Ian felt, there was never a strong attempt to get their wives to get paid employment. This is generally the rule for old dads, who identify with their role as provider. In contrast, there is the case of Martin, a superdad who will be highlighted in a future chapter. Martin once took on the provider role for the sake of his family. While he felt criticized for working two jobs, he would have preferred to work less:

> I got blamed for not being there, but I was working two jobs and I was working a shift that your body isn't meant to work. I was working. I wasn't out drinking. I wasn't out at the bars. I was at work. I wasn't playing golf. I wasn't doing anything that I didn't think I wasn't supposed to be doing. . . . I would have rather been at home with the kids while she had a part-time job than work two jobs and not ever seen anybody.

Martin wanted his wife to get a job, even if part-time, to help pay the bills, but he struggled unsuccessfully in this area. When his wife would not get a job, he took a second job. Now Martin is a single dad with full custody of his children (see chapter 7).

It's Not That Tough

While some old dads felt their provider role created stress, others did not see a conflict between their work and family roles. Eugene, the political consultant told me, "I don't think it's a struggle. Maybe I'm different than other folks, . . . but I don't feel like it's that tough." This lack of conflict felt by these fathers is likely due to the idea that working is part of their job as a father. In this sense, work and family go together. The worker role and father role take the shape of the provider role.

Some old dads do acknowledge a lack of balance but do not necessarily feel it as a source of conflict. These fathers generally find their work particularly rewarding and are career driven. Vernon, a bank supervisor who works 11-hour shifts from midafternoon to midmorning, does not want to change anything about his job:

I'm glad I have a job that I like going to. Most people want a job, you know, wish that they had a job that they loved going to. Vanessa wished her job was like that. But, I mean, luckily I found a job, you know, that I love. And, I mean, that's why I hope everything continues to progress like it does for me, and I hope I'll be there for a long time.

Vernon told me that his wife wants him to change shifts and complains about his work hours and how much he loves his job. In finding his dream job, Vernon has been willing to work long hours, but the combination of long hours and having a job that he loves causes a bit of friction in his relationship with his wife, who expresses some jealousy.

Harvey, an airline operations supervisor, also loves his job and explains how his long work hours are not a problem: "I don't feel like they're balanced because I probably work more than I should. I work hard, but not to the degree that there is a source of tension, because I enjoy what I do and I constantly include my family in what I do." Harvey recognizes that he is a workaholic and that his time at work overshadows his time at home. At another point, Harvey estimates that he has accumulated 300 hours of vacation time: "I never take time off. I work all the time." But he is okay with this situation for two reasons. First, as he mentions, he really likes what he does. This means that he does not spend time worrying about how some work task is a waste of time that takes away from the time he could be spending with his children, as Joel does. Second, while his schedule means he leaves really early in the morning (some would say the middle of the night) and works long hours, he still gets home relatively early in the afternoon, which allows him to spend quite a bit of time (relatively more than other fathers) with his children. He also often takes his children to work with him on weekends, and they enjoy it (he works at an airport). When questioned further, he did admit to some feelings of guilt: "Sometimes I do [feel guilt]. Sometimes I feel like I work too much and it's not fair to her [his wife]." But this sense of guilt is directed at his responsibilities to his wife and the extra burden she takes on when he is not home. It is not in relation to time with his children. This distinction between lack of balance and presence of tension is interesting. This case shows how a lack of balance may not necessarily result in tension.

In other cases, there may be some tension, but work may still win out. Chase, a high school teacher and coach, got into coaching because of his love of the sport. He admits that teaching is his job, and the coaching job is "extra pay for extra duty." In other words, he did not have to coach. This created some conflict with his wife when their children were younger: "It kind of strained, you know—there was a strain on Michelle as far as having three little ones at home, and I'd roll in about 7 or 8 o'clock at night. But you know, she let me have it, you know, a few times, and we kinda worked through it." For Chase, however, his coaching role literally became his father role. His three sons grew up wanting to play the sport for their dad. They eventually went to watch practices and games after school, and now the two older sons play on his team. Chase was able to resolve the issue by incorporating his sons into his work.

Some fathers provide conflicting images of ideals and accomplishments. These fathers say they do not want to work long hours but find themselves feeling fulfilled by working such long hours. Ian experiences a pendulum swing in his prioritization of work and family. While he enjoys spending time with his family on the weekends and may even go to work late on Mondays, he starts placing more and more weight on work through the week. He becomes enmeshed in "work mode" as he shifts his emphasis from family to work. It is as if being at work feeds the desire to be at work. He realizes that there is a lot of work to be done and wants to actually increase time at work. In applying identity theory to fathers' involvement, Rudy Ray Seward suggests, "the higher the identity salience for a given role the more likely it will take precedence over a role with a conflicting but lower salience."[28] In other words, the role that is enacted will take priority over other roles that are important but not enacted. Therefore, fathers who work a lot (enactment) are in fact giving preference to their provider role over their nonfinancial father role.

I'm Still There

Several fathers knew that they did not have an ideal arrangement but felt they were making the best of their situation. Putting together work hours and commute time, Art, an operations manager, is gone about 12 hours a day during the week. Still, he feels as though he makes a good effort to be there for his daughter: "I kind of try to work the early end of things instead of the later end. I try to be home for some of Madelyn's waking hours every day and, on purpose, and weekends, and I generally have tried not to travel very much." Given that his daughter goes to bed around 7:30, he wants to make sure he has about an hour or so with her. He makes a point of eating dinner at home each night and is generally in charge of his daughter's bedtime routine. Similarly, Eugene, the political consultant, emphasizes that he does not travel and is home "almost every night." For fathers who may miss dinner and even their children's bedtime, the focus moves to the weekend. Howard, the executive manager, emphasized his availability on weekends: "I do not work weekends. I very rarely work them. If I have to, it's because I just absolutely have to, but weekends I reserve for my family and my children." By carving out some time that is reserved for the family, these fathers can still claim to be involved dads. They simply squeeze their involvement into a few hours.

Old dads also highlight the positive aspects of their limited involvement. Joel, the government agent who is mandated to average ten-hour days the entire year, tries to put a positive spin on his situation:

I guess the balance is a little off for me. But it's not bad, I still have the evenings when I get home and almost every weekend, which some people don't have. And I have a wife at home there with the kid, and I know he's fine, and I don't have to worry about him. So if you look at it that way, it's like, okay, it's a little off, but you know what, there's a lot of positive things that comes out of it—kinda offsets it.

Joel explains that the ten-hour average is in place to cover days when he has to travel or the need for irregular hours. But it also means that sometimes he is just in the office to put in his hours. Even with these complaints and a feeling that things are not quite balanced, Joel tries to focus on the bright side. As with the other fathers, he draws attention to the fact that he is home at night and most weekends. He further points out that some fathers are not able to be at home during these times.

Some fathers go even further to suggest that they do more than other fathers. Erik, the landscape architect who took a new job so his wife can stay home, talks about his son's bath routine:

When I take him out of the bath, Claire's usually there putting his clothes on, you know. I'll put his diaper on. It's really a team effort. I mean, it's—I see other fathers who just sit around and don't do anything. I'm not like that. I like to, you know, get in there and do everything too, so we're on and off with the bath routine, you know. We've discussed it. It's kind of my time to bond with him since he's always going to mom for everything.

Even for fathers who work quite a bit, there is always a point of comparison to those who work even longer hours. And if these fathers can say that they do more than other fathers, they can feel better about their situation.

Changes—Will They Ever Happen?

Several of the fathers talked about their long hours as temporary, something that would change once they got to a certain point in their career. Howard, the bank executive, recently started in a new position and estimates that it will take a few months for him to get a feel for the work, the place, and the people, but he thinks it will get better: "I'm working a lot of hours now, but it's just because I feel like I'm new here. It will recede some after I get a little better traction on how things are going on here. So when that happens, I'll have a much more positive work/life type of balance for my family." Yet, based on our discussion of vacation, it seems as though Howard is in a perpetual state of trying to advance at work:

I haven't been able to do that [take all of his vacation time], because I've been trying to advance my career. So I've spent about three-year stints in each elevated job level that I've gone through—starting with the first group for about three years, and another group for the first year on level three, and then with another group for about two years, and with another group for about two and a half, and then I moved away. I was with that group for about three years and then was with another group for almost three more, and then I got to here. It takes a good year and a half, two years to get into the full cycle of those types of things. I haven't been able to fully take all the vacation time I've been allotted.

101

The fact that he never uses all of his vacation time reinforces the idea that work is his primary focal point. Howard explains that "vacation becomes more of a penalty" for employees at his level. Since there will continue to be work and he will continue to have the same responsibilities, whether or not he takes vacation, he knows he will have to work even more either before or after a vacation. So he chooses not to take much vacation time at all. The other important point is that he is continually working his way up, and to advance to each level he needs to put in a lot of time at work. Furthermore, he has switched positions at intervals that seem to ensure perpetually long hours of adjustment. For fathers like Howard, it is always a matter of a couple more years of hard work and sacrifice. However, as seen in Howard's example, each advancement brings with it a new timeline for further advancement that pushes family time to the side.

Fathers also suggest that their families, or at least their wives, have agreed to make sacrifices so that they can advance at work, though usually the assumption is that these sacrifices are temporary. Harvey, the airline operations manager, talks about his discussions with his wife:

> Sometimes I feel like I work too much and it's not fair to her. But one of the things that we did, we talked about—and especially moving from Atlanta here—we knew that for the first two, three years, I'd be working a lot until I get to the next level. And once the next level of promotion comes, a lot of the things that I do now I won't have to do. And all the time that I put in I won't have to put in, so we agreed to make the sacrifice.

Harvey justifies his long work hours as a means to an end, and yet he admits it is unfair to his wife. He is particularly mindful of how unfair it is for his wife because of the sacrifices she has made with regard to her career goals. He describes his wife as career oriented, though she stays at home with their children. She had not been planning on staying home, but their first child was premature and required close monitoring for much of the first year. Perhaps because Harvey knows his wife wants to work so much, he is persistent in saying that his long hours will subside once he gets his promotion:

I really would like to be able to spend more time at home and not have to work as much. And only because of the position that I'm in that I do work the way that I work. And I say all the time, "Guys, we're going somewhere." And once this—and actually probably in the next two or three months, the promotion will come. And I knew that I had to put my nose to the grindstone—that was one of the stipulations. And then there were times when I guess I didn't second guess the decision. I just was wondering, "Man, these are a lot of hours." I work a long schedule. But then I'd always look at the flip side, and know that I knew that coming in and, just, it will be fleeting. And again, probably two, three months away from a promotion, and then my schedule will really just—my hours will probably be cut drastically and probably be more a Monday through Friday type thing and no weekend work at all.

The only problem is that Harvey makes it clear everywhere else that he is a self-described workaholic. He likes working long hours. He cannot get enough work. He could not see himself staying home and argued with his wife about who would make career sacrifices (and won). Therefore, again, it is questionable whether Harvey will in fact reduce his hours once he gets the promotion.

I opened the chapter with Matt's story, one of long work hours and little time for family. Matt's job as a delivery driver meant leaving home early and getting home late, after everything that was going to happen at home already happened. While he enjoyed his job, he really did not like the long hours. But once his first son was born and his wife quit working, he was left to earn all the money for his family. Now he is in a position to make some changes. He has almost accumulated enough time at his company to retire with a pension, and he plans to begin a new career as a firefighter:

My goal is to retire next year. I can draw—start drawing a retirement, pension. And to get a job with a municipal fire department—and not only do I enjoy that kind of work, but their schedule is they work 24 hours, a 24-hour shift, and then they're off for two days. So to me, being someone who has worked the way I have for 20 years, working a day and getting two days off is like working a day and getting a weekend. I could do that standing on my head for the rest of my life if I lived to be 100.

Matt has already begun education and training to become a firefighter. He thinks his new occupation will provide a much better work schedule. The thought of working just two or three days a week means Matt will have much more time to be at home with his family. Although he thinks it might be too late for his two older sons, he has hope that he may yet be a better, more involved father for his youngest son.

Conclusion

While attitudes and gender roles have changed, there is still nostalgia for traditional roles, ones based on old ideas about what men and women should do at work and at home. After all, the male breadwinner has been a central component of hegemonic masculinity for decades, and the image of the good provider still pervades American society.[29] The notion that a father is supposed to provide for his family is one that is taken to heart by the dads I described in this chapter. Several patterns emerge among these fathers. First, old dads occupy a range of occupations from blue collar to professional. However, while their emphasis on providing for their families is similar, they differ in the urgency they place on this role. While many professionals work long hours for career advancement and luxury items, blue-collar dads often point to the need to work a certain number of hours for basic necessities. There is a consciousness that each hour means more pay.

Second, old dads tend to work long hours. While long hours are often imposed by employers and a broader workplace culture that supports working long hours, most of the fathers do not complain about these hours, and some increase their hours to make sure they can get everything done, which actually is seen as a strategy for reducing work-family stress.

Third, wives play a big role in both fathers' desire to provide for their family and their ability to focus on the provider role. On the one hand, wives who want to stay home sometimes pressure their husbands to work more hours or to take on a better-paying job. For men who cannot provide completely for their families, there is often a sense of failure. On the other hand, old dads generally prefer that their wives stay home because they do not like the idea of someone else "raising their children," or they think it does not make sense financially. However, when wives stay home to care for children and handle other household responsibilities, it allows men to focus more on work, achieving the goal of ideal worker. These men rarely consider staying home themselves, and once their wives are at home, any consideration of the wives' employment is expected to work around the children's and the fathers' own schedules. A few fathers did express concern about the pressures of breadwinning and their concern about being the only means of support for their families, though this was more common among working-class fathers.

Fourth, old dads often do not feel there is a conflict between their work and family roles. They either say outright that they feel like work and family are balanced, or they acknowledge that the balance tips toward work but suggest that this is acceptable because they really like their work or they think it does not negatively affect their family. This finding also confirms the idea that if providing is a form of paternal involvement, then work and family are not mutually exclusive realms and therefore do not create a sense of conflict.[30] Indeed, old dads generally still feel as though they are present and available for their children. This is often achieved by focusing on the time they do have with their kids, whether that involves a bedtime routine or weekend family time. While most old dads were not looking to make big changes to their work lives, beyond climbing the career ladder, some did talk about cutting back work hours. Yet the fathers who talked about reducing their hours often also talked about work habits that made it unlikely that they would actually work less. An exception to this pattern was Matt, whose story opened and closed the chapter. Matt's story shows that old dads can change and become new dads or perhaps even superdads. The next chapter focuses on the experiences of new dads.

FIVE

"New" Dads and Partial Solutions

While some fathers stick to a more traditional view of their role as father, most of the fathers I talked with see themselves as involved dads. They are not completely dismissive of their monetary contributions to their family, but they do not define themselves as breadwinners. With a continued sense of financial responsibility for their families and a desire to be highly involved in their children's lives, these "new" dads make an effort to combine their work and family roles in a way that the "old" dads do not. Whereas the old dads tended to maintain the same work schedules as before having children, the new dads tried to make some adjustments to their work lives in order to better balance work and family. However, new dads are not revolutionaries but rather work within the system, taking advantage of flexible work schedules already in place or making small changes that have a limited impact on the workplace environment. In fact, new dads are the norm today. While our society still holds on to aspects of traditional fathers, the simple fact is that their numbers have declined dramatically, and in their place new dads have increased.

As fathers attempt to better balance work and family, it is important to consider the concept of work-family balance or fit. Rosalind Chait Barnett, a psychologist and women's studies professor, defines work-family fit as a process whereby workers adjust their work conditions and sometimes their own characteristics in order to meet personal needs and others' needs. Barnett sees this process as occurring within a social system in which individuals consider their connections to others. Importantly, adjustments or strategies are implemented in order to gain a sense of work-family fit.[1] Furthermore, family adaptive strategies may be defined as "the actions families devise for coping with, if not overcoming, the challenges of living and for achieving their goals in the face of structural barriers."[2] These strategies may prevent conflict, reduce existing conflict, or encourage balance.[3]

In this chapter, I examine new dads' strategies for reducing work-family conflict. Some of these strategies require limited effort. As mentioned already, some of these fathers already have family-friendly jobs. These new dads do not make any work adjustments but instead recognize the advantages their jobs provide in allowing them to spend more time with their children. Other fathers, particularly professional workers, also benefit from having jobs with a high degree of autonomy, which allows them to exercise greater control over their schedules. Another strategy is to lower one's career expectations. By downplaying opportunities for advancement at work, these fathers can focus more on their family life. Two seemingly opposing strategies involve some attention to scheduling and the extent to which fathers are willing to separate or combine their work and family roles. On the one hand, some fathers make a considerable effort to completely divide their work life from their family life. While this involves some restraint in leaving work at work, it is more of a mental strategy. On the other hand, fathers may blur the lines between work and family, bringing work home on a fairly regular basis, in order to reduce their stress levels. This strategy allows fathers to come home a little earlier to spend time with their children while picking up work after bedtime. Some fathers become new dads more through their role at home than at work. Often this involves some adjustments in response to a wife's job. These adjustments may be fairly minor, such as leaving work a few minutes early, but often act to throw off fathers' sense of work-family balance. Finally, I consider whether these strategies are effective. While new dads seek a better work-family balance, they often experience more work-family conflict than either old dads or superdads, and their solutions are only partially effective in helping fathers to increase their time at home.

The Perfect Job

Some fathers have just found a really good fit between their work and family lives. It is not necessarily that they have made major adjustments to their work lives but rather that they find themselves in positions that are amenable to family life. Ross, a 34-year-old school psychologist, is one of those fathers with a family-friendly job. He has had the same job since he finished college and says he cannot see himself being any happier in any other position than he is in his current position. His wife works part-time as a nurse two days a week. They have an 18-month-old son and are in the process of adopting another child. During the school year, a friend watches their son while Ross's wife works, and then his wife watches their son and the friend's child on the days she is not working. During the summer and on breaks, he will stay home with their son when his wife is at work. Ross explained the school schedule:

> My calendar is 195 days, is what I'm contracted to work: 180 days of school attendance and then 15 days of in-services and whatnot. And you typically have to be there for the 180 days that the kids are there. Those other days, they're somewhat flexible. So they allow you to work with your calendar. So it's very fortunate if something comes up health-wise or appointment-wise for my son. I've been able to take my lunch and go.

Being on a school schedule means Ross only works for about nine or ten months during the year. He does not take many of those days off, but he gets the summer and various school breaks and holidays off. In addition, the service days that he works are more flexible than the school days, which means he can take care of their son if he gets sick. While his wife only works part-time, the nature of her job makes it more difficult to take time off when she is scheduled to work. While Ross has not changed his work schedule since his son was born, he takes full advantage of the short hours and work year. Even with the short days, Ross makes an effort to go home for lunch every once in a while on the days when his wife is at home with their son. On the days when his son is in daycare, he often goes to visit him during lunchtime.

Curtis, a 33-year-old firefighter and father of one, works about ten shifts a month. This leaves him with about 20 days, including many weekdays, when he can be home with his son:

I think it's a lot different just because of the job I have. I think it's great to be a parent and be a firefighter. I mean, granted, when I'm gone, I'm gone; I'm not coming home for 24 hours. But when I'm home, I'm home for the entire day, so I get to see him, you know, throughout the day. You know, a lot of people they come, you know—fathers come home, they get home 5, 6 o'clock at night. Just in time to feed their kid, maybe hang out with them for an hour, take a bath, and go to bed. And that's all they get. And then they get up early in the morning and they leave. Whereas I come home, it's 8 in the morning, he's just getting up, you know. I get to feed him breakfast, put him in the jogger, go out for a run, or, you know, have lunch with him, play all afternoon. So I don't know, it's great. And then on my four days—I have four days, like right now—I have four days to hang out with him, so it's cool.

Curtis did not choose to be a firefighter in order to have more time with his son, but he certainly benefits from the family-friendly schedule that comes with his job. And he specifically acknowledges that his job is a great one for parents. It allows him to spend more time with his child than fathers in other, regular jobs.

Garrett, a restaurant manager, also has a job that he considers to be a good fit for his family. While he admits that "most restaurant hours are just crazy," he works in a restaurant that only serves lunch. The restaurant is open from 10:30 to 2:30, but the main rush is more compact, between 11 and 1:30. During this time, he works hard, but the time goes quickly. And the upside is that the restaurant is not open at night or on weekends, leading Garrett to claim, "That's the best restaurant hours you'll ever see." Again, Garrett has not made any adjustments to his work schedule since his son was born, but he knows he already has a really good schedule:

I mean, I don't know how it would be if Brook didn't get off 'til 5 and I didn't get off 'til 6. That would be a whole different scene. But you know, I've always gone in early and gotten off early, so, I mean, it kinda works out better for us than maybe it does for other people. It's been about—I mean, ever since Brayden has been born, that's kind of our schedule. I mean, she would take him and I'd pick him up, and I'd take care of him. And when she gets home, you know, I feed him, and then she'll go bathe him, and you know . . .

Similar to Curtis, Garrett realizes that "other people" do not have the same ease he does, as they generally have to work until 5 or 6 at night. Given his early schedule, Garrett can generally pick up his son in the afternoon and still have a couple of hours alone with him before his wife gets back from work. This flexibility contributes to work-family balance.[4]

Autonomy—A Middle-Class Benefit

While some jobs do not automatically provide family-friendly work schedules, they may include characteristics that are family friendly that new dads would be likely to take advantage of. An important job characteristic when considering work-family balance is autonomy. Fathers who have jobs that offer a good deal of autonomy may use this to arrange better work schedules for themselves. However, autonomy is a trait that is mainly confined to professional occupations. Indeed, higher-status workers have greater flexibility within their jobs than lower-status workers, and this work flexibility can allow fathers to spend more time with their families.[5]

Walter supervises a variety of service employees at a university. When asked to describe what he does, he started talking about working with different types of people and different types of services but had a hard time providing a succinct explanation: "It's a real grab-bag of stuff. I consider it job security. If they ever want to give me a pink slip, I'll just pull out the list of things I did, and they'll probably reconsider because they won't find anybody that does all these different things." He says he does not have a typical day, and that just suits him fine.

I don't have a really hard, ya know, real structured day either. Outside of some regular meetings, I get to kind of choose what I'm going to do when I come in, ya know, what project I'm going to work on. . . . And I have a whole lot of freedom too in that . . . I tend to be . . . I have regular meetings with my VP, but beyond that I'm only going to be in touch with her, ya know, by phone or in person if something really dramatic has come up or it's something in-between that can't really wait for our meeting but it's not really urgent. Then I'll send an email, and we feel comfortable communicating that way. But as far as I do each day, I've got a lot of free time, which comes in handy when it comes to dealing with an 18-month-old and a 5-year-old.

While Walter admits that his current position is not his "dream job," it offers a considerable amount of autonomy. He really enjoys the flexibility in both his daily work tasks and his need to answer to his boss. It means that he has control over what he does and when he does it. As he suggests, this freedom is particularly useful for a father of two preschool children, and he takes advantage of this flexibility when his family needs him. While Walter's official hours are 9 to 5, he does not feel the need to strictly adhere to those hours.

As long as I'm not doing it at a time when I'm really needed at work, then I don't have any regrets about that. But it's just the kind of—"I am going to take off a little early and go pick up Colton, and we're going to go to whatever." And I'm pretty forthright about that. I don't just say, "I've got a meeting off campus; I'm going to go home from there." I mean, I really . . . I tell them what I'm doing, and I always seem to get pretty positive reinforcement. "That's great." "That's so super." I mean, I don't think there's any hostility about that at all. But so it's really me working on me more than anything else. But no, there's no accountability. I mean, frankly, . . . I don't know, I mean, if I just started taking two and three hours off every afternoon, I guess at some point it would come home to roost. I think there would be some . . . I can't imagine that . . . but I guess what I'm saying is not on an everyday basis but on a semiregular basis, I'll show up to work at 9 instead of 8 or 8:30 or leaving at 4, 4:30 instead of 5. I think I'm still able to get my job done and get it done well.

When Walter needs to leave early for a family reason, he is upfront with and feels supported by his employees. Because he is the boss, however, it is unlikely that people would complain. After all, most of the people he supervises are hourly employees who do not have the same autonomy over their work tasks or schedule as he does. Walter makes it clear that he arrives late or leaves early on a fairly regular basis, but he qualifies this schedule flexibility in two ways. First, he thinks it is a reasonable amount of time that he is trimming, 30 minutes to an hour here and there. He questions whether he should be at work "eight or nine hours a day because that's what you're supposed to do." Second, and related, he makes sure that he does his job and successfully accomplishes everything that needs to be done. Walter feels as though he can complete his work in less time than the typical eight- or nine-hour day. Walter also suggests that his ability to spend less time at work, while related to his increased family responsibility, is also a result of a natural progression in his position.

> It had less to do with family, well, for several reasons. . . . Family responsibility certainly had contributed to the amount of time I spend at work, and I'll put it that way—the amount of time I'm here on campus. But it was also I think a natural aspect of my job. If I were to change jobs, then I would think there would be much greater tension because I would just . . . I can't imagine that I would be at a new job that I wouldn't have to devote a lot more time to. So I think that part of it is I've kind of matured in this job.

In other words, having two preschool children is not the only, or perhaps even main, factor that drives him to spend less time at work. Having occupied his current position for ten years, he feels as though he "matured" in his job, meaning he knows how to accomplish things more efficiently. Nevertheless, Walter admits, "I probably am pushing . . . kind of pushing the limits on the amount of flexibility I'm exercising in my job." In addition to his narrower day based on beginning and end times, he often goes home for lunch. As he mentioned, he thinks that coming in late, going home early, or taking long lunches any more than he already does would be a problem. However, it is still not clear whether anyone at his workplace would notice.

Rather, Walter suggests he would not be able to handle being too idle: "I would probably be just kind of . . . ya know, I would be flogging myself, ya know, mentally on that." While Walter enjoys exercising his autonomy, he also is aware of work norms and therefore puts limits on himself, suggesting some external influence on his work habits.[6]

In addition to an institutionalized reduced work schedule, Ross, the school psychologist described earlier, feels a good deal of autonomy in his workday. Here he describes a "professional day":

> It's what's considered a professional day; that's how it's termed. So you put in the work that you need to. Kids are there between 8 and 3, 3:15. The expectation is that you'll be there. And then we schedule meetings. A lot of the meetings—I mean 99 percent of my meetings are with parents in that capacity. So if they need to be there at 7 to go to work, then I'll show up at 7. If they need to stay 'til, you know, 4 and have the meeting, then we have the meeting at 4 and stay 'til whenever. So the days that you come early or stay late—on another day if the kids get out at 3:15, then at 3:15 if you don't have anything going on, you can leave.

This professional day basically means that his employer trusts him to do his work. Similar to Walter, Ross has a fair amount of autonomy in his daily work. In fact, Ross describes his supervisor as a "part-time boss" since he only sees him a couple of times each week. Furthermore, the superintendent is his ultimate boss, but they rarely meet. With little supervision and short days on a regular basis, Ross is able to spend a lot of time at home, especially in the afternoon, when other fathers are still working. As with scheduling flexibility, autonomy contributes to work-family balance.[7] Particularly on days when fathers work fewer hours, they are able to use their greater decision latitude to spend more time with their children.[8] While both Walter and Ross choose to use their autonomy to help them spend more time at home, it is important to point out that autonomy, as with the family-friendly schedules described in the previous section, is a characteristic of the job, not the individual father. And so these new dads are still working within the system that is in place.

Limited Career Expectations

Mothers often change their career aspirations in response to the contrary demands of work and family life.[9] There is less expectation that men will make the same career sacrifices. Yet the fathers I talked with referred to choices, and some saw limiting career advancement as a reasonable option. Several fathers talked about their jobs as utilitarian. They did not define themselves by their work and had limited career expectations. For example, Walter said, "I don't think I've really ever been one of those folks who has felt defined by my work or like that I have to be successful in my job in order to feel like I've had a successful life." These fathers often liked their jobs but admitted they were not in their dream job.

Gary provides an interesting example of how a father's attitude toward his career can affect his work effort. Gary is a 38-year-old service manager for a fitness equipment company. Although he went to school for engineering, his career path has had some twists and turns, leaving him in a job that is completely unrelated to his degree. Gary describes his work environment as "pretty laid-back," which is likely fostered by the absence of a direct supervisor, who is located in another city. While Gary's current schedule is Monday to Friday, 9 to 5:30, he talks about a change in work habits since his son was born:

> Before he was born, I really didn't work a lot more, and it was only to make sure that I got the job done. It wasn't, you know, aspiring to get, you know—I'm not necessarily a ladder climber, not really; that's never been my thing. I haven't done it to get all the recognition and move up in my position. But hey, if it comes with the job, and it certainly should—I mean, you need to do your job and move along with it—but I used to just burn the candle at both ends, and I don't do that anymore. . . . I mean, before I was at home, yeah, you know, I need to go in and work, since I'd been setting my own scheduling. Basically, I was the one making myself work all that time, but now that extra scheduling doesn't happen because I'm being—I need to be at home; I need, you know, I need to spend time with my son.

Gary makes a few important points. First, he used to work longer hours and was more driven to work, sometimes trading home for work on weekends. Since his son was born, he works a more regular schedule, which means fewer hours, and he appreciates time at home, including time with his son and extra sleep. Second, Gary was in control of his own schedule. He was not pushed to work by his employer but rather pushed himself to work those extra hours. Now that he feels a greater need to be at home, he does not schedule any extra hours. Third, Gary contradicts himself when talking about work hours and career advancement. He begins by saying, "I really didn't work a lot more," but then later says, "I used to just burn the candle at both ends." It is likely that he did actually work more hours before his son, but his work ethic and ensuring that the job got done may have masked the change until he thought about it further. He also initially says he is not a "ladder climber" but then admits that moving up should be standard if you are doing your job. While there are some inconsistencies in his story, Gary's diminished motivation for his current work has made him reevaluate his willingness to work late: "There are lots of things that I could do, and I could stay and work every night until, you know, 7 or 8 o'clock, but just, there comes a point where I'm just not willing to do that." While he is willing to work late every now and then, something he did not think much of doing more often in the past, he now insists on drawing a line on the number of hours he is willing to work on a regular basis, and this is prompted by his reduced career ambitions.

Roger, a merchandising manager, also felt more driven in the past but noted a decline in his career ambitions since having children:

> I'll say in the last year or so, I think just in my mind, I settled down a little bit in the sense that, you know—not that I'm—I'm still very ambitious, and I'm on my fourth job at this company in five years. So you know, I'm doing different things, but I don't *have* to absolutely get to this next level by the week after next, like I used to feel that way. I don't know what it is. I've settled down on I guess financial expectations to a degree and those kinda things.

Roger had risen fairly quickly upon joining his workplace but has slowed down and reevaluated his expectations over the past year. Often there is a sense that climbing the career ladder means less time with one's family. It is widely known that more advanced positions are less family friendly.[10] While having a school schedule allows Ross to achieve a nice balance between work and family, his attitude toward his job also helps:

> I love my job and I want to be very good at it, but it's—I don't see myself as a career-centered person. It's definitely a big part of my life, but it's not a job where you say, "Oh, I've gotta put in the extra hours," you know; luckily it's education. You pretty much are guaranteed your job regardless. Now there's an intrinsic motivation to be good, but it's not one of those things where I bring work home with me and I do all these things. I make a conscious effort. I very rarely *ever* bring home work. It doesn't work.

There are two points worth mentioning. First, Ross is not particularly career driven. While he wants to make a good-faith effort, he feels as though he does not need to spend all his attention on work. As mentioned in an earlier section, some of the ease he feels is due to his undemanding schedule. He gets home between 3:30 and 5 at the latest, does not work weekends or summers and does not bring work home. However, a second point is relevant here, and that is that Ross has good job security. In working in the school system for over ten years, Ross has little worry that he will ever be fired. So while he experiences "intrinsic motivation" (and rewards), he also feels quite comfortable walking away at the end of the day. For fathers who have low or reduced career expectations, there may be a slight change in schedule, but it is likely that these fathers simply work a standard schedule, forgoing extra time and effort.

Keeping It Separate

Going back to the ideology of separate spheres, sociologists refer to the public domain of work and the private domain of family. These spheres may be conceptualized in spatial terms, with different physical spaces for work and home.[11] Susan Halford, a British sociologist and codirector of the Work Futures Research Centre at the University of Southampton, suggests that this spatial distinction has been used to maintain separate roles for women and men. As men attempt to add the role of good father, or involved father, to their role of good worker, a paradox is created in which being a good worker means more time at work (and away from home), while being a good father means more time at home (and away from work).[12] Nevertheless, some fathers use this physical separation to emphasize their father role when at home.

Russell's Story

While Russell has been in education his whole career, he has changed jobs twice in the past year. He started out teaching in a private school in New England for about ten years and then spent the next decade coaching at a small southern university, but as he started getting older, he began to reevaluate his choice of career:

> I just couldn't see myself doing it in this environment much longer. I'm 51. I said, "Yeah, I can do it at 50. Can I do it at 55?" And the answer was maybe. Can I do it at 60? Certainly not. Certainly wouldn't be able to do it at 65, but with a young child, I'm not gonna retire. So I had to start thinking about career-wise, something, another career.

For one, coaching college sports is a physically demanding job, one that gets more difficult with age. Russell talked about college coaching as "a six- and a seven-day-a-week job." Even in the off-season, he spent a lot of time on recruitment, both traveling to see recruits and organizing events on campus for recruits. During the season, he said, "It was like, you traveled and played on the weekend, and of course you give the kids a day off. But if it's a weekday, you don't take a day off, you go in to work [laughs]. So I'd go, and you'd have your stretches where there's 15 to 20 days in a row without having a day where you didn't go in at all." Another factor, also related to age, was that Russell did not feel as effective as a coach as the age difference between him and his players grew. Finally, while his older two sons are in middle school and high school, he has a 3-year-old son, too, and this greatly influences his thinking when it comes to career longevity. Given these factors, Russell switched back to teaching temporarily, taking a year to teach at an area high school, and when we talked, he had only been in his new position as dean of students at a private school for a few months. Perhaps because the transition was still new, he often made comparisons between his previous job and his current job: "I don't necessarily have to do much on the weekends, so that's been a huge—that's probably the biggest difference between working at the college and working in the job I have now. There's much more the walk-away factor." Russell still works fairly long hours, estimating 45 to 50 hours per week, and has a fairly rigid schedule, but being able to walk away at the end of the day has changed Russell's attitude toward work. He is more able to leave work in its place at his current job, whereas when he worked at the college, he found it difficult to get away from work. This difficulty probably stemmed from two factors. One was the types of tasks involved in his former job, things that required him to spend a lot of time with students during evening hours. The second factor was that he lived close to campus and found himself going back to work quite a bit, something he avoids doing now, save for special events. He further explained that he consciously makes the effort to leave work at a reasonable time:

> So I'm making that decision, or making sure that while I have a desk full of work, it's now time to go home. You don't stay that extra hour, don't stay 'cause I've got responsibilities that I need to take care of going home. And am I doing the job to the best of my ability? Well, if I stayed an extra hour, I could probably do more of the work and get more done, but it's still gonna be there the next day. Nothing that's gonna change significantly. So yes and no, the job could be done better. But I—I'm not gonna be married to my job.

Russell refuses to let work consume him. Instead he talks about leaving work while he still has "a desk full of work." This suggests that working until his desk is clear would entail working too many hours. He acknowledges that he could get more done at work, but then he also realizes that the work will always be there, and it is up to him to walk away. In the end, he chooses family. By expressing, "I'm not gonna be married to my job," he raises the possibility that people can be so consumed with work that the work becomes their family or spouse. He knows that he wants to spend time at home with his family and that he has to actively make that choice, just as others would make the choice to stay that extra hour at work. While he still finds the balance between work and family difficult, he thinks it is quite a bit easier with his new job:

> That was one of the things that was nice about coming here is I could start new. I could start with a clear separation between work and—between work and family life. . . . And I think the physical separation makes it easier. . . . Now it's like getting in the car and driving over is a physical act that separates me from . . . from—separates the two worlds.

This physical separation between workplace and home allows him to feel as though he is really leaving work. While he sometimes returns to school for evening events, he explains that he is not likely to go back unless he has "an extra good reason." In this way, Russell uses a strategy of separating his work role from his family role.

Walking Away

Many fathers are not able to directly adjust their work schedules in order to spend more time with their children. These fathers use a strategy of mentally separating their work role and their family role. Over and over, I heard fathers talk about leaving work at work. In these conversations, there was a real sense of getting the most out of their time away from work and that that was only really possible if one completely disassociated oneself from work, physically and mentally. Oliver, an operations administrator, talked about this separation: "When I walk out the door, I don't even know I work there. . . . At 5 o'clock, I'm not even thinking about that place; it doesn't cross my mind until I go back in at 8 o'clock the next morning. And that's—that's a good situation for me." For Oliver and other fathers like him, the distinction between work and family was clear. Many of them felt they had no conflict between the two because they separated them so thoroughly. They were able to do this because they had straightforward schedules with typical hours, which meant no nights, no weekends, and no overtime. And they held jobs that allowed them to leave work at work.

Other fathers specifically addressed the issue of bringing work home. They avoid bringing work home as if it might contaminate their home life by having work seep into home. Kenan, a merchandising assistant, separates work and family by leaving work in its appropriate place and does the same for home: "Once I leave work, whatever problem I had is gonna stay at work. I don't ever bring my work home. I don't bring my laptop home and work on anything. I don't do anything about work. I don't do it at home, anything from home. I don't do it at work." This arrangement means that he leaves the physical materials of work (his laptop) and mental issues ("whatever problem") in the workplace. And he makes the same effort not to do anything family related at work. Because he is at a lower level, it is easier to fall back on the idea that he is not expected to take work home:

> [My boss] knows that I'm not gonna take anything home, so I don't think he expects me to, 'cause he knows that I put in—I mean, it's like I usually never take an hour for lunch, and sometimes I don't even take a lunch. I just work through lunch, so I get all my work done. So he knows that I'm working hard, so I'm appreciated. He's like, "Kenan's a hard worker, so he's not gonna take anything home." I mean, so I'm not gonna take anything home.

While Kenan generally does not stay late or take work home, he has limited flexibility with his hours. In his last position with the same company, he worked extra hours Monday through Thursday so that he could work just four hours every Friday. In a sign that his current position is higher up than his previous position, even if at a relatively low level, he says, "I could do that in [my last position], but my job is more—more demanding for me to be there. So I know that, so I don't need to do it." Furthermore, Kenan suggests that at some point he will probably be expected to take work home if he is to advance in his career.

Blurring the Lines

Unlike those fathers who try to keep a rigid separation of work and family, other new dads use the strategy of combining work and family, often by bringing work home. Some sociologists argue that it is no longer tenable to make such clear distinctions between family and work spheres when there is more fluidity and shifting of boundaries.[13] Halford questions this distinction and its consequences for involved fathers: "In a world where paid work and family life remain spatially separated, living out new forms of fatherhood remains more of a hope than a practice (Ranson, 2001). Although relations between the 'good father' and the 'good worker' are intertwined (as they have been in the past) this is on specific terms, underpinned by the spatial separation of home from work."[14] Therefore, new dads who blur the lines between work and family disturb the spatial separation to which Halford refers, potentially encouraging more involved fathering. This is evident in the fact that almost one-half of American workers regularly bring work home.[15]

Henry's Story

Henry went to school for industrial design and recently started a job at a large home-improvement company. After his last employer refused to give him a raise, Henry quickly found a job that he thought "was meant to be." He arrived in a division of managers, and much of their work had been sent out to outside design agencies. In an effort to keep more of the work internal to the company, they hired Henry, who now occupies the sole junior-level design position. This means that the six managers, who each "have a hefty work load," all turn to Henry to get him to do some of their work. This has meant that the first few months in his job were very hectic. Henry married his high school sweetheart during college, and they had a son shortly after he finished college. His wife is a legal secretary who works full-time and is also taking online courses in order to finish her degree. Tired of working for lawyers, she is hoping to transition to a career in human resources. Henry and his wife try to share childcare responsibilities as they manage their hectic schedules. Since she leaves earlier than he does for work, he takes care of their son and brings him to daycare. On the other end, she gets off work earlier and picks up their son on the way home. At night they trade off job and school work with family and childcare tasks:

> We'll eat dinner right when I get home. Then we'll both start work-
> ing. I'll be at the kitchen table working on my computer, and she'll be
> in the office on her computer, and then our son will be in the living
> room playing with his cars. Our living room and kitchen are like one
> big room. So I'm in the same room with our son. He . . . obviously a
> 3-year-old demands attention, and he's really good playing good with
> cars. He's kind of . . . I don't want to say a loner at all, but he's very
> content to play just by himself, even at school. He has friends, but
> he's very content just to stand at a bookshelf and play with cars, and
> at home he's very into cars right now . . . race cars. He covers our cof-
> fee table with his racetrack, and he has about 20 of the quarter-scale
> NASCAR cars, and he's all about that right now. How we're working
> on that is like . . . I'm more of a night person anyway, so if I have to
> stay up late, it's not that big of a deal for me, so she gets . . . we like
> to get her work done, her homework done, because she has a year
> left, so we need to get that done. "You need to focus on that. I don't
> have to work at home." My report . . . they tell me to stop working at
> home, but these projects just have to get done. I have deadlines, and
> if they don't get done, that looks bad on them. They have to get done,
> so that's why I do them. So, I was saying, Christina will get her work
> done. She might get done at 8:30 or 9 o'clock. I'm working in the pro-
> cess . . . working and playing. Carter will sit on my lap, and I have this
> tablet that I can actually draw into the computer. It's called a tablet,
> so he'll kinda sit on my lap, and I'll draw him a racecar in the com-
> puter, and he'll get all excited and stuff. I'll go over and just play with
> him and tickle him and . . . normal stuff. And go from there, and then
> when Christina's done, she'll take him upstairs and get him ready for
> bed and everything. I'll just continue to work until I'm done and meet
> them in bed.

The situation that he and his wife have arranged involves them both working at night (and sometimes on weekends). In order to leave work and get home at a reasonable hour, Henry postpones the work until later at night. In bringing work home, there is an attempt to fit it into the family schedule, which often involves spending time with his son while working. This situation results in blurring the lines between work and family.

Henry feels a lot of pressure to get work done even though he admits that his employer actually told him not to work at home. Part of it is that he has only been at his current workplace for three and a half months, so he would like to make a good impression. But he does not like what he is turning into:

> I'm just trying to make a good impression at work and show them that I have a good work ethic because I know I'm a good father. . . . I can take my work home with me, and I'd rather be at home with my family. I really value my family time. I don't want to say I'm becoming a person I don't like, saying I work all night. I don't like— but there are projects that require—there are more intense projects. I don't have those all the time. If it's one week out of the month, I don't mind. But I don't want to do it all the time. I don't want to be that person.

The first part of this quote highlights his perceived need to show his employer and co-workers that he is a good worker. He already feels that he is a good father and does not need to prove this to anyone. And so work has taken over a good part of his waking hours. He tries to compromise by taking work home with him since this means he still gets to spend some time with his family, and the type of work he does allows him to do it while his son is playing or after he has gone to bed. It should also be noted that he gets his son ready and takes him to daycare in the morning since his wife is gone before their son wakes up. Unfortunately, he finds himself working most nights, and he sees how his work is starting to consume him. He thinks it would be okay if the extra work was only occasional, but doing it all the time is turning him into "that person." He does think that working at home all the time is just a phase, but he must have some sense that it will continue since he also says he would like some kind of credit for the hours he works at home, either comp time or other remuneration, since he has worked so many hours at home. He finds himself wishing he could work *just 45 hours*, something he considers normal (rather than 40). Henry also notes that his late-night work was particularly prominent in the week leading up to our interview because he had missed three days of work a couple of weeks prior and was "kind of cramming three days into two weeks at night." Again, this was partly due to his family since his son was sick for a week and he and his wife each took off two days from work (the third day he himself was sick). Here Henry is a new dad, making efforts to be involved with his son and share childcare with his wife. Yet, as a new dad, Henry has also not made any more permanent changes to his work schedule. Instead, he has responded to the constraints of his work demands by bringing work home and extending his work day with his family.

Bringing Work Home

Other fathers also attempt to manage their work and family schedules by bringing work home. In bringing work home, there is often an attempt to spend more time with kids. This can be accomplished in two ways—fitting in time with kids after coming home from work and before doing work at home later at night or spending time with kids while working at home. Just as Henry tries to incorporate his son into his work time, taking play breaks and showing him daddy's work on the computer, other fathers also try to make their work at home more suited to spending time with their children. Claude, a barber who also manages a few properties, says that he and his son do "homework" together:

> When Trevor comes home, he has a little bit of homework to do, and so I bring out my work and we sit at the kitchen table together, and I say—I just tell him, "I've got my homework, too." And so he does his, you know, little math problems, and of course he can certainly ask me at any point if he gets stuck on a problem. I'm able to help him because I'm right there with him.

Claude is able to organize his time so that he and his son "work" together. He also brings Trevor to work sometimes. On days when school is out, he usually works half a day and takes Trevor to the salon or to his rental properties to clean up or mow a lawn. This combination of work and family is almost necessary for this father since he is the only parent involved in his son's life. The overlap of work and family duties can help fathers achieve a healthier balance between these two domains.[16]

Gary, in contrast, does not want to compromise time with his family. Therefore, he leaves work at a reasonable hour and spends time with his family before continuing to work at home: "When I do have to juggle the two, I usually will just—if I have to do some work at home at night, I usually stay up late, and I make time for being a dad and for being a husband so I spend time with my wife as well." This strategy means that he will work late at night, which then affects his sleep and the way he functions the following day. It also means that the number of hours he spends working is not as affected as his personal balance since he makes up for less time at work by working at home. In other words, as with the other fathers who blur the lines by bringing work home, he still manages to get his work done, but it infringes on family time, personal time, or sleep time. These fathers' "integration of previously separate spheres" means they can have a greater presence in their children's lives. But it also highlights the shifting of home out of its former private space.[17]

Compensating for Lost Time—Darius's Story

Other fathers who have less control over when and where they work sometimes use a strategy that involves trying to make it up to their family. This is the case with Darius, a 42-year-old housing program manager. He has been working in affordable housing for several years, though he started his career at a law firm and took a break from housing to work in the community development department of a bank for a few years. Earlier in his marriage, he had ambitions to make enough money so that his wife could stay home with their two children. However, his passion was for nonprofit work: "Even though it's a lot of work and you don't get really paid a lot, it's a lot more rewarding than some of the other things that I've done. It took me until I'm 40 years old to realize it's not all about making a whole bunch of money and all that kind of stuff. The thing is that I enjoy what I do, and having a positive impact on people's lives is a good thing." For Darius, it is a bit personal as well since he never lived in a house while he was growing up. It was not until he and his wife bought a house together that he fully understood the significance of owning a house, and now he enjoys giving back by helping other people and families achieve home ownership. Nevertheless, his job does not pay enough to support his family. And while Darius had notions of a more traditional arrangement, he might have been a stay-at-home father if not for his wife. Darius's wife is a computer analyst and earns significantly more money than Darius. However, because she wanted to stay home, he says she could not have handled going out to work every day while he was at home with the kids.

With regard to work adjustments, Darius started in housing counseling, which kept him home more when his two children were younger. As a program manager, Darius is more directly involved in building affordable housing, but it also requires a lot more travel than in the past. While his children are now teenagers, Darius tries to minimize the impact of long work hours or travel time on his family:

> I'm trying to stay married. It's tough on my wife when I do have to go overnight. So what I try to do is really get up real early that morning and when the kids are going to school and travel during the day. And I'll get back early evening, middle evening at times, so that I don't spend full nights away. And the beauty of it is that I have a little bit more control of my schedule. And I can tell the people I'm working with what I'm trying to do, and nine out of ten times they're accommodating.

In other words, Darius tries to schedule his travel to have the least negative impact on his family. Over time, Darius has figured out how to please his family as well as his employer. His children have become more active as they have moved into their teenage years, and he wants to be as involved as possible. When he cannot avoid missing one of his children's activities, he tries to make it up to them. For example, he will take a comp day during the week after he has to work on a Saturday: "And those are the days when I really have to make it up to my family because I missed something or couldn't do this or do that. So when it infringes on my time, I try to get it back during the following week." Darius explains that while nonprofit work does not pay a lot, it provides more flexibility than other types of work. In particular, he can build up what is called "comp time." When he works more than 40 hours in a week, he gets the equivalent time back as comp time. For example, if he works 45 hours in one week, he gets 5 hours of comp time. Darius estimates that he earns 10 to 15 hours of comp time each week. While he does not mind working those extra hours, and it is unlikely he could even use the full amount of comp time he has accumulated, he does make an effort to use this time on a fairly regular basis: "I always made a point of actually taking one full day off per month for—either for me, sort of a mental health day, or obviously the kids, the teacher workday or especially for the dentist or doctor's appointments and stuff like that. And to be perfectly honest, there's been a couple times we just played hooky because we just wanted to play around a little bit." Because of this comp time and the lack of flexibility in his wife's work schedule, he is generally the one to stay home when the kids are sick. In fact, he is eager to have an excuse to take off work:

All I need is a reason to take the time off. And my employer knows that. They know how I feel about my family. Nothing comes between them. And besides I have enough comp time built up by working as much as I do that it won't even cause a problem anyway. If it was gonna threaten to snow, the kids are outta school, I'm staying home. And if my kids are sick or whatever, they know that nothing is gonna come between that.

Darius tries to make up for lost family time when he is working long days or traveling, and he emphasizes the positive impact of comp time on his flexibility and availability for his children. Some studies do show that perceived flexibility, even in the face of long hours, can improve work-family balance.[18] For example, a study of IBM employees found that an increase of one point on a perceived flexibility scale had the same effect on work-family balance as a reduction of 11 work hours per week.[19] Nevertheless, Darius still wishes he could work a normal schedule: "I would love to work the normal 9 to 5, come home every day at 6, and do the typical routine. But unfortunately that's not the hand that was dealt, and so we just kinda make the best way of doing it." Darius provides yet another example of a new dad making do with what he has got, working within the system.

Adjustments Related to Wife's Work

Some fathers' work adjustments are in response to a wife's job or career. By the beginning of the 21st century, the dual-earner family was the norm, with both spouses earning income in 70 percent of married couples.[20] In most of these couples, the husband earns more or the husband and wife earn about the same amount. Yet there is a small but growing percentage of couples in which the wife earns more money. Not only has there been an increase in dual-earner couples, but there has also been an increase in the prevalence of dual-career couples.[21] In dual-career couples, both partners are not only earning money through employment but also committed to achieving success in their careers. This often has consequences for the husband's work schedule. Most commonly, fathers take over caring for kids in the morning and/or afternoon while their wife works. Marshall, a college administrator, gets his kids going in the morning while his wife works:

> Both are at an age now where they can get themselves ready. But you know, they still need a drill sergeant to get them outta the door. So you know, with my son, I take him to school and I pick him up. My daughter rides the bus. And you know, typically my wife's working or getting ready to, you know, go out and meet clients and things.

His wife works at home, so she is often available—for example, if he is late in getting home for his daughter's bus—but she also travels a lot. He lives very close to campus and finds it easy to go back and forth to take care of kids or to start dinner or other family/home tasks.

Frank's Story

Frank is a 40-year-old design manager for a home-improvement company. He works in the trend and design department so it should not have surprised me when he asked to take a closer look at my office doorknob.

Although it had been in place for decades in a building that had been converted from an infirmary to offices, Frank assured me that it was a very modern look. Frank came to his current job after taking a break from design in order to earn an MBA, a degree he had hoped would position him to move more into management, though his most recent attempts to move up were not met with success. And so he works 8 to 5:30 at a growing company he hopes will eventually offer him an opportunity to advance in his career. Frank is also married with two young sons. His wife is foreign-born and very successful in her career, two things that attracted him to her. She works for a foreign skincare company with its headquarters in another state, which means she travels 50 percent of the time and works from home the other 50 percent. Frank admits it is not an ideal situation. Because of his wife's high-powered career, Frank is generally the one to make adjustments to his work schedule when a family situation arises. Because his wife travels so much, it affects his work tardiness on a fairly regular basis. He describes the consequences of being responsible for getting his infant son to daycare by 9 and his 4-year-old to another school: "I'm late for work more than half the time. And that isn't good because I'm, ya know, running to daycare, dropping . . . On days that I have to bring both because my wife's out of town—she travels a lot—I'm going to be late for work. I just can't get everybody out, fed, dressed, in the car, dropped off."

While Frank has not officially changed his schedule, the fact that he is solely responsible for getting his kids ready and dropped off means his work schedule is not the same when his wife travels. While the difference in time might only be about 15 minutes on either end, he has noticed some unfavorable responses from his co-workers: "And the others that don't have kids or are single, ya know, they kind of look at you like 'I had to be here at 8, ya know, and you're not.'" Frank infers that other parents might understand when he arrives late or leaves early, while employees without children do not really appreciate the cause of his tardiness. He also suggests that there is a bit of a divide between parents and nonparents: "There's really a difference of those that have children and those that do not in terms of . . . You go out to lunch with colleagues and sometimes talk about kids, and the ones that don't have kids just kind of sit there, and they don't want to hear about it [*laughs*]. So that's a little rift." This further demonstrates the perceived lack of identification that childless employees have with co-workers like Frank who have kids.

It may be co-workers' reactions that make Frank more sensitive to the fact that he was not offered an advanced position for which he recently applied. At various times during our conversation, he wondered aloud whether he could have advanced further without kids. We talked right before Columbus Day, a school holiday that is also a workday, and he anticipated having to take off work. Being completely responsible for his sons causes quite a bit of stress. Here Frank describes a typical day when his wife is gone:

> The mornings are the worst because, ya know, it's . . . getting some food on the table, and it's taking care of Levi, getting him some food and some, ya know, milk, getting everybody all dressed, getting the bottles for daycare, getting everybody's shoes on and everything. So then I'm going to be late. I just can't fit that in. And it doesn't make sense for me to get up at 6; they're not going to be awake anyway. It just doesn't work; I'm going to be late. Then another really bad thing about this, and this is when the kids suffer, I really am supposed to be there until again 5:30, and both schools close really at 6. And so, ya know, maybe I'll leave at 5:20. . . . I sneak out and then go fast as I can to go pick up Sebastian. "Come on, Sebastian." And it's no fun, either. I'm not really fun or engaging to his teachers when "Come on, come on; we got to go pick up Levi." And that's the worst thing is picking up Levi, the little one, ya know, at 5 minutes to 6—one of the last ones there. Sometimes he's actually sleeping, like evening sleeping. . . . He's been there since 7:30. It's 7:30 to, ya know, 6 o'clock. That's just harsh. And that's what, ya know, is the biggest, I think, negative point I could express. So I pick him up, and then it's house to home [*sic*], or sometimes we go out to Chili's or something just to make it easier. And then it's—I have to bathe them, feed them, and put the little one to bed first, and then try to get Sebastian into bed. And it's a lot of stress those nights. And it's often too, so I think the kids suffer a little bit because they're at daycare so long, and then

dad's a little stressed out because there are so many things I've got to do to get them to a certain point, and they start getting tired and whining. And I try to be fun, but I'm not as much fun on those nights as I am other nights.

As he relayed this snapshot of a typical day without his wife, the stress was palpable. Again, the effect on work may be limited, leaving a little early, but his sense of balance is completely thrown off by feeling like he is in overdrive all day. It is the constant rushing to get his sons up and ready, dropping them off, working, leaving early to pick them up, feeling bad they have been in daycare so long, getting them fed and cleaned and ready for bed at night, and trying not to let the stress affect how he interacts with his sons. In summing up his feelings about his responsibilities while his wife is away, he said, "It drives me a bit nuts sometimes because sometimes I feel like I'm a single dad because she travels a lot. . . . So then she'll be out for, ya know, for sometimes four, five days. . . . Then it's all—I'm doing the whole thing. I'm like a single dad when she's gone." To make matters worse, Frank confessed he has pangs of jealousy when his wife travels.

She's been out doing her thing, and ya know, I've been doing my thing. Of course, she's meeting new people and kind of experiencing . . . She's going to go to a big trade show this weekend in Texas. So meeting those people . . . and you go to a trade show and you have dinner and things like that, so you go to restaurants and conversations, and ya know I'm racing to get to daycare at 5 minutes to 6.

While Frank appreciates his wife's financial contribution to their family and supports her career ambitions, he is also cognizant of the fact that she is having fun while he is busy taking care of the kids. Frank sees travel as exciting and would like to be the one to go on trips every once in a while. However, he qualifies this desire to travel: "I wouldn't want to be gone 50 percent of the time because I don't like to spend time [away from] the kids—just every so often." He also knows there are costs when one parent travels, since it leaves the other parent with all the responsibilities.

Temporary Disruptions

Some men's work/family balance is more sporadically affected by their wife's work. Men whose wives have secondary jobs or activities, or whose wives travel for work, find themselves adjusting their own schedules when necessary. Kenan, the merchandising assistant, finds himself adjusting every other week. His wife works a second job in which she cleans an office building. She has split this job with a friend, and so they switch off, with each taking on the job every other week. When it is her week, she goes to the office directly after her first shift job, which leaves Kenan with solo childcare duty:

> I have to leave work at 5 so I can get both of them by 6 because traffic is backed up so much. We get home, you know, I tell them to get out their homework, and we go over homework. . . . Then, okay, after we do homework, we get home about 6:15, 6:30, we do homework; it probably takes us probably like an hour. I start cooking around about 7:30. I might get to finish cooking like 8:30, but then in the meantime while cooking, I will go ahead and give them a bath, let them play. Then about 8:30 then, they will eat, about 9 o'clock we'll read a book, and then they'll go to bed. It usually gets, on those weeks that she works late, they usually get in bed—'cause their bedtime is at 9—they usually get in bed by about 9:15, 9:20.

With this schedule, his wife does not get home until near bedtime every day for a week every other week. While Kenan does not need to make a huge adjustment with his work, he has little flexibility in the afternoon. He feels as though he can get away with not staying late at this point in his career but acknowledges that he might need to stay later at some point in order to advance his career. Right now he appreciates the extra money his wife brings home. But it does mean rushing out of work to pick up his kids and being the one to "take care of everything else" half the time. On the other weeks, he still does quite a bit at home but not everything. When I asked Kenan about balancing work and family, he admitted that his wife's schedule makes it more difficult: "Well, I mean, it's hard, managing work and family, especially like on, like I said, on those weeks that Aaliyah has to—when I have to do everything."

When a partner travels, the disruption is a bit more sporadic but still can have a large impact on men's work/family balance. It often results in men cutting back time at work or trying to cram more into fewer hours. Gary, a service manager, finds himself shortening his work days at both ends when his wife travels:

> I had lots of nights where, nights and mornings she would be gone for three days, and I had to wake him up, get him ready in the morning, get him off to school, go and pick him up. And so the commute in between—so it means I'd get to work late, and I'd get home early, you know. So I'm like slimming down my days, and then I have to work after he goes to bed.

Gary feels guilty because he is getting to work late and leaving work early, but it seems to affect his personal balance more than his actual work time since he finds himself working at night after he has put his son in bed.

Being Involved Dads

Many fathers judge themselves based on what they do when they are at home. Although the total amount of childcare might not be shared equally with their wives, they pride themselves on being equal participants when they are at home. Walter works full-time but makes an effort to share housework and childcare once he is home:

> Typically I can be home by 5:30, 6 at the latest. And at that point, I would say that my role is really equal in terms of, ya know, attention to the kids and playing with them and discipline and so forth. I say equal; I shouldn't say that. Alicia does more of that than I do, but my opinion is that I'm—and I think she would agree—that I'm present and that I'm involved with the kids.

His wife, Alicia, works part-time, so she is home more and takes on a greater share of the childcare tasks. He acknowledges this when he backtracks on his statement about an equal division of tasks, but he also sees himself as a full and equal participant when he is at home. Fathers whose schedule allows them to be home at least some weekdays are more aware of the daily routine. Curtis, the firefighter, talks about sharing duties in more detail:

> I change as many diapers as she does, and you know, I clean the house just as much as she does. And I mean, she kinda has a set schedule as far as, you know, take him out, taking him out for—she takes him out in the jogger like every single day so. And that's basically his mid-morning kinda nap time and get some fresh air. She goes for a walk or jog or whatever and does that with him pretty much every morning. And it's hit or miss whether I go or not, so . . . And then [*long pause*] basically I don't know. When I'm there, the duties are pretty much shared equally, I think.

While making a similar point, Curtis has a schedule that allows his "equal sharing" to be more extensive than Walter's sharing. Some fathers make a direct connection between separating work and family and being involved at home. Roger, the merchandising manager, takes his work seriously but switches gears once he leaves the workplace:

> I'll start as early as you want and probably go as late as you want, but when I'm done, I'm done kinda thing. . . . I'm involved. I'm very involved too when I come home. . . . I mean, I have to say looking back to—I wasn't alive then, but in the '50s, early '60s, what you might say is the more traditional, where the guy did his five days a week and the woman did *everything* else . . . That's definitely never been us. And I never wanted it to be myself. My wife sure wouldn't allow it either, you know.

He specifically does not want a more traditional division of labor. He wants to be involved and do "everything" that his wife does. And his wife wants him to as well.

Darius's view of parenting is also one that is more nontraditional. He prides himself on being "a good father," crediting his mother with helping him to develop housekeeping and childrearing skills:

And that's how my mother reared me, that, you know, in order to be able to be more than just a provider, I needed to be able to take care of my kids. And feeding them, washing clothes, iron their clothes, help them with their homework. To doing whatever there is. It's not so much certain roles that my wife plays versus I play. We are in this together, and I gotta be able to do just as if she wasn't there, and vice versa.

For Darius and other new dads, providing is not their primary role. Rather, part of being a parent entails taking care of their children's daily needs. Perhaps because of the hardships of Darius's childhood as well as the values instilled by his mother, he feels he needs to be prepared for any situation, including the possibility that he is left alone with his children.

Ross also has a more egalitarian view of domestic tasks. It is important to Ross that he and his wife do not model traditional roles for their son: "I don't want him to see like the traditional, 'Well, Dad goes to work, and he comes home, and you don't bother him for a while,' you know, that kinda thing. I'd like him to kinda think that, 'Hey, you know, these are my parents, and they both do things.'" Perhaps because he is a psychologist, he is more aware of the potential effects of gender roles on child development. Ross talks about this in relation to the disciplinary role, saying he and his wife make a conscious effort to share this role and others that have been traditionally assigned to one gender or the other. Ross is also sensitive to the work that goes into caring for a child:

If she is taking care of Owen all day, how on earth could you just come home and put your feet up and do nothing? That would just boggle my mind. 'Cause I know, I've watched, and maybe it's the perspective of—I've taken care of Owen as the sole provider for a day here and a day there and then the whole summer. And I went, "Oh, my god, being a parent is hard." It is waking up and breakfast, and he throws it, and he gets so frustrated, and he never does what you ask him to do—you know, all these things. Well, my day's easy. Going to work is a piece of cake.

He further explains:

When I watch the kids, I know what it's like, so I try to be real cognizant of the fact that it is pretty draining watching one and/or two
kids for a whole day. When I've done it, I can't wait for Kim to get
home, so I can just go and veg out for 20 minutes and just not be hy-
peraware of everything. So I try to ensure that when I get home, I just
go get changed real quick and then say, "Go lay down. Go read."

Because Ross spends so much time with his son and occasionally watching their friends' child, he is attuned to the high demands of the caregiver
role. As such, he considers his wife's need for him, and he makes it a point
to take over for his wife on days when he is working and she is at home all
day. Ross is obviously a highly involved dad, but his advantages come from
his chosen career.

The Unexpected "New" Dad—Clay's Story

Some fathers were new dads without planning to be. When Clay, a media
relations director in stock car racing, walked into my office for his interview,
he started off by telling me that he had a story, handed me a schedule with
all the races he had traveled to with his son, and proceeded to talk at a swift
pace. He wanted to talk about his experience trying to be a new dad in a
race world: "We traveled this many races with Wyatt when he was brand-
spanking new, an infant—that many races, that many weeks, that many hotels, the whole deal." His wife is a newspaper reporter, covering the races.
Given that they both had good jobs, ones that they loved, he wanted to
make things work. This meant that they had to figure out how to continue
in their jobs, which involved traveling four days a week, while raising a baby.
Clay recounts, "He is literally born into a situation where we've all got stuff
going on. And it's not like in our situation, it's not like you go to work in
an office down the street. We go to work in Atlanta, Georgia; Darlington,
South Carolina; Talladega, Alabama; Pocono, Pennsylvania; the town beach,
Florida, the whole deal. I mean, we work—our job is on the road and gone,
you know, so he's born into it." The general practice was for them to leave
on a Thursday and come back on a Monday. Clay realized early that "everything had to be organized; you had to know exactly what everybody was do-

ing every single minute." There were some bumps along the way, most notably with his son getting sick, changes in babysitters, and feeding issues. The first race they took their son to was difficult because they left him with a babysitter in a hotel, and when they called to check in, they were told he was not taking the bottle. So they jumped in their car and worked their way back and forth through traffic so his wife could nurse their son and they could get back for the race. The next race they tried bringing his mother to watch their son. This was not much easier, as his son developed a fever and Clay had to run around town looking for medicine after a 12-hour day at the track. It got to the point where he viewed his work as more relaxing than his "home":

> I'll tell you how stressful it was. It was so stressful that the most relaxing part, the absolute most relaxing part of each of those days, was when I was at the racetrack running around with my tape recorder trying to talk to my drivers and frantically typing to get my quotes and notes and stuff out for the deadline meeting. That was the most relaxing part of the whole deal, which was mad.

His colleagues, and his own mother, told him he was crazy. And, in fact, Clay told me, "You feel like you was beat with a stick, like somebody had absolutely taken a baseball bat and beat you" by the end of the scheduled season. And so Clay and his wife found a good babysitter and packed their bags each week. They spent a lot of time driving to and from races, and they spent a lot of time in hotel rooms. While others saw it as crazy, Clay developed a real sense of pride: "There's a lot of pride in what we're doing. I mean, we're really proud of that. We've made millions of sandwiches on the floor of a hotel room with the lights out so we didn't wake up the baby, you know, and that's what we do. But you're together, and that's the whole point of it: you're together." Clay thinks it would have been harder if one of them had quit to stay home and raise the baby. He feels as though there would have been a distance between them. Instead they were able to be together as a family. However, a few months before we met, there were budget cuts at Clay's company. This has resulted in less travel for him, something that has been integral to his job. At the same time, his wife continues to travel for work, which means he is at home with his son more than he ever thought he would be:

I have always thought I would be the guy—I'd be gone. I just sort of mentally prepared myself to miss a lot, you know, because that's the way it is, you know, and she has always wanted to be with the kid and said, "Okay, well, I'm not going to go, and the heck with this, and I'm going to stay here and be with the kid." And that was perfectly okay with me, and everything's a-okay. Well, now it's like our roles some-how got reversed to where I'm staying home with the kid for four days, and she's gone—like she was gone this weekend for four days, and I'm home with Wyatt for four days, and I never realized how dif-ficult it was being at home with a kid by yourself for four days, to try to keep a 2-and-a-half-year-old occupied and everything, I told them it's the hardest work I've ever done, I was raised on a farm, and it's still the hardest work I have ever done by far, because you are respon-sible for everything, you know, and you look at—everything's a lot different when you're there by yourself, mano a mano, hand-to-hand combat for four days.

Clay loved his job and was used to long hours. He had planned on things being different and is now trying to figure out how to stay home and raise a child. He finds himself a bit frustrated, not only with his "hand-to-hand combat" but also because he misses being at the track. Because the travel is a key part of what he does and because everyone else in his workplace is gone Thursday through Sunday, it means his hours have been reduced substantially, and he is generally at home those four days. He talks about coming to terms with his new role:

It took me a long time to finally realize that you've got to focus on the kid; don't focus on being bitter that you're sitting there on the couch. And I had to work through some bitterness [laughs], you know, because what I worked on professionally, you know, it was gonna be reduced. And you're just like, "uhh," and then you're thinking, "Well, is it gonna come back or not?" you know. And I had made a conscious decision this year, because of those changes and because of those frustrations, to put things in order more on a personal side and say, "Okay, well, to heck with the job. Focus on the kid for four days, okay.

138

And then when you get back to the office on Monday, worry about what happened at the track."

Even though it was not his choice, and he might jump at the chance to go back to his old schedule, he is starting to accept his reduced work role and focus more on his son. For him, it is important to make a "conscious decision" to focus on that time with his son.

Conclusion

New dads are the largest group of dads today. They engage in what many social scientists have labeled involved fathering. As they try to make more time to be involved fathers, they face challenges in balancing work and family. Often, these fathers make small but significant adjustments to their work schedules. Larger visions of keeping work in check seem to have an impact on fathers' strategies, yet these strategies often do not require much change at all. For fathers who have family-friendly jobs, it is a matter of taking advantage of the work schedule already in place. This may mean having the same school hours as one's child or having a lot of nonwork time during the day. Similarly, fathers who experience a good deal of autonomy in their jobs are able to bend their schedules to fit their families better. In both cases, these fathers enjoy a privileged position, one specific to the job rather than the individual. Other fathers adjust their career expectations in a way that allows them to focus more on their families. Several fathers talked about drawing a line in reference to the number of hours they are willing to work. While this attitude prevents these fathers from being overcommitted to their jobs, it often does not result in large changes to one's work. Many of the fathers I talked with use the strategy of mentally separating their work and family lives. This is achieved by refusing to bring work home or even to think about work at home. While a good way of keeping their home life pure, this strategy does not affect their work schedules. In contrast to separating these two domains, other fathers actively seek to blur the lines between work and family. These fathers achieve more family time by doing some of their work at home at night. Some fathers attempt a bit of separation by first spending time with their family and then working after bedtime, while others work while spending time with children, attempting to involve their kids in their work lives. For fathers who are not able to make these kinds of adjustments, one strategy is to minimize the negative impact of work on family. These fathers try to compensate for lost time by taking off work days to spend time with family. What unites all these fathers is their attempt to be involved dads. But while these fathers have strategies for balancing work and family, they are incomplete strategies with limited results. In sum, new dads are the norm, the typical father. Because they are trying to be highly involved with their children while meeting the continued expectations of being a breadwinner, they face a lot of conflict in balancing these two demands. New dads are not less committed to nurturing their children than superdads are, but their efforts to be more involved are only partially effective because they do not challenge the system.

SIX

Superdads

While much of the previous research on fathers and employment finds that fathers work more hours than men without children do, supporting an emphasis on the breadwinner role, there is mounting evidence that the relationship between parenthood and work hours is not so simple.[1] Some studies show that the effect of a first child on a father's work hours has weakened among more recent cohorts of fathers.[2] Other studies show that married fathers do not increase their work hours.[3] Furthermore, other studies show that some groups of fathers, namely, men with continuously employed wives and egalitarian fathers, actually reduce their hours of employment.[4] In fact, a recent report by the Families and Work Institute finds that, in general, men's work hours fell more between 2002 and 2008 than women's work hours did, resulting in a smaller gender gap in work hours.[5]

We already know that lots of fathers experience work-family conflict, and balancing work and family is a challenge for men as well as women. We have seen "old" dads who fit the description of breadwinner, making little adjustment to their work lives and facing little conflict as they align their worker role with their father role. We have also seen "new" dads who struggle quite a bit and make small adjustments to their work lives, often working within the system to take advantage of benefits they already have, such as consolidated schedules or autonomy, or making the most efficient use of their time by separating or blurring their work and family roles.

Now we come to the superdads, those men who make large changes to their work lives in direct response to their role as father. Among their strategies, these fathers quit jobs, change careers, change positions, start their own businesses, adopt flexible work schedules, take on shift work, and work from home. Among couples who are trying to share parenting, flexibility is crucial in choosing jobs, and shared parenting is on the rise, as almost one-half of men and one-third of women report an equal or male-skewed division of childcare.[6] For superdads, shared parenting and greater involvement with their children drive their decisions, especially when it comes to changing jobs and careers. These fathers also make use of workplace flexibility, the most commonly mentioned family-friendly policy.[7] However, flexible scheduling looks quite different for professional fathers compared to working-class fathers. Among fathers with professional occupations, arranging part-time work and flexible start and end times is a good strategy for balancing work and family. On the other hand, shift work is a common strategy among working-class parents as it allows for reduced daycare costs and increased time with children. In fact, 32 percent of American preschoolers with employed mothers are regularly cared for by their father, and this number itself is a notable increase over just the past few years, from a figure of 25 percent in 2005.[8] Finally, while older studies have found that women's but not men's decision to work at home is influenced by their family responsibilities, this may be changing as more men become involved fathers.[9] This chapter focuses on married and cohabiting superdads, while the next chapter focuses on single superdads.

Jacob's Story—Quitting

As soon as I sat down to talk with Jacob, he brought up the fact that he works around his kids' schedules. With two children in elementary school, one of whom attends half-day kindergarten, Jacob generally does not have more than two or three hours at a time to work during the day. As a writer, he has the flexibility to set his own hours and place of work:

I work at home, and I typically work in the morning, take my kids to school in the morning, work, pick my kids up from school, play with my kids. Then my wife comes home. We deal with dinner stuff, put the kids to bed, and then I usually work at night. So I'll work from 8:30 in the morning—usually by the time I get back home, I'll work from 8:30 to 11:15 in the morning, and then I'll work from 9 to 1 a.m. Then I get up and start it all over again.

Jacob uses his flexibility to work at times that are convenient to his family. Jacob has always had a passion for writing and ignored earlier advice to "get a career" and put his "writing on the back burner." Yet he taught English at the high school and college level for many years in order to have a steady income. During this time, Jacob engaged in both teaching and writing "relatively full-time," which meant long hours. However, once kids came along, this double duty "became impossible." For Jacob, it was a matter of juggling multiple roles and coming up short in his role as father. When he realized that he could not manage teaching full-time and writing full-time while also being a good father, he decided to quit his teaching job. In his mind, Jacob chose to be a good father. He is quite deliberate in his ordering of priorities, admitting that his role as father takes precedence over his role as husband. Nevertheless, in choosing writing over teaching, Jacob is also able to follow his passion for a chosen vocation. As with fathers who switch careers or jobs, he took a financial risk to make this change, but found this risk acceptable. Now Jacob schedules his writing around his children so that he writes while they are at school or after they go to bed. This allows him to be involved in their daily routines before and after school to a degree that was not possible before he quit teaching.

While his wife works as an elementary school teacher, Jacob has come to be the primary caregiver for his children. After dropping his kids at school, he can work for a few hours in the morning. However, his son's kindergarten schedule means he is back at the school by 11:30 to pick him up. Even this daily task can remind Jacob of his strong feelings for his kids:

I'll pick my son up at 11:30 like he doesn't know I'm there or thinks I'm not there, and I look at his face, and he's just distraught, about ready to cry. And then he looks at my face, and then all that tension and fear washes away out of his face in an instant. He's happy, a beautiful moment, a kinda thing that you live for in a way. There are always moments in every day where I feel that with my kids. I just adore my kids.

He then has about three hours to feed and play with his son and maybe fit in some work during his son's naptime, before returning once again to the school to pick up his daughter. Jacob spends the rest of the afternoon alone with both children until his wife's arrival between 4 and 5. Jacob enjoys spending time with his children and being a dad. Again, he sees his role as dad as being "extremely high priority." His commitment to parenting also comes out when talking about his parenting style. He has particular views about parenting that he recognizes add to his time commitment. He emphasizes what others have coined "democratic parenting" and what he calls "rational parenting":

[It] is the idea of bringing your kids into a rational discussion process about what the group needs in order to be able to move forward and get things accomplished, while at the same time you're also acknowledging their needs. But they need to recognize where their needs fall in this group, this family. And it works extremely well. It's very time consuming. It also tends to create kids that are very verbal because you are constantly talking to them about things. I don't say, "because I said so." What I say: "I understand that you want to go play in the front yard right now, but it's getting dark, and I'm making dinner, and I can't watch you." You know, you go through a whole explanation of it. And of course then it becomes this discussion [*laughs*], which is maddening. . . . But it's a great way to raise kids because it raises kids who are intelligent and verbal and know how to engage with adults. But it also tends to be highly labor intensive because you aren't taking a short cut to a decision. You take the long way around.

Through democratic parenting, Jacob is able to emphasize the communication skills that are such a big part of his own vocation. But he also knows that it means more time and effort in raising his children. And all this time with his children and effort to balance work and family means that he feels as though he is being pulled in both directions.

Jacob craves uninterrupted time, both for his work, so he can think and write, and with his family, so he can spend time with his kids without thinking about deadlines. In other words, he wants to be able to devote full attention to his work and full attention to his kids. Jacob's goal is to separate work and family more, which he thinks will be possible once his youngest starts school full-time.

> [Working at home] is good because it's flexible and I can pick my kids up from school every day, which I love doing, and spend time with them in the afternoon. But it's difficult because I do work at home, and so it tends to feed my already hyperdeveloped workaholism, and I'll tend to go to work whenever I want. . . . I have a tendency to work whenever I can, which means the kids are occupied, so I can go upstairs and start writing.

But he also tries to combine the two sometimes. He says he can do some "less needy" tasks while his son hangs out with him in his office. But he usually just focuses on his son when he is around. This attention and his choice to work from home is what distinguishes a superdad who admits to having a "hyperdeveloped workaholism" from old dads. While Jacob may enjoy working and feel the drive to work whenever there is a spare moment, he controls these urges and opts to spend his time and attention on his kids. Once his son goes to first grade, he will have an expanded writing schedule and looks forward to keeping his writing focused in one time period and his family the rest of the time.

* * *

Unlike Jacob, Reggie had no immediate backup plan when he quit his job as an electronic technician. Reggie was basically fed up with how his employers were treating him. At the time that he quit, Reggie was the only technician at the factory working second shift. His hours were supposed to be from 2 in the afternoon until 10 at night; but he was regularly called in early or kept late, and he worked every Saturday, making it a six-day workweek. Reggie relayed an instance in which a machine broke right at the time of the shift change, resulting in him getting off work hours late:

> I say, "Well, you know, this machine's down." He'd say, "Well, it broke down right at 10 o'clock, so you need to go fix it." So I'd go and fix the machine, and then my wife would call and say, "What time are you gonna be home?" I say, "I'll be home—I'm due to get off now." Then I'll start working on the machine; the next thing I know, it's 12 o'clock, 1 o'clock in the morning. Then I get home and everybody's asleep. . . . "You hired me from 2 to 10, not whenever you want me to come in." Sometimes they'd call me in at 10 o'clock in the morning, I'd work to 2 o'clock the next morning. And just, I didn't like that. . . . You know, we in financially—in pretty good financial shape. We're not in the best, but we can get just about anything we want. Or go any way we wanna go. You know, it's not like I'm burdened down with bills or anything. And you know, I told him that. I told him today, "I'll go bag groceries," and they didn't believe me for the longest time. . . . And so I left.

For Reggie, the particular job was not as important as having time with his family. His boss did not believe that he would really "go bag groceries," but Reggie saw it as just another job. He had tried to tell his boss that he needed more time at home and church, but his boss was not responsive. Reggie said, "It was wearing me down, and I didn't have no family time, so I let them have it." A few days after he quit, his boss called him to come back to work. Reggie was able to negotiate and change to the first shift with half as many Saturday shifts. As with other superdads, Reggie felt it was important that his boss understood how important his family time was.[10] Now he works 7 to 3, so he is able to spend time with his son after school. His boss also lets him leave for functions at his church.

Luis's Story—Changing Careers

So you don't compare yourself to other fathers?

No, definitely not. I compare myself to what I view as not necessarily the ideal but what my son needs and deserves. That's what I compare myself to, which is more of an idea, not a model from some other person. So I definitely compare myself to that and strive to be that. It's something that I guess I construct on my own.

The most extreme decision a father could make, short of staying home or quitting one's job, was to switch careers. This occurred when a man's career was particularly problematic for family life, and he saw the need and opportunity to change. Luis was a bit unique in that he was constructing not only his own vision of fatherhood but his own family-centered world. He was the only person to completely dismiss my question about balancing work and family:

> I don't seek a balance. A balance is not something that I'm concerned with. My concern is spending as much time as possible with my kids and paying the bills, so that's why I worked real estate. I tried to, you know, just hang out with my family and still, you know, possibly make enough money to pay the bills.

Luis is extremely family centered. In talking about his kids, he said, "They're my life. They're why I do everything I do." He mixes a bit of traditional and egalitarian ideology as he talks about his wife's role and his own: "I don't mind if she works. I just want her to spend enough time with the kids. I want that to be the primary focus, and so do I. That's why I went with real estate, so I could stay home with the kids as well." Like traditional men, Luis wants his wife to be at home with their children as much as possible, and he feels an obligation to provide for his family (e.g., paying the bills). At the same time, Luis possesses a distinctly egalitarian view in his desire to stay home with his children, too. He does not expect only his wife to focus primarily on the kids but expects the same of himself.

Luis has worked in casinos for about eight years. He has been in school on and off since graduating from high school, about 12 years ago. He admits that finishing school has taken longer than expected. In an effort to finish school and move closer toward his career goal, Luis needed to find a job that could pay the bills while providing flexible hours. At the time, the area was experiencing a real estate boom, and so Luis seized the opportunity to switch jobs, allowing himself to make money, go to school, and spend time with his family. Luis describes the change in schedule and the reason for this change:

> My work schedule has changed from the mandatory hours that I worked at the casino to real estate, where I set my own schedule. . . . With respect to my kids, they're the reason I did that. They're the reason I changed my schedule and try to stay home as much as possible. . . . In real estate, you set your own hours. So I definitely stayed home more.

Luis's decision to quit his job at a casino and try real estate was based on spending time with his children. When we talked, he was spending two or three hours each morning with his kids before getting on with the tasks of the day, which included real estate business and studying for the law school entrance exam. Luis's ultimate career goal is to become a lawyer who will be able to make good money and set his own hours, goals tied back to his children. He sees law as a way to become the type of father he wants to be, one who can be there and one who has stable, professional employment. In choosing a law school, his decision-making process has been very much in line with other education and employment decisions as his role as father takes center stage. While there are two accredited law schools in the area, one school only allows full-time students. This would not fit with Luis's other responsibilities: "I'm a working father. I can't work full-time, go to law school full-time, and spend any time with my family." This means that he has one option for law school. He notes that there is a big difference in the ranking of the two schools, but this does not matter: "My goal is not to go to the best school possible and get on with the best firm and work my way up. I want to be home with my kids, so it's not that big of a concern at all to go to such a prestigious school." Luis pictures a future in which he works flexible hours, is financially comfortable, and spends a lot of time with his kids. He thinks the best way to do this is to have his own practice. Again and again, he expressed that his primary goal is not to make money but to spend time with his family. In this sense, he is open to working for a firm as long as it meets his requirements of flexibility.

> I say work for myself because I am assuming that that will be more flexible hours. If I work for a firm that allows me to have time with my family, I won't necessarily need to work for myself. That's just the way I envision it as the most flexible schedule so I can be with my kids, go to his games, go to my daughter's whatever. I want to have more kids.

Through all Luis's decisions about work and school, it is clear that he is thinking about his kids. It is as though he sees the world through dad-tinted glasses.

* * *

Some fathers felt as if they had had enough of their old jobs, and in these cases, the men were almost pushed out of jobs or careers. Charlie, who is in the process of changing careers from hotel management consultant to real estate, came to that point when he realized his travel was keeping him away from his two young daughters for extended periods of time: "It was tough being away. . . . I knew that going into it; however, he said that it would be, you know, two and a half months, and it turned into three and a half to four. . . . And that's one of the reasons I'm in real estate school now, because I want to stay home, you know, and work from home and not do that as much or at all." Charlie did not necessarily blame the structure of consulting for hotels but came to the conclusion that this type of work was not conducive to family life. He no longer wanted to be away from home for months at a time and instead decided to switch careers to one in which he will be able to work from home and therefore be around his daughters more. Blake, now a supermarket manager, came to his decision a little later. After working several years in restaurant management, he decided he was missing his daughter growing up:

> All of a sudden I looked up and said, "Wow, the higher up I get, the more travel, the more nights, the more holidays, the more weekends." And my daughter was . . . she was 6, she was starting first grade or started kindergarten . . . and I just said, "This has gotta go. My wife and my kid have a day job, and I've got this crazy job, and I'm like the roommate that pays the bills, so to speak." I'm really not feeling connected *nearly* to the point that I wanna be. It just wasn't what I was about. So I career transitioned. That was hard financially. And I probably still pay for it a little bit. But it's been awesome, though, as far as all of the things that I can do now and having a regular sleep schedule and, you know, everything else—it's been great. So it's been *well* worth it.

When Blake was working in the restaurant business, he compared his wife to a single mom. He let her down several times and found it difficult to keep his word regarding when he might get home: "As much as you want to keep a commitment, you just couldn't many a time." This meant that he might not get home until 9:30, even after telling his wife he would be home at 6. As with other fathers, Blake's decision had economic repercussions. Still, Blake's only regret is that he did not switch careers sooner. He feels he has escaped the plight of many fathers who look up when their child is grown and say, "Where have I been?" While he admits that time flies, he says, "I can remember that time. I know what we've done for the last five years."

Greg's Story—Changing Positions

Greg met his partner ten days after she gave birth. He recalls how they met at a friend's apartment while he was on a break from college and how they just clicked. As soon as he finished school, they moved in together and have been a family ever since. While his son's biological father used to take him every Sunday, there is currently no regular schedule, and Greg says he cannot remember the last time his son visited his biological father. Greg emphasizes that he himself has been there for his son from the beginning: "I mean, he has grown up with me as dad in the household. And that's the way it's always been." Greg has an egalitarian outlook and is very offhand about the division of labor with his partner:

> We've always shared responsibilities, so I don't want it to seem like she's done more than me or I've done more than her. But in my eyes, it's kind of been an equal thing. Ya know, those duties have just really been shared. I don't think one of us did more than the other—in my opinion. Again, I've dressed him up, bathed him; I mean, it's normal. I guess it's a normal-as-normal-can-be lifestyle.

Greg works in a community organization and is devoted to this kind of work. He talked about how he used to work long hours, either opening or closing the center (and sometimes both) and going in six or seven days a week. But as his son got older and started school, Greg felt as though he was missing out on family time, being at work or in bed whenever his son was home during the week. He describes his choice to switch from one department to another at his workplace:

> My desire to get away from membership was because my little boy at that time had just started school. So six or seven days a week, open to close, just didn't suit the family lifestyle. For me, it was more—I just—with Isaiah starting kindergarten and me not being there either in the morning to see him off to school or at night before he went to bed, I just couldn't deal with it anymore. . . . Truly that decision was based on the fact that Isaiah had started school, and I was

missing him. I was missing, ya know, him starting to grow up in kin-dergarten. I was at work. I was at work when he went to bed. I was at work when he woke up in the morning, I was in bed. So I was missing those things. And again, it was six and seven days a week, so there was no weekend time either. Mom was getting all the joy and the fun, and I was missing it. And I didn't like it, so I made that decision.

Greg was able to find a fulfilling position within his work organization as an after-school director. He took a pay cut in changing positions but said that money was not a factor in his decision. First, he did not grow up with money, so it is generally not a driving force in his decisions. He knows how to get by, how to spend money and save money. Second, his partner makes more money, enough to live comfortably. Therefore, he could base his deci-sion on what kind of work would "suit the family lifestyle."

Besides a four-hour window when he needs to be at work, Greg has quite a bit of flexibility in his schedule:

I pretty much make my hours. After school goes from 2 to 6. I am al-ways going to be there from 2 to 6. Now the flexibility comes in the morning or after 6. Mainly I'm at work between 8 and 9. Isaiah's off to school at 7:40, so he's gone, and I am usually going to work. So the flex-ibility is wonderful because I don't have to be at work at any set time other than the fact that I'm always going to be there between 2 and 6.

Along with his personal change and effort to be more involved in his fam-ily life, Greg feels there has been a shift in attitudes at his workplace, and he talks about himself and his younger co-workers as the new generation:

This new generation, . . . we want to serve our members. We want to serve the community. However, we understand that we have a family life that we cannot neglect. Ya know, it is . . . because it's very easy to get sucked into work. . . . You could spend well over 13, 14 hours and not even realize it because you're just engulfed in what you're doing. But the newer side of the staff that's in our branch, ya know, we know that when it's over, work is over. It's over. . . . You're giving work your all for two hours to ten hours, but when I go home, it's family time. You still have to take care of and nurture your family.

So this new generation of employees wants a better work-family balance. They are passionate about the work they do in the community but also want to be good parents. Given Greg's ability to change positions and the positive work environment, he speaks about his organization with great praise:

> Luckily enough for me, I am at Comcare, because I know a lot of parents—a lot of the parents that I see in our program are in the banking industry, so they spend a lot of time away from their kids. We probably spend more time with their kids than they do, especially during the week. So I could not imagine a better job for a mom or a dad than Comcare because of Comcare's flexibility in their schedule. . . . There's an opportunity somewhat for time for you to spend time with your child while you're at work. And I couldn't imagine working anywhere else.

He continues by noting how the flexibility he has allows him to take off when his son is sick:

> I love having flexibility because nine times out of ten, I'll take . . . I mean, because . . . it's easier for me to leave work, especially when I don't have a meeting in the morning. It's just easier for me to leave than it is for Alexa. . . . So it's just easier for me just to do it. And I have that flexibility. So it's great. Not an issue. Any time he is sick, I'll take him. Unless mom just wants the day off from work, then she'll take off. But nine times out of ten, I'll just take off. It makes more sense.

Now Greg is able to walk his son to the bus stop, meet him for lunch occasionally, check in on him in the after-school program, and take him home when his shift is over. He feels that he is in sync with his son: "And then my little one is in after-school. So now he's there and I'm there, and when I leave at 6, he leaves at 6. So it's nice to be able to spend that time with him and work with him, and then also I'm home to help with homework and to help with dinner and those things. So that's a blessing." Greg has come to the ideal place. He is only really apart from his son while his son is in school. Otherwise, they are both at his workplace together, or they are both at home together.

* * *

Andrew, an underwriter, also changed jobs in order to spend more time with his children. He describes why his current job is the right one for him:

> It's a good job in the fact that you kind of—well, what you should do is when you have kids, you need to kind of rearrange your priorities. I took a step down from management when my wife decided to go back to work. The reason I took the job I did was for the hours. . . . This job—I like this job because to me, money isn't everything. Yeah, I'd like to make more, but what I have to give up isn't worth it. So for where I am and what my needs are, it suits me fine.

Andrew had been in management working 55 to 60 hours per week. When he applied for his current job at a local bank, his employer thought he was overqualified. However, Andrew convinced his boss that he wanted this job and would do well at it. Andrew engaged in a "new type of conversation" before taking the job, one that emphasized his priority on family.[11] Now he is able to stagger the workday with his wife so that he goes in earlier while she takes their daughter to daycare, and then he gets off earlier and picks her up in the afternoon. As a result, he can be the "hands-on father" that he wants to be. It is important to note that Andrew takes full ownership of his decision. He feels strongly that "people make their own decisions for what they want to do." What he wants to do is be there for his daughter, and this meant switching jobs and reducing his work hours so that he could be home more. Greg and Andrew represent a small but significant trend of new fathers with employed wives and/or egalitarian attitudes who decrease their work hours when becoming a parent.[12]

Nik's Story—Self-Employment

After working in the furniture business for several years, Nik started up a moving business. He does mainly local residential moves and specialty-item transportation. He enjoys the work and helping people over short stretches of time. Though there are occasional disputes over broken items, Nik likes that he can avoid long-term entanglements with customers. On the family side, Nik and Lauren had a rocky start. After living together for a couple of years, she got pregnant and he ran off. Nik had been using drugs since he was a teenager, and at the time his addiction took him to "a dark place." With Lauren's help, he made an effort to break his addiction by going through a treatment program, which he still attends. Once clean, Nik and Lauren got married. At the time, Lauren was taking their son, Julian, to a daycare near her work. When Julian turned 2, they found themselves in transition with daycare, so Nik decided to stay at home with his son for a couple of months. At that point, he stopped advertising and limited his business to a few word-of-mouth clients. Now business has picked up a bit more but is still pretty slow, so in between moves, he works on projects at home as they prepare to sell their house and build a new house. His son is in a local daycare, and Nik explains their family schedule:

> Lauren's the main breadwinner now, so her schedule's first. She goes to work, she gets to the bus in the morning, . . . catches the bus at 6:30 in the morning. I get Julian up. I try to wait for her to leave sometimes before I get him up, . . . have him awake and dressed by 7—latest he sleeps is 7 o'clock—have him dressed and ready to go, fed, teeth brushed, trying to potty train, all that kind of stuff in the morning. Then we leave, take him to daycare, and then depending on what I have going on, I need to go to work or I go back home and work, and then pick him up every afternoon. And if I can't pick him up, . . . Lauren is able to get up here. She gets to the early bus, and she's able to get up to where she can get to daycare by 6, and if everything goes out of whack, then I fall off and I go do what I got to do, take care of family.

Lauren works in a bank and earns enough money to support the family. Nik has come to terms with this, apart from a bit of a bruised ego in the beginning, and readily admits that he works around his wife's schedule. His attempts not to disturb her in the morning when she is getting ready to head out to work show his attentiveness to his wife's needs. Nik also accepts the fact that he is the one to drop off and pick up his son. In fact, when things go "out of whack," Nik is the one who drops what he is doing to get his son. He sees his role as being there for his son, which includes keeping his schedule open enough so that he can manage his son's daily routine. He even jokes that there is some gender bending in his household:

Right now I'm more—I'm more the mom, I guess [laughs], because my work, you know—I work when I work, and if something comes up, you know—we know we're going somewhere, she's taking off a week's vacation from work, and we know we're going somewhere, and something comes up for me or somebody asks, I can always turn the job down. My job's easier too, so I'm the floater kind. If the child's sick, she can't miss time at work. I can always pick him up, most of the time.

In addition to taking care of his son in the morning, Nik spends most afternoons playing with his son and making dinner, the "mom" role. Nik also jokes that his wife has a boss, and he has got her as a boss. But Nik seems to have come to a good place in his life. While he used to take every job that came up, he now feels comfortable turning down jobs because of his wife's salary:

We can live off of her salary. We don't like to, and it's tight, but we can live off of her salary. And with me working, it's just a good situation right now. My schedule's so flexible that I don't, you know—before I used to say, "I've got to take this job. I'll do anything for the jobs," you know, gung ho business, and I was, you know—if I had to do three moving jobs in a day, I would just do something, just be making the money, and I was controlled by—I was obsessed. But now that's not as important anymore, least for me. It's not as important for me. I'm happy with myself. I'm content with myself. . . . I know what I can do. I know what I can't do. And I'm happy with myself. And it's become all about us being happy and Julian happy.

Nik schedules jobs so that they fit within the hours his son is at day-care or makes arrangements with his wife to come home early. Because his wife has limited vacation time, the family plans around her, and he will not schedule any work for whatever time period works best for her. Because of this arrangement, he has learned to gain satisfaction from other nonwork tasks, particularly caring for and spending time with his son.

* * *

Maurice, a married father of three young kids, recently started his own business in which he installs fire alarms, security systems, and camera systems. He was motivated to become self-employed so that he could limit his work hours and days. When he worked in construction, he got paid by the hour, and there was a tendency to stretch jobs out to get paid more.

So, you know, now it's like he gives me the whole job, and you get it done. You can get it done in two days, you can get done in two weeks. . . . It's like this past week I finished the two jobs I had, and I've been outta work since Thursday. And I'll go back Monday and, you know, work Monday and probably through Thursday, the end of next week. I just do so much better on my own. . . . And it's just a matter of just doing it, you know; once you've done it, you go home. You get so much done in the day, you go home. You spend time with your family.

Maurice enjoys having control over his time, a family-friendly benefit of self-employment.[13] Since he gets paid by the job rather than by the hour, he can now make more money in less time. Instead of stretching out work or falling under someone else's rules, he can focus on what he needs to do and get it done. Maurice limits his work week to four days: "If it can't get done—to me if it can't get done before Thursday, then you done something wrong, and it'll be there on Monday. It'll be there on Monday." He is also clear about planning his schedule to the hour:

It's like I said: plan your work, work your plan. I know how much time I'm gonna spend on that job today. I know what I wanna get accomplished. I know when I want the thing to end, so you know . . . Granted, I could probably stay there Monday and Tuesday, like two long eight-hour days, and get it all done, but you know, I want to take the kids; I wanna stay at home with them.

Maurice has tailored his work around his children. While he does not drag out jobs, he also is mindful of how long his workday is. With two children in elementary school and one in preschool, he likes to have time to take them to school, to visit their classrooms on occasion, and to hang out with them most afternoons.

Sean's Story—Flexible Working

Sean may be the poster father for flexible working arrangements. He and his wife are both government lawyers. They met in law school, and she was the first to acquire a job in the state office where they currently work. After a bit of persuasion, Sean saw that working for the state might be the best option for a lawyer to work a regular 9-to-5 schedule. In fact, Sean has taken full advantage of the flexible working options. Now with three children under 6, he uses three flex options. First, both he and his wife recently went to a part-time schedule. They each work 30 hours over three and a half days. Second, he and his wife each work one day from home. While they used this option in the past, it has become integral to their work-family arrangement with three young children. Third, he switched his schedule so that he goes in early (6 a.m.) and gets off early (2 p.m.) so that he can work around his kids' schedules. These options allow Sean to structure his work time rather than having a set schedule determined by his employer.[14]

A chart of the couple's schedule is shown in table 6.1. At the same time, they manage three children's schedules. Their oldest son goes to kindergar-

Table 6.1: Sean's and His Wife's Work Schedules

	MONDAY	TUESDAY	WEDNESDAY	THURSDAY	FRIDAY
Him	Off	Work	Works at home	Work	Work (6–10 a.m.)
Her	Work	Off	Work	Works at home	Work (10 a.m.–2 p.m.)

ten from 8:30 to 11:30, their middle son goes to daycare from 8:30 to 2:30, and their baby stays home. Sean walked me through his week:

Mondays I'm off, and my wife has a similar schedule, but she's off on Tuesdays. So Mondays she goes to work. And on that day, I'll have all three kids in the morning. And then I'll take all three kids to kindergarten, drop off the oldest at kindergarten. Then I'll take the middle kid to daycare. And then I'll have the baby with me. And then at 11:30, I'll pick up my eldest, and we'll hang out for a few hours. And then my wife will get home around 3, picking up the middle kid from daycare. So that's my Monday, and I don't have to work at all. Although I'm finding with telecommuting on Wednesdays, I'm not able to get all my hours in, so I'm working a little bit on Mondays, in between the baby's taking a nap and everything. . . . Then on Tuesday, I get up at 5 and leave the house at 5:30 and get to work at 6 and work until 2, pick up my little kid on the way home, and then everyone else is home, and we just hang out. Wednesdays are a little more tricky because I work at home, so Wednesday we're having a sitter, and she's coming at a quarter to 8, and she's going to watch the baby, and I'm going to take my oldest to kindergarten and my middle kid to daycare. And then she's going to be there until 2, and what I'll do is I'll go to a coffee shop with my laptop and work from there. Then I'll pick up my son from kindergarten at 11:30, and what we've been doing—what we did is, once we'll come home, he's old enough now that if I give him an art project or drawing or reading, for probably about an hour and a half, he could be fine. We'll go into my room sometime. We'll tell the babysitter—we won't let the baby know, because once I get home, he'll want me. And we'll hang out, and I'll work a bit. And then my wife comes home at 3, and she'll watch the kids while I finish up working.

And then on Thursday, I go into the office with that same Tuesday schedule, and on Friday, I only have to work four hours to make it 30. And what I do on Friday is I work from 6 to 10, then my wife has taken the kids to school, has the baby, drives into work, meets me out front. We gotta get the baby out of the car. I drive home. She takes my car, which is then home. I get home about 10:30, and I pick up my oldest from kindergarten, hang out with him. And then my wife picks up the middle one from daycare.

It is a complex schedule, and timing is quite important. For example, when Sean goes into the office, he works through lunchtime, eating at his desk, so that he can leave at 2 to pick up his middle son from daycare. At this point, he and his wife only pay for daycare until 2:30, so the schedule is "incredibly tight." But it does allow Sean and his wife to juggle their work and family responsibilities while emphasizing caring for their children, including "rigidly scheduled family responsibilities" such as picking up children and preparing dinner.[15] Because they each have one full day off, they each work from home one day, and they split a half day of work, someone is always home.

Things have worked quite smoothly at Sean's office, with the exception of his immediate supervisor, whom Sean describes as "kinda more old school." Sean says that his supervisor discouraged him from going part-time, and he speculates that his supervisor, who has a stay-at-home wife, could not understand Sean's desire to change his work schedule. Yet flexible work options are quite common among his female colleagues.

Every woman, younger woman, who has had kids in my office have all come back and worked three-quarters time, every single one of them. So when I asked—well, I did not have to ask him; I told him. But there's someone above him that makes that call, a female. I was prepared to have a fight on my hands, because he says he wasn't sure if I was going to be able to, and we both found out, she says, "Oh, sure, no problem." So then I had all these reasons lined up, and I probably would have sued them through my union if they wouldn't have let me, but fortunately I didn't have to do that.

While Sean found little resistance in the end, he acknowledges that prioritizing family could delay his career advancement and affect how his male colleagues view him:

> If I'm branded as a bad worker because I'm doing too much with my family, fine: I'm not going to get fired for it. I'm a lawyer. I have an obligation to court, and I make all my deadlines. I'm going to do a good job, but the family is higher on the priorities right now. I think it's very well documented and well aware in my office and some people that are my age have said, "Well, what if you never make 4 [work level]?" And I say, "Well, I hope I do. I think I deserve." But you know, I have to do what I have to do, not what I want to do. I think I'm a little atypical from the people that I work with, the men that I work with, but I think it's well worth it. My kids are going to grow up having me be there for a lot of important stuff, and I volunteer periodically at kindergarten to help with the kids and go to all the field trips. I'll be the dad that will take them and stuff. Taking them is something I like doing.

He knows other dads outside his workplace also talk about him. He says some friends call him Mr. Mom, and his father thinks he does too many things his wife should be doing. But he does not care. He enjoys the reputation. Sean epitomizes the superdad. He works around his kids' schedules. Sean has plans to go back to work full-time in a couple of years. By that time, his middle child will also be in school, and he will plan on working the early schedule so he can pick up both older sons from school.

* * *

Other fathers reduced their work hours significantly, though perhaps not under the label of part-time work. Vincent, a veterinarian, switched from working in a day practice to working in an emergency practice a couple of hours from his home. While his schedule is not ideal, it allows him to spend more time with his family while making more money than he had in the day practice. Vincent views his choice as a trade-off:

I don't like being that far away from home on a regular basis, but it's a choice. I can do day practice. . . . But that usually involves being gone every Saturday, and especially when the kids were young, it's a lot harder to be gone during the day all the time. And this allows me to be gone for two to four days in a row, but it allows me to be home for long stretches. It allows me to be more present.

Vincent's schedule over a month is to work two days, four days, two days, and then have off a week. On a typical two-day week, he will drive to the animal hospital in the afternoon, work the night shift, sleep there during the next day, work another night shift, and then drive home. This means that he only really misses one full day as he is home most of the day he leaves and most of the day he returns. The four-day work week is the hardest, but in any given month, he has a full week off and two other weeks in which he is home five or six days. When calculated over a month, it is the equivalent of working 24 hours a week. This trade-off allows Vincent to work long shifts a few days a month in order to have more time for his family on other days.[16] Vincent has been unable to find comparable work in his own town, and the emergency night shift pays so much that he is able to work a fraction of the days he would work in a day practice in town. It also allows his wife to continue working part-time, which has kept his family together. Before he took the job as an emergency veterinarian, his wife worked "all the time," and they wound up separating for a few months. Similar to Luis, Vincent wants his wife to spend as much time as possible with their children, and he holds himself accountable as well. While he may be gone for up to four days for work, he is home the rest of the time, and he prides himself on being an involved father.

Cliff, a pilot, changed his schedule so he would avoid being gone for several days in a row and could spend more time at home:

I used to fly three four-day trips—12 days. And I liked that. You'd go out and fly hard for four days and come home and work 12 days a month, and you're off for the rest. But for four full days, you leave at 6 in the morning and then get back about 10 o'clock on the fourth

162

day. That's too long, so I don't do that anymore. You know, you miss too much. . . . It just doesn't work well with kids to be gone four full days a week.

His current schedule guarantees him 11 days off each month. The rest of the days he is on call, but he often gets to stay home for long stretches. And even during busy months, he works less than when he worked the three four-day trips, which is effectively like part-time work. This change in schedule means less pay but allows him "a significant amount of time at home, sometimes an enormous amount of time" that he gets off. He gets to spend lots of time, whole days, with his children under this schedule. All these fathers are quite intentional in choosing a work schedule that allows them to be active in caring for their children.[17]

One thing these fathers all have in common is that they hold professional occupations—lawyer, veterinarian, pilot. As indicated earlier, fathers with higher-status positions tend to have greater access to family-friendly policies including flexible scheduling.[18] Middle-class fathers also engage in more public activities with their children, which is particularly evident in their presence at formal events and involvement in children's school, something Sean, Vincent, and Cliff all take pride in.[19]

Seth's Story—Shift Work

Seth works as a security officer in a department store warehouse. He is a sweet man. There is no other way to put it. He held a smile throughout our interview and laughed frequently. I really enjoyed our conversation as he reminisced about meeting his wife on her front porch and serenading her with a song he had learned when he was 3. They have been together since that moment 20 years ago, and he still likes to surprise her by asking her out on a date every once in a while. He sees the bright side to everything. He talked about struggling financially, living with various parents or in a mobile home, both he and his wife being unemployed at times, and scraping together to pay the bills and buy groceries, but he still had such a positive outlook, emphasizing how fortunate he was to have such a great wife and son. He also really likes his current job because of his schedule and his co-workers, being able to joke around with them. And one thing was clear—Seth lives his life for his family. His decisions about work have been made in an effort to coordinate schedules with his wife so they can take care of their son. When his son was first born, his wife only took two weeks off work, mainly because she was forced to slow down after her caesarian section. Seth had been unemployed and was using a government grant to go to school. So when his wife went back to work on the third shift, they were able to cover childcare themselves:

> So by the time I went to school at 8, she would come home and watch him for a little bit. And then whenever I would get out of college about 12 or so, I'd come home, and she'd sleep a couple hours, and you know . . . So we kind of basically watched after him best we could. We didn't really have much daycare. Had a woman that lived in the mobile-home park right there close to us watched him every now and then, but it wasn't very often.

Seth and his wife were living with his father at the time but did not want to rely on him to watch their newborn as he was gone so often. Along with their tough economic situation, they had to rely almost entirely on themselves. Seth took the third-shift job he has now in order to work around his wife's changing schedule, although his wife has recently become unemployed. Now he works Friday from 4 a.m. to 12 p.m., and Saturday, Sunday, Monday, and Tuesday from 12 a.m. to 8 a.m. He really likes his schedule, which he says "creates" an extra day:

> When I get off of work Tuesday morning at 8 o'clock, I come home, take a nap. I've done got paid for Tuesday. So it's like me having an eight-day pay, eight-day week, because when I get up, I still got all day Tuesday left. And then I get Wednesday and Thursday, and then I come back in on Friday at 4 a.m. So it's like we have an eight-day week, which I like.

Like many other low-income fathers, Seth works a different shift than his wife and takes on a considerable share of childcare duties.[20] He enjoys being at home during the day, especially being there for his son: "Usually when I come home, I go to bed and I get up, and my wife goes and gets him and brings him home or whatever. And you know, by the time he comes home, I'm usually getting up about then. So he knows I'm there just about all the time. I'm there for him for anything he needs." Once his son gets home, the routine is for him to make his son a snack, monitor him while he does homework, watch a little TV together, and play outside together. As previous studies have shown, working-class fathers may not be as publicly visible, interacting with their children in public spaces, as middle-class fathers, but they often arrange their work schedules in a way that creates extended periods of time with their children.[21] While this allows for extended periods of time together, these fathers' lack of financial resources often means this time is spent in home-based activities.[22] Seth feels that the third shift allows him to spend maximum time with his son, and so he feels strongly about *not* changing his shift. The following is an exchange we had about his desire to keep his schedule:

I needed to be on a certain shift so I could work around being with him, and then at another point, I had to change around. That's the reason I'm on third shift now, because I had, you know—I had to work out what I could so I could be with him while Hailey was at school. And now with being on third shift, she's wanting me to get back on second. And I'm like, "Un uh. No." I like my third. I like the way everything's working out right now. It's just fine the way it is. I got no problem with it.

So why does it work so well?

I mean, because while he's at school, I'm asleep. I got no problem with it. . . . And by the time he comes home, you know, I'm well rested. I can play with him. Everything's just hunky-dory.

So and if you went to second shift, it would—

If it went to second shift, I would have to be at work at 4 o'clock. I would have to leave by 3. I would never see my son. That ain't gonna happen. And I can't get the first shift [*laughs*]. First shift I would work from 8 in the morning to 4 in the afternoon. Which means I would be coming home about the time he's getting home from school. And then I would be tired, and just I wouldn't like it. I like it just the way it is.

Seth is very happy with his job and his schedule. He might be hesitant to change things because he has found just the right combination. In the past, he has had various jobs: cleaning, festival work, car sales, a couple of factory jobs, and other security jobs. When he lost one of his factory jobs because the company moved overseas, he got a grant to pay for college. At that time, his wife was working a third-shift job (from 7 at night to 7 in the morning), so when she got home in the morning, he would head off to school. He would come home around noon and let her sleep while he took care of their son. All this shows a pattern of coordinating around their son. Seth has always been around for his son and thinks that is the way it should be. After going to college for data entry, he could not find a job in that area and wound up back in security. He is not particular: "If it's a job, I'll work it." So he views work as a way to pay bills and actively arranges things around his family. For fathers like Seth, commitment to family comes before any vision of ideal work characteristics or individual autonomy.[23]

* * *

Several other fathers work second or third shift in order to coordinate childcare with their wives. Most of these fathers are blue-collar workers and choose shift work because it helps reduce or eliminate daycare costs and allows them to spend more time with their children.[24] This usually involves coordinating schedules with one's partner. For example, Trevor, an electronic technician, and his wife have always worked different shifts to minimize childcare issues. With their first child, he worked second shift and she worked first shift, while with their second child, he worked second shift and she worked third shift:

[With the first son] I was there with him in the morning, and then I'd take him down to my grandmother's house. And I had to be at work at 2 or 3. Then she'd keep him until my wife—I think my wife got off at 3. So he was just down there an hour.

[With the second son] I'm thinking she was on third shift, so she'd get up in the morning and I was with the baby. You know, I'd get up early in the morning. . . . She'd get home at 7 and making breakfast. Then I'd get up with him and, you know, take care of him. And then by sometime— well, she'd be awake by the time I get ready to go to work I believe. Or sometimes I would take him down my grandmother's house. Then when she got up, she would go get him and take a nap or whatever at my grandmother's house. And you know, it worked out pretty good.

Other studies have found that fathers spend more time with their children and take on more childcare responsibilities when their wives work at night.[25] By arranging different shifts, Trevor and his wife were able to take care of their children most of the time, and then they used his grandmother for smaller amounts of time when shifts overlapped or the need arose. Working mainly second shift, Trevor was able to care for his children in the mornings and early afternoon. He was also laid off and out of work for about 18 months at one point. During this time, he took his sons to school, picked them up, and spent lots of time with them. He also cooked and took care of things at home. Fathers who work second or third shift and whose wives work first shift are often responsible for daytime tasks such as the ones Trevor described doing, and couples who work different shifts share household tasks more equitably than those who work the same shift.[26] Trevor's high degree of involvement in household and childcare tasks led his wife to want him to stay home. When he quit his current job recently, she did not want him to go back to work. Meanwhile, she has worked throughout their marriage except for short breaks when each son was born, and they have worked different shifts most of the time. Maurice, the fire/alarm-system installer, also adjusted his schedule to limit childcare costs. With his first child, his wife was working two part-time jobs, and he was working full-time, so his aunt watched their baby. But then he switched to the third shift so he could watch the baby in the morning and then switch off with his wife.

Darryl, an administrative assistant who has worked various jobs in the past, worked various shifts in order to work around his wife's education and work schedule: "When she started going for RN, then we changed a little bit, because that's one of the reasons that I worked at night: to take the kids to school. I would be there when they got home from school, and then I'd go to work." As his first three children got older and went to school, he did not need to work third shift and switched back to first shift. But then when their fourth child was born, his wife worked nights, so she took care of the kids during the day while he was at work, and then he took care of the kids at night while she was at work. They switched again when they had their youngest child. Darryl again worked at night and stayed home with their youngest daughter during the day. He says that they tried bringing her to preschool when she was 3, but it did not suit their schedule very well because he was working at night and would bring the older kids to school when he got home and then have his youngest daughter take a nap while he laid down. So by the time he took her to the daycare, it was nap time. And his daughter did not want to take a nap since she had just woken up. Because of this, he says, "We pretty much scrapped the whole idea" of daycare, and he stayed home with his daughter. Through five children, he and his wife have worked different shifts and traded off childcare. He thinks that different jobs and different shifts have worked for him and his family, but now that his kids are a little older, he prefers his day shift. He specifically changed jobs to day shift so he could go to his kids' activities in the afternoons:

I tried to get back on days because I didn't want to work nights. I wanted to be there, to be able to go to my kids' activities. They were starting to play the different sports in the evenings, and I just wanted to be there and go to the different activities, band concerts and all that. It was part of my motivating factor to try and find a day job. . . . If I combine lunch and break, then I can be off [early]. And their activities don't start until after 3:30 or 4, so that gives me enough time to get to the games and track meets or if they need a dental appointment. So that makes it possible for me to do all that.

His current schedule allows him to leave work in time to be there for all his kids' afternoon and evening activities or to be there for any other needs such as appointments. Darryl provides a good example of how fathers adjust shifts in order to maximize time with their kids. In this way, working-class fathers redefine the notion of "good father" in a way that emphasizes daily care and involvement over breadwinning.[27]

Hector's Story—Working from Home

Hector, a project manager for a technology company, has a thick New York accent and the attitude to go with it. He showed up to our interview in a leather jacket with a cell phone molded to his ear. As he held a couple of side conversations over the phone, I could hear his brusque, no-nonsense business manner. So it made sense when he told me that his daughter describes him as "always the same, always even, no matter what happens." In Hector's case, it is a very calculated demeanor, which he attempts to hold for the sake of his daughter. Hector's wife suffers from depression, and so Hector says, "I try to be there so that I can be a buffer." He does not want his daughter to be exposed to too much of his wife's negativity, so he physically places himself at home as much as possible when his daughter is home: "I worry that, you know, if my daughter gets home at 4 o'clock, I need to be home not too much after that—not that I fear for anything physical or anything like that, but if my wife's having a bad day, it shows. And I don't like my daughter witnessing a lot of negative behavior." Although Hector's wife's mental health problems only became serious in the past few years, he notes that his wife was always a bit immature. When they first had their daughter, Hector described himself as the primary parent. While a family friend cared for their daughter during the day, he was the one to get up at night and feed and change the baby. As a result, he and his daughter developed a bond so tight that he is still the go-to parent. And so now Hector continues to take on the primary responsibility for his daughter's care, arranging his work schedule around her schedule. He takes his daughter, a third grader at the time of our interview, to her bus stop almost every morning and picks her up almost every afternoon. In the rare event he cannot do it, he says that he has to remind his wife to get up and do it. His wife's illness is the motivating force behind his decision to work from home: "I've had to put her away twice. I've had to sit down with psychiatrists and therapists—major issues. That's one of the reasons I got permission to work from home was because I had to watch my kid. I couldn't depend on her for anything at that point." Working at home allows him to get his daughter ready for school, make her breakfast, pack her lunch, and get her on the school bus. Once his daughter is off, he can decide whether to log in from home or drive into work. Working from home also allows Hector to be there for his daughter when school is closed for holidays or teacher workdays. Working from home means that fathers are there for their children in "a more mundane, accessible and flexible way" than working in an office.[28]

According to the National Study of the Changing Workforce, about one-half of companies permit occasional and one-third permit regular telecommuting in which employees work from home.[29] Fewer employees make use of flex-place than are eligible, about 23 percent of male employees, according to the latest numbers from the Bureau of Labor Statistics.[30] Nevertheless, studies show that access to flex-place can improve work-family balance.[31] Hector feels that his workplace is supportive of his efforts to work from home. In fact, working for a computer company means that his workplace is becoming more virtual all the time: "All my managers work from home. Everybody's virtual. There's no real offices in a lot of places. It's just a virtual office." Employees have access to all the information they need to do their job, and supervisors have access to their workers. This is the direction Hector is hoping to take. At the time we talked, he was applying for a 100 percent virtual position within his company.

Conclusion

These superdads are changing the way fathers face work-family challenges. As many fathers do, they claim family as their first priority. However, they go beyond what has become the common situation of new dads to directly confront those challenges by making large, sometimes life-altering, changes to their work lives. They have not stumbled onto family-friendly jobs, nor have they chosen the path of least resistance. Rather, superdads take action to change their careers, jobs, positions, and schedules so that they can be better dads. Their desire to be more involved fathers is the reason and driving force behind their work adjustments. These adjustments are related to type of job and flexibility in work time and place. In this chapter, we saw examples of fathers who quit their jobs, changed careers, changed positions, and became self-employed. All these fathers sought a better work situation, one that allowed them to care for their children. Sometimes this meant extreme strategies such as quitting or changing careers, in which case fathers were able to choose more family-friendly careers. Others stayed in the same line of work but changed positions, negotiating a better schedule and often fewer hours. In the case of self-employment, fathers were able to set their own hours, working around their family's schedule. We also saw examples of fathers using flex-time and flex-place to choose their schedule and workplace. There were class differences in scheduling flexibility, with middle-class fathers having more control over their start and end times and working-class fathers having less control but choosing shift work that would accommodate their wives and children. An important point is that these superdads achieve a better balance between work and family than new dads do. Other studies have found that fathers who are family-centric, more focused on their family than on work, experience less work-family conflict.[32] Superdads may be the new "new" dads. Although all superdads are defined in relation to their reason for making, and the extent of, work changes, those who are not married face special challenges. In the next chapter, I focus on the special case of single superdads.

SEVEN

Single Superdads

The number of single fathers is increasing at a fast rate. Much of the literature on single fathers focuses on nonresidential fathers.[1] However, the growth of residential single fathers also deserves attention. In 1970, there were 400,000 single fathers, while in 2010, the number was up to 2.8 million. Just in the past decade, the number of single-father families has increased by 27 percent.[2] Men now constitute 19 percent of single residential parents.[3] Men are more involved in raising their children and as an extension more interested in custody following divorce.[4] This is paired with changing custody preferences in the judicial system, from one in which judges preferred sole custody and avoided split-week custody to one in which joint physical custody has become more popular, even if remaining a minority arrangement.[5] Perhaps we will see further movement toward joint custody as studies show children in these arrangements experience much higher adjustment scores than those in sole custody.[6]

On the one hand, single residential fathers, almost by definition, are more involved with their children than married fathers are.[7] On the other hand, single fathers spend a little less time than single mothers caring for their children.[8] Nevertheless, there are few differences between single mothers and single fathers in their parenting style, and instead similarities may be created by the heavy demands of single parenting.[9] However, single fathers are less likely to receive child support from their ex-wives.[10] This may create differences in how single fathers and mothers adapt to the competing demands of work and family.[11] In addition, fathers are still seen as breadwinners, which may contribute to the greater work-family strain experienced by single fathers.[12] This may be particularly relevant for single fathers with custody, as custodial fathers identify more with their father role.[13]

Given the increasing importance of balancing work and family roles for men, this chapter focuses on single fathers' attempts to keep their father role central while also providing for their children through their work role. Specifically, I focus on the phenomenon of single superdads, men who prioritize their role as father and change their work lives in order to better balance their time with their children. Single fathers in this study face unique challenges as they attempt to gain custody or raise children on their own. Divorce directly leads to career changes for many of the men going through this process. Other divorced fathers are pushed to change jobs or positions due to the demands of their original job. Single superdads are different from married fathers in both their path to becoming a superdad and their enactment of the role.

Becoming a Superdad through Divorce

Some single superdads were not superdads when they were married. These fathers often took on more traditional provider roles, which meant their involvement in family life was shaped by work rather than the other way around. However, in the process of separating from their wives, these fathers realized they could not sustain their focus on work and be good single dads.

Larry considered himself a "typical father" when he was married. He worked long hours on his way to becoming a crew chief for a race car driver while his wife stayed home with their daughter. However, when they separated just six months after getting married, he was faced with a decision about whether he wanted to be a "one-day-a-week daddy" or a real parent to his 18-month-old daughter:

173

I looked at my life, and I thought, "Okay, I'm at a crossroads here. I can keep going the way I'm going, have all these great things, but I'm not gonna be able to have a relationship or I'm not gonna be able to have my daughter." I can't—you know, with where that would have been taking me, that's—there would be no time for it. I would have been a one-day-a-week daddy, you know, see you when you can, give you a call when you can, and I—it was very simple—I just, in my heart, no, I don't want to. I want to be a parent to this little girl. . . . So I told my company I'm done. I can't go on this—this path.

That was when Larry stepped off his fast-moving path and took a position as a fabricator in order to ensure that he would be there for his daughter, consistent with the child-centered ideals of the couples in Scott Coltrane's book *Family Man*.[14] This allows him to stay in the shop making cars rather than traveling every weekend to the racetrack. It also means he works fewer hours and has more flexibility in his day-to-day schedule. He makes only a fraction of what he estimates a crew chief makes (though it is still "good money"), and he cannot really move up further at work in his current position:

Basically with what I do, you know, I'm soon to be maxed out, you know. I've climbed to the top of the ladder, you know. If I wanted to go any higher in my business, I would have to go back on the road, and that'll never happen, you know, because of what I want to be for my daughter. And that's okay, you know.

Although he sacrificed his career for his daughter, he feels he has made the right choice. He shifted his source of achievement from his work to his daughter. Being at "the top of the ladder" also has its advantages: "I'm very respected in the company and pretty much can do what I need to do for my family, for my daughter. So I got it made. I really do." Larry trades seniority for work-family flexibility, something he acknowledges other fathers in his workplace do not have. As indicated in chapter 6, higher-status employees and "high performers" such as Larry are granted greater access to flexible work arrangements.[15]

Other divorced fathers made big career changes in order to spend more time with their families. Some struggle more than others with this decision, but most if not all feel a great deal of satisfaction in being "a good daddy." Similar to Larry, Todd, a 41-year-old father of three who works in marketing, experienced a transformation when his wife told him she wanted a divorce.

> I didn't know at the time—I knew that I didn't wanna be without the kids, but I didn't know if I could handle three children. My job here is—is a great job. . . . But I travel. It's a demanding job in many ways. And so is raising three kids. And the youngest was still in diapers. She was only 2 years old at the time, or just barely 2. And it took me a couple of weeks thinking about, "Can I do this?" or "Should I just let her have 'em?" She told me how much child support was going to be, and I thought, "I don't make that much money." Um, "Am I doing this for financial reasons? Am I doing it because I think I can be a single dad?" And I finally sorted it out in my own head as to the fact that I really needed the children. And I thought that they needed me as well.

Todd was honest about his doubts, never claiming he knew the answers from the start. His situation was even more difficult because his wife had an affair, and when he confronted her, she had already made plans for a divorce and her future life with her boyfriend and children. She assumed he would simply sign off on the papers and allow her to take the children. Instead of reacting immediately, Todd took a couple of weeks to do some soul searching and decided not to sign the papers. This meant that both he and his wife had to stay in their house (he at night and she during the day) while they were sorting things out, being careful so that neither could be accused of abandonment. However, after two months, his wife came to him and said she wanted to move on with her life. That night she moved to another state with her boyfriend, eventually marrying him. At that point, primary physical custody went to Todd, and he realized he would need to make some changes to his job:

I went in right away to the manager I had at that time and said, "Hey, I'm going through a divorce right now. I really can't travel. I need to be there for my kids." So they were able to change my job because I've been a good employee here for a lot of years, so they were willing to sort of reinvest in me and keep me here and say, "All right, we'll work around that. If you can't travel, or you have to take care of the kids and you need to be at home, you can work from home," at that time. So my job has been very flexible to me.

As did Larry, Todd decided traveling was not compatible with being a single father. He also kept his job and changed his position, benefiting from his long history with the company.

Similar to Larry and Todd, Roy took on more of a traditional role while married and changed jobs once he and his wife separated. While married, Roy and his wife argued about work. They moved from upstate New York to a small city in the South for his job. She went through periods of part-time work and staying at home. While he encouraged her to work, he was dismayed when she worked more and more hours. At the same time, he was offered a promotion that would mean moving back to New York. When she refused to move, he wound up traveling several times a week. He felt as though his wife did not have "the team mentality" needed to keep their family together. His constant traveling and time away from his kids resulted in him being "totally stressed out." Disagreements about how to raise their kids added to the tension over work, and they separated, arranging half custody. Roy then decided that he would need to change jobs:

You think it's hard doing it here. Try to get out of town and get to an appointment on Wednesday, you know, when you've got to drop the kids off at 8, you've got to be somewhere, you can't be anywhere on a flight until noon, so you got to—then you've got to be back by Friday. So I just couldn't do my travel schedule, so I left the company I was with to do it this way. So this is a little more stable.

Again, we see that work-related travel becomes a major obstacle for newly single fathers. Sometimes it is just not possible to coordinate travel for work with being there for children. Roy changed jobs because he found the travel too difficult to manage with his custody schedule. He realized that being a single father meant planning around his custody schedule and maximizing his time with his children. Even though he did not have his kids on Wednesday and Thursday nights, he had problems trying to squeeze all his travel into those two days. Unlike many other married fathers, Roy did not have a cushion in terms of time. If he had to get his children on Friday after school, he could not risk any delay. He considered traveling less, but it was not going to work with the job he had. So he decided it would be easier to change jobs. This initial decision has had longer-term consequences on his career since he thinks of it as leading to a larger change in the way he views his work. Roy sees it as a mental change, one in which he has made a choice to put his kids first. This means that he will do his job, and pretty well as he sees it, but will not push it.

When I first talked to Adam, he told me that being a single father "forces you to be a better parent." Adam has increased his custody from 4 of 14 days when he was first separated to 6 of 14 days and was in the process of negotiating complete 50/50 custody when we talked. Adam never wanted to be a "weekend warrior" but instead wanted to have his two children on school days as well as weekends. He feels that he has proven himself as a responsible parent, that he can do anything a parent needs to do with regard to daily caretaking as well as academic and extracurricular activities. Part of proving himself has involved what he does directly with his kids, but it also meant changing jobs in order to spend more time with them. Adam no longer travels, saying, "I feel that because I'm not traveling I can be a better parent." He feels successful in that his kids are "happy and healthy" when they are with him and that it is his kids' goal as well as his own to have true joint custody.

Whereas Larry and Todd were able to switch positions and remain working for the same company, Roy and Adam, who experienced the same dilemma of trying to reduce or eliminate work travel postdivorce, felt pushed to change jobs. This is actually similar to what many of the women whom sociologist Pamela Stone talked with felt. Stone wanted to understand all the attention given to a seeming trend in professional women quitting their jobs to stay at home and care for their children full-time. While much of the press surrounding this issue focused on women's choice to "opt out" of the work world, Stone found that many working mothers were pushed out by inflexible employers and partners rather than "opting out."[16] While Roy and Adam did not quit their jobs to become stay-at-home dads, they too felt a sense of being pushed out of their jobs. When they could not figure out how to reduce their travel and hours within their jobs, they took the step of finding new jobs that would better accommodate their children's needs.

While these fathers did not necessarily hold an egalitarian outlook toward childrearing while married, the possibility of losing their children altogether created an awareness of their responsibility as a father. This meant that work decisions could no longer be separated from family decisions. And so these fathers experienced a transformation to being superdads.

Becoming a Superdad to Be Near Children

Some fathers made decisions about work based on being physically close to their children. Bruce, a 34-year-old producer, learned that the show he was working on was going to be canceled the same week his wife told him she wanted a divorce. Before that, he had been offered another job with the same network in another state. As Bruce puts it, his career and marriage fell apart in a matter of a few days. Without much thought, Bruce turned down the position and went freelance in order to stay in the same town as his daughter and share custody with his ex-wife:

> I would have not in a million years—I am not gonna live someplace different than where my daughter is. And I've said since the beginning, since this happened, that if Stacey remarries and moves someplace, then that's where I'm moving too. Because I am going to be where my daughter is, come hell or high water. . . . I mean, I know guys who have kids in New York and in a different state, but how can you not be there? I mean, this is your kid. This is more important than your job. This is more important.

Bruce said he would be "sick to death" without his daughter, a common psychological response of fathers to the potential loss of children following divorce.[17] Furthermore, Bruce seems to think decisions about residential location are more in his ex-wife's control, and yet he shows no signs that this bothers him. In Bruce's case, his feelings of powerlessness may have been exacerbated by the fact that his divorce was "kinda outta left field," imposed on him rather than chosen. Now his focus is on being near his daughter regardless of what this means for his career.

For those fathers who were not awarded custody, changing jobs could mean the difference between seeing one's children weekly versus monthly. Justin, a 48-year-old divorced father and mechanical engineer by training, sacrificed his career in order to be near his children. After ten years of marriage, with two young children, Justin's wife left him. Their initial separation agreement gave her primary custody and him two evenings during the week, every Saturday, and every other weekend. However, soon after the divorce, his wife accepted a job in a town about two hours from their home and moved with their children. He told me his reaction: "And alls I could think—man, my heart just sunk into my stomach, and I said, 'My goodness, I'll never see the kids.'" At that point, Justin went to court, but the judge granted custody to his ex-wife while giving him visitation every other weekend: "Going from every other day, I saw those kids every other day and had them every other weekend, the whole weekend, to seeing them every two weeks." This change in custody and location of his children transformed Justin's view of work and family. He spent two years waiting for the transfer that would locate him in the same town as his children. During this time, he passed over other jobs and promotions.

As soon as Samantha was able to move up there, I put in for a transfer at, okay—and they told me, "Look, we have plans for you down here. We want to get you into engineering and get you high up. You could be a district manager. There's a lot of things you could do here. You're educated, you know how to deal with people, you have an engineering degree. We're looking for people like you who can excel." And so I said, "Well, I gotta do what's right. I wanna be with my kids." So I put in for this transfer.

Justin's request to transfer was delayed as the company waited for an opening in the desired office. In the meantime, he was offered other positions that involved moving up in the company. Justin's supervisors were operating under assumptions of Rosabeth Moss Kanter's "masculine ethic" that connects masculinity not only with providing but also climbing the workplace hierarchy. This "masculine ethic" suggests that men will push aside their personal issues in order to focus on work.[18] As such, Justin's supervisors did not fully take him seriously when he said he wanted to transfer but instead kept pushing other opportunities, with the assumption that a man with his education and skills would want to pursue career advancement. Yet Justin continued to turn down other positions so he could get the transfer request. When the transfer finally came through, it involved selling natural gas rather than using his skills as an engineer. Now Justin works at a lower tier than he might have, in a small office at a job that is a bit removed from his original occupation.

> I ended up not being at the corporate office. I ended up not going that route and ended up going far away, kind of out of their reach now, in a small little district where there's only like eight people in the office. We're kind of way out there. So, you know, if you're not under the radar, they're not gonna see what you do and stuff like that so. But it doesn't matter to me, as long as I'm with my kids.

Since moving, he has been able to increase the amount of custody he has and sees his children much more frequently. He also works long hours on the days he does not have his children so that he can leave early or take off the day when he does have custody, a common strategy for other divorced fathers with partial custody. Indeed, Justin displays the most important characteristic of a superdad: "My life, as you can tell, revolves around seeing my kids. My job revolves around—was chosen so I could see my kids." He is in the process of seeking shared custody with his ex-wife and hopes that all his efforts to be close to his children will be taken into account in the custody decision.

Letting Your Inner Superdad Shine Through

While less common, other single superdads were already on the path to becoming superdads or were superdads before getting divorced. These fathers were already making adjustments to their work schedules before their marriages dissolved. Martin, who has full custody, was very involved when he was married and always considered his children when making work decisions. Before children, he had a series of odd jobs, but he took his current job working in a hospital pharmacy in order to get health insurance for his children. When he and his wife separated and she became addicted to pain medication, Martin responded to his children's needs even more.[19] Even within this job, he has arranged his shifts according to what would be best for his children:

> Up until a month ago, I worked third shift all my daughter's life. Which gave me a lot of free time and flexibility during the day. Which really made life hard. It was hard on marriage. But it was better for the kids and better financially, and which gave me a lot of flexibility, like I said, to be home with them if they were sick or anything like that. But recently it's been a little bit harder since my daughter started kindergarten. That third shift wasn't working out because I would have to sleep while she was at school, and then—and I would only see them for a couple of hours after school. So I had to switch to a first-shift job, a daytime job. And my son is in daycare, and my daughter is in kindergarten. I'm still getting used to that balance of things, but structurally it is much better right now. It is so much better that I'm with them every night to feed them and give them baths and read to them. It's just much easier for everybody mentally, I think.

It is clear that Martin took his job and then changed shifts in an effort to do what he thought would be best for his children. He admits that his job at the hospital is not his "dream job," but he needs it. This is part of the strategy that single fathers follow in order to maintain stable work while also having enough time to take care of their children.[20]

Getting Custody

Many single fathers think that child custody decisions favor mothers, with greater emphasis being placed on gender rather than the best interests of the child(ren), and there is a general sense that American society is more supportive of single mothers than single fathers.[21] Justin was one father who thought he "didn't have a chance" when it came to custody. As mentioned earlier, his ex-wife moved their children to a town two hours away from their home, leaving Justin with limited visitation. When I asked whether he had tried to gain joint or primary custody, he responded,

No way I'd try that. The courts aren't going to give me primary custody.

Why?

Because the children are not in danger. There's no—there's no reason why I should get custody because the mom is not showing any neglect, any negative effects on the children. So there's no reason why they would ever give me custody.

He further speculated that being an engineer with a 9-to-5 job put him at a disadvantage compared to his wife, who worked part-time as a doctor and still made more money. Justin's fears echo the concerns of other single fathers about the general cultural insensitivity to single fathers who want to raise their children and the perceived antimale bias in child custody hearings.[22] There may, in fact, be bias among judges in custody settlements, with a preference toward maternal custody.[23] Bruce, the independent producer, was a bit more optimistic about his chances initially, only to be discouraged by lawyers:

I would have thought that I would get, having never experienced divorce before or any of the typical legalisms of it—I would have expected 50/50. I'm every bit as much her parent as her mother is, so I would have expected, "You get her half the time. I get her half the time." At the outset, she said, "This is my plan for how often you'll see Savannah." And at first I was not happy with that at all. I was very much considering, going for, in the court, half. And my lawyer told me, he says, "Well, you can do that if you want to, but that might be a gamble. You might end up with less than what she is offering." He basically told me, "You're getting a pretty good deal here. You might want to just think about taking it." And so I did.

While initially expecting joint custody, Bruce wound up with the deal his ex-wife offered, which was 5 of 14 days. His lawyer, thinking the standard was closer to every other weekend, persuaded him not to challenge his ex-wife in court. It is important to note Bruce's contention that he is "every bit as much her parent as her mother." Previous studies of single fathers' attitudes show that they tend to agree that children need their mothers as much as their fathers but disagree that children need their mothers *more* than their fathers.[24] Larry, the fabricator, also made it clear that he felt strongly that children should have both parents in their life. In talking with him, similar themes about parental importance and lawyers' input came up:

> I was told that, you know, you're underhanded just going in, and I said, "Why?" Said, "'Cause you're a man, and she's a woman, and you have a daughter, you know. The general consensus is the daughter needs to be with her mother, and her mother needs to make decisions," you know. So little things like that, I just feel like, you know, that because of a lot of deadbeat dads that there's a lot of men that don't have respect of what they are. And we're equal, you know: a mother's no more important than a father, and a father's no more important than a mother, but make it equal. Don't—don't disregard the father, you know.

Larry and his wife had several problems going into their marriage. They met while she was still married, and when she got pregnant, he felt he should do the right thing and marry her, though they had to wait until her divorce was official. Just months into their own marriage, they started experiencing problems, including his wife's unfaithfulness. Perhaps because of the guilt from this affair and the notion that he would not want half custody, Larry's wife offered joint physical and legal custody. Though Larry was not completely confident in his ability to care for his daughter on his own, he jumped at this opportunity, never regretting his decision. He also has no doubts that the custody should be shared rather than primarily his. Even given their rocky relationship, Larry admits his ex-wife is a good mother and thinks it is important that they split custody.

Roy, the father who changed jobs in order to avoid travel and works from home once a week, was more active in gaining shared custody:

I said, "Look, all I'm expecting is this: I want 50/50 custody of the kids. There's no reason why I think you should have more than I should. . . . If it's not at least 50/50 to me, I go to the mat." I said, "We go into World War III." I said, "I'm not dealing with 'I'm the father, so I don't get it.'" I said, "I'll fight for more if you take me to the mat, and you know, who knows what happens." But it just isn't in the guy's favor. It just isn't, you know. No one's telling you, you know—no one ever says, "Hey, you'll get 60/40." They usually will say, "You could get 50/50," so to me it was 50/50's fair.

Even though he realized custody battles are generally not in the father's favor and did not expect to get any more than 50/50, he was willing to fight for an even split and threatened to ask for primary custody if pushed. While his wife wavered a little, and he speculated this was based on the fact that she could get more money with more custody, they came to an agreement relatively quickly.

Some fathers continue to face legal challenges as they attempt to gain more custody or hold on to the custody they have. Adam, the father who worked his way from 4 of 14 to 6 of 14 days, is hoping to move officially to 50/50. His two sons have been asking to spend more time with him, and he has unofficially taken more time; but he wants to get a written agreement to ensure this arrangement remains:

My kids have expressed for a year now that they want it to be 50/50. We have maintained a 50/50 agreement both legally and physically to this point. And that's part of the agreement, and the other part had the kids legally staying with their mom. But I think that will need to change. I have proven to myself that I can keep kids. Whether it be academic or extracurricular or maintenance, I have managed to do it. And the kids are happy and healthy when they are around me, and they have asked for more time. I've even changed jobs to be able to spend more time with them. Both the kids' goals and my goals are to make it a true joint custody.

Adam is a scout leader, and as his sons have become more involved in scouts, he has arranged his schedule to be more involved, too. When his sons started eating dinner and getting ready at his place before meetings and fixing uniforms at his place after meetings, it seemed pointless to take them back to their mother's place on scout nights. Based on his actions since the divorce, Adam feels that assumptions about fathers and best interests of children have not played out in his case, as he has proven that spending time with him is in his sons' best interests. Adam went so far as to express that he would love having his sons full-time, but he thinks that sole custody for either parent would be unfair to his sons.

For single fathers with a greater share of custody, there are often lingering fears about custody challenges from their ex-wives. Todd, the father of three who wound up with primary physical custody when his wife left with another man, is concerned that his ex-wife is plotting to take his children away:

I slowly, and by my attorney's advice, let her have more and more time with the kids. She picks 'em up now every day after school, sees them every other weekend, spends a lot more time with them—*much*, much more time with them than she ever has, probably pretty close to 50 percent of their waking hours are spent with her now. And I had actually agreed once to say, "Well, let's just put this into writing, that we'll continue what we're doing now." And she said that wasn't enough still, so that's when our negotiations broke down this summer and we decided to go to court. So I think that my six years of having done very well with the kids, having for the most part: good grades, seeing their same friends, living in the same house, going to the same church—I mean, everything's been very stable in their lives—that I oughta get some credit for having done that and not have the kids be yanked away from me.

While Todd has welcomed his ex-wife's involvement with his kids, he does not want to lose custody. After moving around quite a bit over the past few years, including moves to other states, his ex-wife appears to have settled down not too far from their home. However, Todd has his doubts that she will stay in the area permanently. For one, her current husband still lives and works in a neighboring state. She also has maintained her out-of-state driver's license and car registration. With an unstable job history and rental status, it seems clear that she would not be given full custody of the children. Yet fears of bias against fathers and an unwarranted Department of Social Services visit around the time his ex-wife said she wanted to challenge his custody have left Todd in an uncomfortable position.

Making It All Work

While these single superdads try to balance their roles as worker and father through changing jobs, positions, and schedules, they also find a need to juggle daily schedules. The need for daily management of work and family schedules is more critical for single fathers than for married fathers. Some fathers arrange to work from home on certain custodial days. Roy, the regional manager who changed jobs, talks about how he arranges his schedule around his time with his children:

> You just start planning your week around knowing you don't have a lot of morning flexibility and you got to get back, so you got to know that on Mondays and Tuesdays are tough days because I have both—bookends on both sides. So that's why I do the Tuesdays at home. So I know in the morning I can get them up, get them dressed, get them off to school, go back to my house, which is only a couple of minutes away. And then I'm still there, so I can pick them up after school.

Roy picks his children up from school on Monday and drops them at school on Wednesday, and his ex-wife picks them up from school on Wednesday and drops them at school on Friday. They alternate weekends. By working from home on the full day he has his children, Roy is actually able to get more work done since he is not spending his time driving to and from work. Eliminating commuter time is a commonly described benefit of working from home.[25] Roy is also able to get more done around the house when he works at home:

> I get more out of my workday 'cause I'm not driving an hour on both ends. It's a two-hour commute for me, so now I save two hours. And I'm on the phone doing laundry. I'm doing all that stuff at home. So today I've emptied the dishwasher, I cleaned up from Halloween last night, I got all their costumes, put them in the bags while I'm on conference calls and doing—talking to my reps. I'm walking around throwing loads of laundry in and sweeping up the floor. So I get a lot done on Tuesdays.

Along with routine parental tasks, such as taking kids to school, working from home allows fathers to accomplish household tasks.[26]

Unlike other fathers who leave the bulk of caregiving to mothers, single fathers have no other option but to provide daily care for their children. They are generally on their own in attempting to balance work and family, and this can become problematic when children have appointments, become sick, or have school holidays. Larry, the fabricator, told me that his daughter's needs affect his vacation time:

> My vacation time is pretty much dedicated to Rebekah. I get three weeks a year but actually physically tangible to use at my discretion two weeks and two days 'cause we have to take three of our days and use them for the week we have off for Christmas. So therefore, excuse me, I take Rebekah on vacation one week out of the year. That's her—we've done Disney World, we do the beach, you know, things like that. And the other week are pretty much saved for her days, you know. I have to take a day off 'cause she's got a doctor's appointment or snow days or whatever. I mean, her mom can help me out and stuff, but I don't feel comfortable—daddy going to the Bahamas or Jamaica or something like that—because I need to save that little cushion of one week.

As a single father, Larry plans all his vacation time around his daughter. He thinks it is important to take her on vacation, but he also uses vacation days for any of her other needs. While he can plan some days, such as appointments and school holidays, he also likes to be prepared for unplanned events, such as snow days. Other single fathers talk about the impact that sick children have on their work schedule. For example, Roy talks about improvising when one of his children gets sick and he cannot get out of a work obligation:

> I have a rep up in Jonestown, big meeting I've got to present at, okay. Kids are with me. Kids get sick when with dad. Dad's gotta deal with it. . . . I throw his butt in the car with a, you know, with a plug-in TV, and he drives to Jonestown with me, and he sits in the back of the room [*laughs*], and this is how we do it.

While he sees the positive aspects of spending time with his son and his son seeing him work, Roy suggests that his flexibility is more limited than his female colleagues'. He thinks that it is not as acceptable for him to miss a meeting for a sick child. And it turns out that working around sick children is a common theme for single fathers. Adam also talked about being able to quickly adapt when the kids are with him: "When I have custody and they get sick, everything has to stop because I have no one to turn to. So when Jake got sick—he got strep—I have to take off from work and take him to the doctor. I tried to do some email from home. So my schedule changes when I have the kids." Furthermore, having a workplace that allows flexibility, especially in making arrangements with sick children, is a big reason some fathers stay in their jobs.

> For some reason, I can't leave this place. But, I mean, if you think about it, it's flexible enough to where you can take days off if you have sick kids and then still take days to go backpacking for yourself. Especially as a single parent, that is invaluable. You could make more money other places, but the cost emotionally trying to figure out what to do with your kids would be unbearable. (Adam)

I have had offers for more money to go to other companies, and I have turned them down just because of the fact that I know that if I'm working and Rebekah calls me and she don't feel good—"I got a tummy ache" or "I want this or that" or "I need to do this"—I can go do it. (Larry)

Both Adam and Larry mention that they could make more money in other jobs, but the flexibility in their current jobs is seen as invaluable, particularly because they are single parents. Knowing that they can take off when their child is sick allows them peace of mind.

Satisfaction with Work Changes

For the most part, single fathers who have chosen to make work sacrifices are satisfied with this decision.

It wasn't a struggle. I think it was a struggle with pride thing more so than the want of the money, you know, because, you know, of course, we all want to have a sense of achievement, you know. And I had to let go of that sense of achievement somewhat, but I think it was very equally replaced with the sense of achievement that I have now knowing that I'm a good daddy, you know. I take big pride in that. I really do. (Larry)

And sometimes I think, you know, "Where could I have been if I were single or let mom have primary custody of the kids? I could have really climbed the corporate ladder a lot more and been somebody." Then I think, "You know, I've got something that my manager doesn't have. I've got three kids who love me and have promised when I get old and I'm in a wheelchair drooling on myself, that they're gonna wipe up my spit for me" [laughs]. But they're gonna take care of me, and I wouldn't trade, you know, what I've lost—what I suspect that I may have lost here at work because I didn't take all the trips that I could have taken and, you know, bypassed some opportunities that may have been good for my career. I think that it's gonna pay off in the long term. . . . I've got something a lot of other people don't. I've got three *really* great kids. And that's helped. (Todd)

Both Larry and Todd are content with their decisions but acknowledge that there is a trade-off. For Larry, the trade-off is a sense of pride and achievement that he might have gained from work being replaced by a new sense of pride in being a "good daddy." Larry's crew work in the male-dominated racing world provided a higher source of achievement, one that might have reached its pinnacle with advancement to crew chief, than his more backstage work building race cars. Todd also speculates about how far he could have gone in his career and refers to lost opportunities. Yet, as with Larry, he comes back to a different "payoff," that of raising children. Here Larry and Todd specifically reject the "masculine ethic," choosing to emphasize their children's emotional needs above their own career goals. In this sense, single dads may construct masculine identity in a way that highlights their sense of achievement from being good dads, which fills a gap that is typically occupied by men's work achievements and identity.

While Roy is ultimately happy about his decision to change jobs and rearrange his schedule around his kids' schedule, he also notes that this situation creates some tension.

I've already taken a big career hit to do this, but that's a decision I made. I'm happy about it, and I've mentally said, "Look, you know, I brought these kids in the world, you know. This is about—it's about them now." So and I'm good with my job, but I'm not pressing the envelope like I used to.

Roy feels he should get more done at work, but he also acknowledges that he made a decision to put his kids first. Again, it appears as though he is not gaining as much accomplishment from his work because he is not going beyond the minimum requirements. Similar to other fathers, Adam, the project manager who changed jobs, says he is a "better parent" because of the changes he has made at work, but Adam also expresses more dissatisfaction than other fathers.

> I feel trapped. I feel like I went off and got a degree, and now I am a cash cow. And I don't feel like I can change my life. I have to say that I have been sentenced to this obligation, so it's almost like you're in prison professionally or somewhat emotionally until the kids grow up. . . . I can't really change anything. And that is exceptionally frustrating. . . . And that's a sad place to be in, to have to make yourself enjoy what you're doing.

Adam has considered his options carefully. One option would be to progress in his current career, which would allow him to be more fulfilled professionally. However, this would involve moving and/or travel, two changes he is unwilling to make because they might compromise his custody arrangements. Another option would be to change careers to teaching, a strong interest of his. However, this would involve a pay cut, which he could not sustain given his child-support obligations. Therefore, Adam feels trapped, unable to make changes to his career that would be self-satisfying but problematic for his family. The constant fulfillment of the worker and parent roles can take a toll.

> Marathon Monday is when I'm in the middle of my five-day period. And for me, you get up in the morning, and you're running until you lay down at night. And you don't have time to sit down and watch TV or read a book. You're just doing what needs to be done. (Adam)

> I mean, there isn't a day that goes by that I'm not either (a) working or (b) parenting. There's almost never a day when I'm not doing one or the other. So, that said, I'm like 34 years old, single, parenting, working. That's it. That's all there's time for. (Bruce)

Adam and Bruce provide a sense of the all-consuming nature of being a single working father. Bruce sees his life clearly in two dimensions, or rather as consumed by two activities, which leaves no time for anything else. Adam further mentions that his only free time is his 30-minute commute and talks about losing himself to parenthood: "I think in this situation you can either sign up to be a parent or you can sign up to be yourself, and I signed up to be a parent. I think that is good enough."

Renegotiating Masculinity—Superdads and "Mothering"

As single superdads focus first on their responsibilities as father, this often means taking on the mother role in addition to the father role. Martin describes his experience as "one of the moms":

> I've been the primary father-slash-mother for about three years. I always had to take them everywhere. I was always the only father at birthday parties usually. When my daughter was in preschool last year, I was one of the only dads dropping their kids off. You know, some of them called me, that I was one of the moms, and I wasn't at all offended by it. I was just doing what has to be done.

Martin echoes Barbara Risman's assertion that being a single parent takes precedence over being a man in that "the clearly expressed need of young children to be nurtured will create behaviors in men that are usually called 'mothering.'"[27] Canadian sociologist Andrea Doucet also took on this issue in her book *Do Men Mother?* Studying fathers who acted as primary caregivers, Doucet did not firmly commit to a yes or no answer. Instead she claimed a "partially affirmative answer" in which fathers nurture their children in similar ways to mothers but also differ in their nurturing *style*. And among fathers themselves, there remained doubts, with even sole-custody fathers feeling "they can never be mothers or replace the *mothering* done by women."[28] However, several of the fathers I talked with did not shy away from being "one of the moms." They feel they are responding to their children's needs in whatever way it takes. Martin has been both mother and father to his children since his wife left and he got full custody. For him, there is no other option, and as with other single superdads, being a good parent is more important than fitting traditional notions of manhood. Martin's gender flexibility in terms of what he is willing to do with his children and the language he uses shows his acceptance of this negotiated sense of masculinity.

Furthermore, masculinity may be challenged by our notions of who is responsible for family work. Much of family work is classified as "invisible work"—work that is critical to the maintenance of institutions but undervalued in a way that omits it from more commonly used but restrictive understandings of "work."[29] While this work is often accomplished by women, men can and do perform tasks associated with mothering. Men "who construct their gendered selves in more 'feminine' terms would be more likely to attribute positive meanings (e.g., loving care, concern, nurturance) to family work tasks that traditionally have been performed by women."[30] In this way, a certain emphasis on care and nurturing and men's ability to assess others' emotions may be an important aspect in masculine identity negotiation.

Some fathers do not necessarily talk about themselves as accomplishing mothering but rather focus on their ability to adapt to the situation. For example, Todd feels that people can generally rise to the occasion when faced with a challenge:

> I thought it would be a lot harder than it was. But I think that—it amazes me that if you put someone in a situation where they have to do something, you can do it. It doesn't matter what it is. It's something you have to do, and see it as your job, or something that you have to fulfill. . . . If you see it as your job, just that something needs to be done, you'll do it. Especially when there's the stakes involved like when having kids. They're just too precious.

Both Martin and Todd make it clear that taking care of their children is what they do. Being the primary caretaker is still seen as more of the mother's role, but these fathers are sure they are just as capable as any mother. Todd emphasizes the situational context of parenting and compares it to a job. When at a job, workers have a sense of responsibility and urgency in completing tasks. This same view could, and Todd argues should, be applied to parenting. When we reconceptualize housework, childcare, and emotional support as work, it becomes more acceptable for men.[31] In this sense, fathers can step into this role when called on.

Conclusion

Single superdads are a unique group of men. While many single fathers disappear from their children's lives, there is an increasing number who want to be involved on a regular basis, including holding joint custody. Single superdads provide a window into what might be. Not only do these fathers choose to stay in their children's lives, but they make every effort to be the best dads they can be, which generally means making changes at work. While single custodial fathers may face fewer problems adjusting postdivorce than single mothers do, fathers still express some difficulty in managing their time and thus their ability to move beyond their two roles as father and worker.[32] Single superdads differ from married superdads in a few important ways. First, the pathway to becoming a superdad often differs for single and married fathers. Single superdads often become superdads in the process of their divorce. Being faced with limited contact with their children and the possibility of being a "one-day-a-week daddy," these fathers make substantial, and sometimes abrupt, changes to their work lives. These may involve similar changes to the ones we saw among married superdads in chapter 6, namely, changing jobs or positions or making adjustments to work schedule or place. But single fathers are faced with a more drastic decision as they try to be involved dads. Second, single fathers must deal with custody settlements and sometimes battles. They face assumptions about fathers' expected roles and in some cases are steered away from equal custody by lawyers or judges. These fathers would argue that they are equal parents and that joint custody is fair to the parents and children. There is, in fact, mounting evidence that joint custody is beneficial for children's adjustment as well as fathers' emotional well-being.[33] Third, single fathers face different issues on a daily basis in trying to make it all work. When they have their children, they have sole responsibility for their care, education, and other activities. Most of these fathers simply claim that they are doing what is necessary, but this can lead to a renegotiation of masculine identity.

EIGHT

Conclusion

Fathering roles and relationships have the potential to encompass most of a man's adult life.[1]

Twenty years after Arlie Hochschild proclaimed that there was a "stalled revolution" when it came to women's rights and gender equality, Paula England spoke of an "uneven and stalled" revolution.[2] Both suggest that the change in gender roles that has occurred has been asymmetrical. Women's roles have changed dramatically, as they currently earn more college degrees than men do and compose about half the workforce.[3] Yet, while women have entered previously "male" spheres, there has been much less movement of men into "female" spheres. Thus, gendered roles continue to inhabit relationships between men and women, and England states, "Women are most likely to challenge gender boundaries when there is no path of upward mobility without doing so, but otherwise gender blinders guide the paths of both men and women."[4] She argues that the asymmetry in the gender revolution is due to asymmetric incentives for men and women to make changes and to gender essentialism. First, it is clear that in a society that values masculinity and masculine activities while devaluing feminine activities, women will have more incentive to engage in masculine activities than vice versa. For example, women have a strong incentive to enter the labor force because of its economic rewards. On the other hand, men have little incentive to leave the labor force in order to take on the unpaid task of caregiving. Second, gender essentialism, the idea that women and men are fundamentally different, is still prevalent in our society. Therefore, ideas about what men can and cannot do shape our notions of proper family roles.[5] Yet fathers are also expected to be more involved with their children, and there is increasing evidence that fathers' own desire for involvement is real. And while change has been slow, the trend is definitely under way, as fathers today spend more time with their children than did fathers of the past. Men are not the only ones to notice this change. Almost one-third of wives report that their husbands take on equal responsibility for childcare.[6]

In order to better understand men's experiences as working fathers, I talked with 70 fathers who represent a diverse range of demographic and occupational characteristics. These men's stories provide a picture of the work-family struggles and strategies of fathers in the early 21st century. What lessons do they provide? First, it is clear that today's men experience a profound change in their attitudes and priorities regarding work and family upon becoming fathers. Confirming survey data from the Families and Work Institute, more fathers are family-centric than work-centric.[7] While fathers in the past certainly experienced life changes when first entering this new role, today's fathers now face the challenge of how to best combine work and family. The first challenge new fathers face is arranging time off around their child's birth. Consistent with other recent studies, most fathers I talked with took one to two weeks off work following the birth of a child, though this varies by class. Particularly important to understanding men's decisions regarding paternity leave is that very few fathers have access to paid leave. Under the Family and Medical Leave Act, leave is unpaid, and very few fathers work for companies that offer paid paternity leave. As a result, new fathers often use vacation days or informal practices in order to take time off. There is some possibility for change, as witnessed by some of the California fathers in my study, and this is expanded on later in this chapter.

Second, and following from the first point, most fathers experience some kind of work-family conflict or imbalance. Again, the numbers are evident in larger-scale survey research, which shows that men are actually more likely than women to report work-family conflict.[8] Understanding this phenomenon requires that we listen to men's stories about this conflict. Men today do not go about business as usual once they have kids. Rather, in addition to the continued pressure they face to provide for their families, there is an added meaning placed on their role as father that emphasizes time with their children. The conflict occurs when fathers are expected to work long hours but are also expected to be highly involved with their children. In their stories, there is a real sense of stress and tension. For many fathers, the result is that they feel as if they do not spend enough time with their children. Added to this is the lack of time with their partners and by themselves. Yet some fathers also feel conflict because they are spending more time at home and think they could be doing more work. The common theme across all those facing work-family conflict is their lack of time. What distinguishes these fathers is how they respond to this conflict.

Most fathers today can be classified as what we have come to call "new" or "involved" dads. These fathers want to spend more time with their children, and they often make some effort to tweak their work schedules in order to be there for important events. Many set aside family time in order to avoid work interference, though this may mean doing work tasks after their kids are in bed. When they are at home with their families, they pride themselves on being highly involved and sometimes equal parents. These new dads have largely replaced the more traditional fathers of the past, what I refer to as "old" dads. While old dads are much fewer in number, they are likely to persist as a category, as some men continue to view their primary role as breadwinner and others simply define themselves as workaholics. However, though these fathers do not spend an enormous amount of time with their children, they also do not generally fall into the "read the paper and drink a cocktail" stereotype of the past. The little time with their children is seen as quality time. Therefore, even this group of fathers is qualitatively different from the providers of the past. Finally, a third group has developed out of the evolving roles of fathers, and these are what I call "superdads."

Twenty years ago, demographers Frances Goldscheider and Linda Waite asked whether changes in male-female relationships would lead to "new families" or "no families."[9] At the time, increasing female employment without a corresponding change in men's family roles, à la Hochschild, suggested that people might opt out of family life altogether. Yet Goldscheider and Waite were obviously pulling for "new families" and suggested there were several trends that supported the growth of these families, from changing gender-role attitudes to pressure on men to share in domestic work to a reversal in the marriage squeeze.[10] The dominance of new dads and the emergence of superdads provides support for the "new families" Goldscheider and Waite were hoping for.

Are Superdads the New Supermoms?

In the introduction, I compared the term *superdad* to *supermom*. Certainly when women, and especially mothers, were entering the labor force in great numbers, there was an effort to label this new phenomenon. They were not content with the traditional female role of staying home, nor were they fully satisfied with focusing solely on work. They wanted to be caring moms at the same time as taking on the added worker role. Similarly, the Families and Work Institute refers to the "new male mystique," in which men try to do it all.[11] This is an explicit comparison between men's and women's work-family transitions. In this way, men's increased participation in the family realm can be seen as parallel to women's earlier increased participation in the workforce. At a most basic level, new dads can be seen as the male equivalent of the supermom. New dads are indeed trying to "have it all" by combining work and family. And like supermoms before them, they are experiencing a great deal of stress as they attempt to balance these two realms. This is because new dads add the active dad role without getting rid of their work role, much as supermoms added the work role without getting rid of their mom role. Perhaps it is new dads who are the new supermoms.

If this is the case, where does that leave us with superdads? Like new dads, superdads have added the caregiver role to their worker role. But unlike new dads, superdads have made changes at work that put their father role ahead of their worker role. This does not mean that new dads are less committed to their families. It means that new dads try to make room for their families largely within the constraints of the workplace, while superdads fit work around their family life.

I should note that there is an important difference between working mothers and superdads, and that is in how their actions are judged. In 2003, Lisa Belkin wrote a piece for the *New York Times Magazine* called "The Opt-Out Revolution." Setting the scene with eight Princeton-alumnae book-club members, Belkin described how college-educated, professional women were choosing to abandon (at least temporarily) their careers.[12] Many social scientists were dismayed at both the unscientific approach of this "research" and the misleading storyline, and this prompted a number of studies that examined the phenomenon of "opting out." Among them, sociologist Pamela Stone found that women were being pushed out of their jobs by inflexible employers rather than choosing to leave. Using national survey data, Princeton PhD student Christine Percheski found that only a small percentage of professional women left the labor force for a year or more during their childbearing years and that labor force participation rates were actually becoming more similar between mothers and women without children.[13] Nevertheless, the image of mothers "opting out" became widespread, and thus working mothers who might have been labeled supermoms lost this moniker when they "chose" to quit, work part-time, work from home, or in other ways shift to more family-friendly hours. Instead they were now seen as "downshifting" or "opting out." So how can we label men superdads when the same actions they are taking would be seen as capitulation among women? As alluded to earlier, the answer is that men and women are making different changes and, rightly or wrongly, are applauded for different actions. Women are celebrated when they make progress in the more public realms of work and politics. So it should not be too surprising when men are applauded for making progress in the more private realm of home life. After all, I would argue that superdads are making progress. Their actions may not be seen as "opting out" because they are not reverting back to a more traditional role when they spend time with their kids. Rather, I claim that these men are "opting in" to family. Superdads are making changes that move them away from work and toward family life.

The Case for Superdads

All the dads I talked with, in their way, are super dads. They are all completely devoted to their families, whether they show it through working extra hard, trying to have it all and share work and family burdens equally with their wives, or fitting their work around their families. But only superdads point the way toward a future for society as a whole of saner work and family policies. Superdads are highly involved, like the new dads, but what distinguishes them is that they specifically make changes to their work lives in order to accommodate their family lives. In this sense, they are like working mothers, who are often the ones to sacrifice career advancement for their families. This is significant for a number of reasons. First, superdads view their caregiving role as more important than their provider role. In becoming superdads, their priorities have shifted to their children and what they view as their children's immediate needs for parental presence. This in turn places father as the primary identity for these men, which means that they gain a sense of confidence and accomplishment from their superdad role. This is good for men's own personal growth and development. Second, superdads move toward gender equality. Superdads have views and experiences of parenthood that are more similar to women's. By highlighting their caregiver role and making adjustments to their worker role, they are making the changes that so many sociologists, gender studies scholars, and feminists have called for. Since Arlie Hochschild talked about the stalled revolution and men's lagging role in the gender revolution, researchers have waited for signs that men are changing. Here is a big sign. Third, superdads offer children another caregiver, someone deeply invested not only in providing or playing but also in caring for daily needs. This is good for children. Finally, superdads are not only good for individual men, women, and children but for the larger society as well.

Benefits to Men

It is important to consider the impact of fathering on men as this role has evolved and become more central to men's identities. Becoming a father may be the biggest transition of men's lives. Yet it is not simply a single transition but offers the possibility of multiple transitions and changes as men adapt to their role as father. When men were primarily expected to be economic providers, stability was crucial to being a good father. With to-day's emphasis on fathers as nurturers, there is greater potential for transitions within fathering.[14] In this book, I have focused on transitions or adjustments to men's work lives in response to fatherhood.

Thirty years ago, sociologist and feminist scholar Jessie Bernard pointed to the negative psychological costs of the provider role for men. Bernard argued that men had all their eggs in one basket, and that one basket was being a good provider. If a man was a good provider, he would be able to get away with a lot of other things, not to mention sit around and drink beers instead of doing housework. The problem was that if he was not a good provider, there was no way he could compensate for this failure.[15] But even among marriages in the 1950s, role specialization increased the likelihood of "empty shell marriages," ones in which couples stay together but are less and less happy with their relationship.[16]

There is a sizeable development literature that draws largely on psychology studies on the relationship between parenting and adult development. German American developmental psychologist Erik Erikson, noted for his theory on social development in which he proposed eight stages of development throughout the life course, asserted that parenthood is a major developmental marker that encourages personal growth.[17] At a time when childhood and adolescence is extending later and later, becoming a father may signal one's full transition to adulthood. While being a father may facilitate personal reevaluation and growth, being a more involved father, and certainly a superdad, is likely to expand opportunities for growth in ways not experienced by less involved fathers. Because being an involved father means caring for a child, with attention to their physical and emotional needs, there is a growth curve when it comes to achieving the goals of involved fathering.[18] In becoming involved fathers, men have the opportunity to learn about themselves. In teaching and caring for children, they learn more about their own values and feelings, and they build important life skills.[19] Involved fathers engage in more self-reflection and self-evaluation, become more oriented toward the needs of others, and embrace Erikson's notion of generativity, which is the task of caring for the next generation.[20] In turn, fathers who are very involved with their children experience greater self-assurance and psychological well-being than less involved fa-thers do.[21]

In addition to psychological and developmental benefits, there is evi-dence that father involvement is associated with better physical health and well-being. For example, more involved fathers are less likely to engage in substance abuse, have fewer accidents, have fewer hospital admissions, and have lower rates of early death.[22] There is even a recent study of Swedish fathers that found that fathers who take longer paternity leave have lower mortality rates.[23] Being more involved and having priorities that center around family also have the potential to improve work-family balance. More involved fathers have greater marital happiness and stability. More involved fathers also experience less work-family conflict.[24]

Benefits to Women

Superdads also have the potential to make women's lives easier, both at the individual couple level and in the aggregate with regard to gender equality. Fathers who make work adjustments for their families enable their female partners to focus on their own career goals more. It seems like a fairly clear trade-off; mothers who do not need to take full responsibility for childcare but rather have a partner who shares childcare tasks will have more time and energy to work. Often employed mothers, especially those with very young children, do not fully commit to their careers because they are con-cerned about their children. This is likely why women are more likely than men to make work adjustments in order to care for children.[25] While we al-ready know that mothers spend more time on childcare than fathers do, it is telling that mothers also spend a greater percentage of their childcare time on their own without their spouse present, compared to fathers, who spend relatively little time alone with their children.[26] Therefore, if men take on more responsibility for childcare, especially on their own time, while their partners work, it will ease mothers' concerns. Indeed, there is evidence that fathers can help working mothers by increasing their own involvement with children. A British study found, "The children of working mothers re-ceive no less active parental interaction than the children of non-working mothers because the involvement of fathers rises to offset lower maternal involvement. This is an important result because it indicates that perhaps the most intuitive mechanism through which we might expect maternal employment to be harmful to children, i.e. a reduction in parental inputs, is simply not in evidence. In addition, it seems that the greater involvement of fathers in child rearing in households where mothers work has strongly beneficial effects on children's cognitive development."[27] In other words, fathers who are highly involved in caregiving eliminate any negative effects of full-time maternal employment. In instances in which mothers work and fathers take over care for children, whether it involves feeding children or playing with children, this involvement has a positive effect on child outcomes. This positive influence outweighs the potential negative effects of reduced maternal involvement due to employment.[28]

Supporting superdads may also have a larger impact on gender equality. In studies of nonindustrial societies, there is a link between the strength of father-child relationships and female status. For example, when fathers engage in more routine childcare, females participate more in community decision-making and have greater access to positions of authority.[29] As with mothers' employment, it just makes sense that mothers will be able to do more nonfamily activities, including community and political activities, if their partners are taking more responsibility for childcare. On the other hand, when fathers focus primarily on breadwinning, as with old dads, and leave mothers to do all the childcare and household tasks, women will have less time and energy to get involved in workplaces, community, and larger public roles. Indeed, there is some evidence that the largest factor in determining the gender pay gap is the unequal division of caring tasks between women and men.[30] In a study of 20 OECD countries, political scientists found that female representation in government and maternal employment are positively related to each other, which suggests that men's participation with children may ultimately expand opportunities for women in both employment and politics.[31] As Scott Coltrane envisioned, fathers who are fully involved in childcare and housework have the power to transform not only themselves but also American society in a way that promotes gender equality.[32]

These ideas go back to prominent psychoanalytic feminist Nancy Chodorow's theory that gender is reproduced in the home, that a gendered division of labor in childcare produces a gendered division of labor (or gender inequality) in the greater society.[33] There are three ways in which greater father involvement may promote greater gender equality. First, when men and women share tasks in one domain (e.g., at home), they are more likely to share tasks in another domain (e.g., in government). This is the basic premise that equality promotes equality. Second, as noted, men's greater participation in home life frees women to participate in public life. Third, men who are more involved with their children are likely to raise girls and boys who have a greater sense of gender equality. In particular, boys will see that they can take on nurturing roles just as effectively as girls can. Boys would see their fathers engaged in nurturing, and they would learn that fathers and mothers share responsibility for the caring of children. This model also suggests that father-child relationships might develop independently of father-mother relationships, allowing more possibilities for father involvement regardless of marital status.[34]

Benefits to Children

When fathers' main role was breadwinner and involvement in daily care was limited, there was an assumption that they would have little direct impact on their children's development.[35] As the rates of divorce and nonmarital births increased, there was much concern over the effects of father absence. Much of the literature does suggest that a child's academic performance, social behavior, and emotional well-being fare better when a father is present. But now that more and more fathers take on the role of nurturer and some become superdads, there is more reason to pay attention to the potential effects of father involvement on child outcomes. While living with a child may be beneficial in itself, all residential fathers are not necessarily highly involved in shaping their children's development. The interactions and relationships between fathers and children are also important. When fathers are more involved in caregiving tasks, the potential benefits to children's cognitive and social development may be even greater.[36] In fact, there is some evidence that paternal employment when children are young, though having a smaller impact than maternal employment, is negatively related to child outcomes.[37]

It seems likely that father involvement may have an impact from very early ages. Several researchers have found that parental leave is positively associated with children's health. On the other hand, mothers who return to work within 12 weeks of giving birth are less likely to breastfeed and less likely to take their infants for regular checkups at the pediatrician, which can affect infant health. Also, infants of these early-returning mothers are less likely to have complete immunizations and more likely to show signs of behavior problems.[38] Among fathers, those who take longer leaves are more likely to continue to be involved in their children's lives even after returning to work.[39]

Eirini Flouri and Ann Buchanan, researchers at the University of Oxford, assert that father involvement should have a positive impact on children's education for three reasons. First, involved fathers tend to actively play with their children, and this contributes to children's emotional and cognitive development. Second, when fathers are involved, mothers also tend to be involved, resulting in two highly involved parents. Third, involved fathers provide a more positive family environment.[40] Studies that have tested the relationship between father involvement and children's educational outcomes have largely shown positive results. According to the National Center for Educational Statistics, children whose fathers are more involved are more likely to take part in educational activities such as museum trips. Highly involved fathers promote children's inquisitiveness and exploration, which leads to better problem-solving skills. In addition, a study of Head Start children showed that children with involved fathers had higher mathematics readiness change scores than those with less involved fathers.[41] Effects of father involvement may be long lasting. A study of achievement through middle school found that fathers' equal participation in child activities was associated with a high level of achievement among girls. At the same time, girls from traditional families with less involved fathers experienced lower performance in math and science.[42] Using the National Child Development Study, Flouri and Buchanan went further by looking at the effect of father involvement and mother involvement at age 7 on educational attainment by age 20. Confirming previous studies, they found that father involvement at a younger age positively influences educational attainment later on. Importantly, the effect of father involvement was independent of mother involvement and had the same effect on daughters and sons.[43]

These benefits extend to children's psychological well-being. On the one hand, Michael Lamb, a child-development specialist, speculated that father's involvement would have a similar influence on child development as mother's involvement.[44] On the other hand, fathers might influence their children differently because of differences in father-child interactions. For example, fathers spend more time playing with their children, especially in physical activities, than mothers do. This might encourage children to develop more competitiveness and independence.[45] Several studies have shown that father involvement contributes to positive child outcomes, including psychological adjustment. Children with involved fathers have greater self-confidence and self-esteem than children with less involved fathers. One study even found that when both father-child and mother-child relationship measures were examined simultaneously, only a positive father-child relationship reduced a son's levels of distress. Adolescents who have a close relationship with their father have lower levels of depression than do adolescents who do not have a close relationship.[46] Other studies have shown that the impact of father involvement extends into adulthood. Having a close relationship with one's father during childhood is positively associated with children's psychological well-being as adults. A longitudinal study based on the National Child Development Study found that daughters whose fathers were highly involved at age 16 have lower rates of psychological distress at age 33 than those with fathers who had medium or low levels of involvement at age 16.[47]

Father involvement also has the potential to affect other child outcomes. Children with involved fathers are less likely to demonstrate antisocial behavior and more likely to conform to accepted values and ethics than are children with less involved fathers. They are also more likely to develop supportive social networks and positive peer relations.[48] When fathers are involved, mothers report less problem behavior among children. This positive influence may be even greater for sons.[49]

Benefits to Society

Finally, superdads have the potential to create a healthier, more gender-equal society. David Eggebeen, a professor of human development and sociology at Penn State, argues that fathers have a stronger stake in children's welfare issues than do men who remain childless.[50] It follows that fathers who engage more directly with their children on a daily basis will have more knowledge and interest in promoting all children's well-being. This focus may be encouraged by fathers' increased interactions with extended family.[51] But fathers also extend their networks beyond family members to other social institutions, including schools and churches, and participate in more community-service-oriented activities. In a study of middle-aged American men, sociologists found a positive relationship between father involvement and community involvement. More specifically, fathers who were more engaged with their children as they were growing up were more likely to develop altruistic social relationships and get involved in organizations with a service component.[52]

It is already clear that Americans support gender equality. In fact, attitudes concerning marriage and gender equality in marital roles experienced major shifts in the 1960s and 1970s, with smaller changes since the 1980s. When asked whether married couples should share household tasks on the basis of ability and interest rather than presumed gender roles (i.e., certain tasks should be done by the husband, while other tasks should be done by the wife), about half of Americans agreed in 1961, whereas almost 90 percent agreed in 1978. By the mid-1990s, almost everyone agreed with sharing tasks. A similar transition occurred in attitudes regarding equality between husbands and wives in family decision-making.[53]

In earlier work, I argued that more egalitarian attitudes among men promote stronger marriages, as egalitarian men are less likely than their more traditional counterparts to get divorced.[54] When egalitarian attitudes are translated into behavior, it is beneficial for marriage, as men who do more housework are more likely to have stable marriages. Indeed, a more equal division of paid and unpaid work reduces the likelihood of divorce, compared to marriages characterized by a single breadwinner.[55] This may be why the negative relationship between women's education and marriage has turned around.[56]

Creating More Superdads

While I have emphasized the differences between old dads, new dads, and superdads, there is one similarity that could stall the further evolution of fathers' work-family balance. The one thing they all have in common is that they do not expect much from employers or government. Almost all the fathers I talked with shared a typically American emphasis on individualism, focusing on their own personal situation and difficulties. For the most part, old dads were content with their work-family balance and did not talk of major changes. They liked being the primary or sole breadwinner, and they hoped to advance further in their careers in order to provide more resources and opportunities for their families. The few who thought they might want to cut back faced other constraints that made change unlikely. Yet, even among this more traditional group, there are signs of change. For one, the old dads are not uninvolved fathers. They generally spend as much time with their children as they can, and though this falls short of the new dads and superdads, it is still more than fathers in the past. Second, Matt's story shows us that it is never too late to change. As he makes plans and engages in training to change his career from delivery driver to firefighter, there is hope for greater involvement with his children. In addition, some of the new dads and even superdads in this study used to be old dads. While I have categorized fathers according to what they were doing when I talked with them, their diverse work and family histories demonstrate the dynamic nature of these categories. Unlike old dads, new dads emphasized their provider and nurturer roles more equally and made some attempts to better balance work and family. Nevertheless, these were largely minor adjustments made within the system, and these fathers still experienced quite a bit of work-family conflict. The fact that many of these new dads achieved balance by separating their work and family roles, both physically and mentally, shows that some of the adjustments were more mental than structural. The sense that there was not a lot the fathers themselves could do because "the job I have is the job I have" was quite common among new dads and emphasizes again the individual as the focal point of any change. Unlike new dads, superdads have taken matters into their own hands in order to effect change in their lives. The uniqueness of superdads that I have sought to highlight in this book is not simply that they make work adjustments or are particularly good at balancing work and family but that they respond to their family's needs and change their work lives because of the type of father they want to be. Nonetheless, while superdads may possess a greater awareness of structural constraints on fathers who try to balance work and family, their solutions are still largely individual ones. And so while I propose changes that individual fathers (and mothers) can make, my larger focus is on the institutions that maintain these constraints and are therefore better targets for large-scale change.

What Men Need to Do

In order to create more superdads, we need more fathers who are willing to put their families ahead of their work. Men need to see themselves as equal participants in family life, sharing caregiving and household tasks with partners, regardless of whether they are married to or cohabiting with or living apart from their children's mother. While most fathers today want to be involved in raising their children, they cannot accept a secondary role in which they "help" mothers. Rather, they need to be equally engaged, equally accessible, and equally responsible for their children. When fathers become equal parents, they will be more likely to question the workplace structures that impede parental involvement. There is already evidence that in Sweden, men are more likely than women to challenge workplace culture that conflicts with their family priorities. Furthermore, men's increased focus on fatherhood has been a critical factor in Sweden's changing workplace culture.[57]

What Women Need to Do

Although I would like to emphasize the role of government and employers in creating change, I cannot overlook the role of women in supporting superdads. By support, I mean that mothers and partners need to allow fathers to take on a more equal role. There has been quite a bit of literature on maternal gatekeeping and its part in suppressing father involvement. Here I refer to mothers who are reluctant and sometimes downright unwilling to hand over half or even some of the responsibilities of childcare. Gatekeeping may come in the form of setting inflexible standards for childcare, defining family roles in gender-specific ways, and looking for external validation of one's mothering practices. It generally results in a more unequal division of family work, with women who act as gatekeepers putting in about five more hours of family work each week. The good news is that maternal encouragement has even stronger effects on father involvement than criticism does.[58]

What Employers Need to Do

Early research on the impact of family-friendly workplace policies on men's work behaviors found that men were often reluctant to use these policies. This reluctance stemmed from a fear that employers and co-workers would think they were less committed to their job than men who did not take advantage of these policies.[59] While women are not immune to these concerns, the fact that men are still seen as providers means that employers often assume they will be even more committed to work when they become fathers.[60] This is unfair to fathers and in the long term to all employees who want to have a life outside work. Therefore, workplace norms need to change, and one of the biggest changes should be the acknowledgment that men have family responsibilities. This will pave the way for more men to make changes in how they prioritize work and family.

Of course, changing the workplace culture is not the only thing that needs to happen. There should be more concrete policies that help all employees balance their family responsibilities with their work responsibilities. The first step is to recognize that working fathers may have particular needs in relation to managing work and family. Therefore, a plan should be implemented to assess these needs, and this should include talking directly with workers about their needs and how the workplace could better accommodate these needs. Second, policies should be designed to meet the needs of working fathers as well as other employee needs.

These policies should include family leave, comparable benefits for reduced or part-time work, and more flexible options for work time and place (see next section on government policies). Family leave should apply to all workers who have been with the company for a certain amount of time and should provide equal amounts of time for men and women. Ideally, it should be paid family leave, at least for a minimum number of weeks. Reduced hours or part-time work should be available to all employees and should result in prorated pay and benefits. Employers should make flex-time available to employees. Given an agreed-on number of hours for an employee, the employee should be able to arrange this time in whatever manner suits his or her family schedule. When appropriate, employees should also have access to flexibility in workplace. Most work can be accomplished from a variety of settings, including the home. If employers are concerned about productivity, they can utilize a results-only model in which employees are compensated and judged based on their performance rather than time clocked. A recent study found that the implementation of a results-only workplace (ROWE) increased employees' control of their work schedule, which, in turn, improved work-family balance.[61] Instead of focusing on "face time" in the workplace, fathers can use this opportunity to have more "face time" with their children.[62]

Finally, in order for these policies to be effective, there should be an effort to publicize these new benefits. Unless workers actually know they exist, policies will not be very helpful. These efforts should be aimed equally at male and female employees. Furthermore, employers should encourage workers to take advantage of existing and new family-friendly policies. Again, there should be an extra effort to let male as well as female employees know that they will not be penalized for using the policies.

Family-friendly policies are good for employers, too. There is evidence that family leave increases retention and morale and decreases turnover.[63] Furthermore, flexible working also can benefit employers by attracting and retaining highly qualified employees. Flexible working may further enhance productivity.[64] In Sweden, a forerunner in family-friendly policies (see the next section), some companies actually offer men financial rewards for taking parental leave, with the notion that these policies improve recruitment and retention. Indeed, there is no evidence that fathers who take leave experience any negative long-term impacts on their career prospects, a sign that Swedish employers are supportive of working fathers.[65]

What Government Needs to Do

Government support of families has the potential to ease much of the stress that working families face. If these policies are implemented with attention to gender equity at work and home, women would be able to increase their financial contribution, while men could increase their family involvement. Here I discuss four areas for policy changes: family leave, work-hour regulations, part-time work, and custody and child support.

Family Leave

The Project on Global Working Families recently released the Work, Family, and Equity Index. Based on data from 177 countries, this report provides a comparative view of the United States in matters related to work and family. According to this report, the United States lags behind other countries in leave around childbearing, among other family-related policies. The United States is one of only four countries that do not provide any paid maternity leave. What are the other three countries? Liberia, Papua New Guinea, and Swaziland. In fact, 66 countries also guarantee fathers paid paternity leave or paid parental leave. Obviously, the United States does not offer fathers any paid leave.[66] As mentioned in chapter 2, the Family and Medical Leave Act (FMLA) offers up to 12 weeks of *unpaid* leave for new mothers and fathers but is infrequently used because most eligible employees cannot afford to take unpaid leave. A few states offer paid leave (see table 8.1), but the majority of American employees must rely on employer policies. Less than 10 percent of employers provide paid paternity leave.[67]

Sweden provides an excellent example of government policies that support both families and gender equality. This is achieved by special attention to men's early involvement in childrearing. Sweden was the first country to introduce parental leave (replacing maternity leave), back in 1974. Then, in 1995, Sweden introduced "daddy leave," in which one month of leave was reserved for fathers only (i.e., if fathers did not take the month, the family lost that leave), and in 2002, the daddy quota was increased to two months. Now 85 percent of Swedish fathers take parental leave, and their share of the total 13 months leave is increasing.[68] The Swedish government also considers the ability for new parents on leave to improve certain skills, such as multitasking, communication, and interpersonal skills, which will transfer to the workplace, making parents better parents, workers, and citizens.[69] It is clear that policies, particularly those aimed directly at fathers, can be effective in increasing men's time with infants.

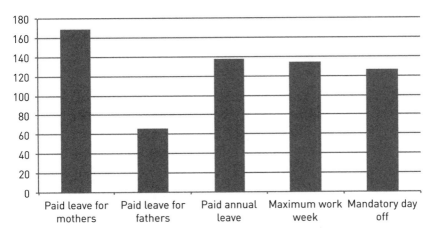

Fig. 8.1. Number of countries with family-friendly work policies. Source: Work, Family, and Equity Index, Project of Global Working Families

While it is preferable for the federal government to pass legislation that will provide benefits to all workers, there are a number of state policies that offer some benefits. The federal government may take some lessons from a few of these states. Five states offer partial wage replacement to new mothers through state temporary disability insurance (TDI) programs (see table 8.2). These states are California, Hawaii, New Jersey, New York, and Rhode Island. Most states allow six weeks of pregnancy-related disability, though this may vary based on birth experience and health conditions. Wage replacement differs by state but is generally based on a percentage of weekly wages. Most of the funding for TDI programs comes from employee contributions, though some programs also rely on employer contributions in addition to employee contributions. These programs mean that much of the required infrastructure for family leave is already in place.[70]

California was the first state to offer paid family leave, passing the law in 2002 and implementing it in 2004. California's Paid Family Leave Insurance Program offers up to six weeks of leave in order to care for a newborn or adopted child (it also includes caring for sick family members—child, spouse, parents—or domestic partners). Wage replacement is partial, with workers receiving 55 percent of weekly earnings up to a maximum of $959 per week (the maximum amount is updated annually based on the state's

Table 8.1: State Laws That Offer Additional Job Protection or Benefits for
New Parents Who Are Private-Sector Employees

	STATES	PROTECTION/BENEFIT
Family leave benefits	California, New Jersey, Washington	Up to 6 weeks paid leave
Medical/disability leave benefits	California	Up to 4 weeks before and 6 weeks after the birth of a child
	Hawaii	Up to 26 weeks
Flexible use of sick days	California, Connecticut (75+ employees), Hawaii (100+ employees), Washington, Wisconsin (50+ employees)	Use of sick days to care for newborn, adopted child, or spouse with pregnancy or birth-related disability
Job-protected family and medical leave	Iowa (4+ employees), Massachusetts (6+ employees)*	Up to 8 weeks of leave for pregnancy-related disability
	California (5+ employees), Connecticut (75+ employees), Louisiana (25+ employees), Tennessee (100+ employees)	Up to 4 months of leave for pregnancy-related disability
	New York	Up to 26 weeks of leave for pregnancy-related disability
	Rhode Island	Up to 30 weeks of leave for pregnancy-related disability
	Connecticut (3+ employees), Hawaii, Montana, New Hampshire (6+ employees), Washington (8+ employees)	Reasonable leave of absence for pregnancy-related disability
At-home infant care	Minnesota, Montana, New Mexico	Benefits to low-income parents to care for infants at home
Other	Colorado, Maryland	Employers that provide parental leave must offer equivalent to employees adopting a child
	Kentucky	6 weeks of parental leave for adoption
	Maine	Up to 10 weeks of family and medical leave (15+ employees)
	Minnesota	Up to 6 weeks leave (21+ employees)
	Oregon	Up to 12 weeks of unpaid family and medical leave (25+ employees)
	Rhode Island	Up to 13 weeks of parental leave (50+ employees)
	South Carolina	Prohibits employers from firing an employee who takes leave for pregnancy disability (15+ employees)
	Vermont	Up to 12 weeks of parental leave (10+ employees)
No additional protection or benefits	Alabama, Alaska, Arizona, Arkansas, Delaware, Florida, Georgia, Idaho, Illinois, Indiana, Kansas, Michigan, Mississippi, Missouri, Nebraska, Nevada, North Carolina, North Dakota, Ohio, Oklahoma, Pennsylvania, South Dakota, Texas, Utah, Virginia, West Virginia, Wyoming	

* Recommends similar leave for male employees

Source: National Partnership for Women and Families, www.nationalpartnership.org

Table 8.2: *State Temporary Disability Insurance Wage Replacement*

STATE	PERCENT	BASE	MAXIMUM
California	55	Highest quarterly earnings	$959
Hawaii	58	Average weekly wages	$510
New Jersey	66	Average weekly wages	$524
New York	50	Weekly wages	$170
Rhode Island	4.62	Highest calendar quarter wages	$671

Source: Fass 2009; http://www.paidfamilyleave.org/pdf/PaidLeaveinStates.pdf

average weekly wage). California's program is an improvement over the federal Family and Medical Leave program because it (1) offers paid leave and (2) covers nearly all employees, including those working for companies with fewer than 50 employees and part-time workers. These two criteria are crucial. First, remember that only about 60 percent of employees are covered under FMLA. Second, based on evaluation studies, a majority of employees who needed leave but did not take it said they did not take leave because it was not paid, and most of these employees said they would have taken leave if it was paid. Therefore, we might expect many more workers to take leave if there were no restrictions based on company size and if the leave was paid. Nevertheless, California's program does have a couple of drawbacks. One is that it does not provide job protection for employees who take paid leave under this program. For those employees who also meet the requirements of FMLA (50 or more employees, working for company for at least one year, worked at least 1,250 hours), they can take paid leave and know that their jobs are protected. However, employees working for smaller companies or working part-time must take a chance that their job will not be there upon their return from leave. A second drawback is that California's program does not require employers to extend benefits, including health insurance, to employees on paid leave. Again, those employees also covered by FMLA will continue to receive benefits, but other employees may not. Therefore, it is important that any paid leave program also offer job protection and continued benefits.[71]

New Jersey passed a very similar law as California's in 2008, with implementation in 2009. Under New Jersey's Family Leave Insurance Program, employees are eligible for up to six weeks of paid leave to care for a newborn (or ill parent, child, spouse/partner). Wage replacement is 66 percent of weekly earnings, up to a maximum of $546 per week (adjusted annually). As with California, New Jersey's program also builds on its disability program in funding the program via a payroll tax. It is also more inclusive than FMLA, covering employees in small companies and part-time workers. However, this state program does not offer job protection.[72]

Washington passed a paid family leave law in 2007 but was delayed in implementing this program. Washington's Family Leave Insurance Program would offer five weeks of paid leave to care for a newborn or adopted child. Washington's program differs from California's program in who is covered and what the benefits are. Under the program, employees who work 35 hours per week or more would receive a flat payment of $250 per week, while part-time workers would receive prorated benefits. Washington's program does offer job protection to those employees working for companies with 25 or more employees who have worked at least 1,250 hours in the past year. Because of budget issues, this program is not scheduled to go into effect until October 2015.[73]

We know that men's use of family leave is positively associated with child and family well-being. Furthermore, longer leaves for fathers promote father involvement even after returning to work.[74] Family leave also benefits women. Employed mothers who postpone going back to work after giving birth are less likely to experience depression than mothers who return sooner.[75] At the same time, women who have access to parental leave are more likely to return to employment and more likely to return to the same job than those who do not have such access. Parents' labor force attachment increases economic security for families.[76] Public-policy researchers Janet Gornick and Marcia Meyers propose three strategies for increasing fathers' use of parental leave. The first strategy is to offer high wage-replacement rates. Since men tend to make more money than women do, when low or no wage replacement is offered, it is more likely for mothers to take leave or to leave the labor market than for fathers to take leave. The second strategy is to provide separate parental leave for each parent. If leave will be lost if not taken by the father, it is more likely for fathers to take leave. The third strategy is public campaigns to increase awareness of parental leave and to change public perceptions about men's role in caregiving.[77]

CONCLUSION

Regulations on Work Hours

The United States provides little regulation of work hours. The Fair Labor Standards Act established a maximum number of hours above which employees must be paid overtime wages. This was originally 44 hours in 1938 and was reduced to 40 hours in 1940. Since 1940, this threshold has not been changed. In addition, an increasing number of workers are not covered by these provisions. Over one-quarter of full-time employees are exempt, which means there is no limit on their hours and no extra pay for any hours over 40.[78] Furthermore, there is a growing culture of long work hours. A recent report by the Center for American Progress finds that professionals often see a 40-hour workweek as part-time and potentially "career suicide." This may be the reason an increasing share of professional men and women work 50 hours or more, on average, per week.[79]

The U.S. policy is in contrast to most European countries that set normal full-time work below 40 hours. Regarding actual hours, 134 countries have laws concerning the maximum workweek, and 126 countries mandate one day off each week, while the United States has no such regulations.[80] The EU Directive on Working Time sets a maximum workweek of 48 hours over each seven-day period, and this includes overtime. As such, there are normal full-time hours and maximum hours. For example, France has a workweek of 35 hours, with maximum working hours of 48. The Scandinavian countries, on the other hand, have set both normal working hours and maximum working hours at 40.[81]

Beyond regular working hours, there is a discrepancy between the United States and other countries on vacation time. While 137 countries require employers to provide paid annual vacation leave, and 121 of these countries guarantee at least two weeks of paid vacation leave, the United States does not have any requirements regarding vacation.[82] There is no minimum number of vacation days employers must offer and no requirement to pay employees for vacation days. In fact, American workers average around 11 paid vacation days per year. In contrast, the EU Directive on Working Time, in addition to regulating work hours, requires that employers offer at least four weeks of paid vacation each year. About half of the EU countries have gone further, requiring five weeks of paid vacation.[83]

Part-Time Work

In the United States, there is no policy on part-time employment, and most part-time work is limited to certain jobs that pay less, have fewer benefits, and provide less job security. Again, the United States differs from its European counterparts. The EU Directive on Part-Time Work has the goal of improving the quality of part-time work by requiring that employers treat part-time employees similarly to full-time employees. It seeks to address equity in training, pay, benefits, and promotions. The Netherlands provide a good example of favorable government policy regarding part-time work. Dutch law allows employees flexibility in increasing or decreasing their work hours. Its intention is to promote more equal sharing among couples, with the ultimate goal of each partner working a three-quarter-time schedule.[84] A comparable policy in the United States would encourage more superdads like Sean, the lawyer who arranged a three-quarter schedule alongside his wife.

Child Custody

For much of this country's early history, fathers were awarded custody in the rare event of divorce because children were seen as property belonging to fathers. Starting in the 19th century, the "tender years" doctrine, with its emphasis on mothers' superiority in parenting infants and children, dominated custody law. This resulted in a legal preference for maternal custody. Most recently, states, while varying in details of their laws, favor a "best interests of the child" doctrine.[85] While this doctrine is gender neutral in language, gendered assumptions about parental roles still exist. As professor of social work Edward Kruk suggests, "decisions prevalent in the arena of family law have reflected the presumption that only one parent, usually the mother, is to care for children, while the other, usually the father, provides financial support."[86] Other studies show that mothers are awarded sole physical custody more often than fathers are and that ideas about traditional gender roles still influence judicial decision-making. For example, interviews with trial-court judges reveal that many judges possess "a worldview that mothers and fathers are fundamentally different and provide different kinds of support and role models for their children." As a result, judges may think a child's best interests are served by awarding mothers custody.[87]

While legal practice seems skewed toward mothers, mounting evidence demonstrates that joint physical custody may be in the best interests of children and parents. First, a majority of children of divorce say they want equal time with their parents and believe shared custody is the best arrangement for children. Second, children in joint-custody arrangements experience better adjustment to the divorce than do children in sole-custody arrangements. Third, the living arrangements of children in joint-custody arrangements are as stable as or are more stable than those of children in mother-custody arrangements. Fourth, children of divorce who spend equal time with both parents have better relationships with mothers and fathers after divorce than do those who spend more time with one parent than the other. Fifth, divorced parents who share custody experience improved cooperation and decreased conflict over time compared to parents in sole-custody arrangements.[88]

Policy Suggestions

Based on my findings and the accumulated knowledge we now possess about men, work, and family, I recommend the following changes:

1. Parental leave should be paid, and it should offer job protection. All employees should be covered, including those who work for smaller companies and part-time workers. At least one month each should be set aside for fathers and mothers.
2. There should be regulations regarding the maximum workweek and paid vacation.
3. There should be more options for part-time work, and this should be paid at the same rate with the same benefits as full-time work.
4. Joint custody should be the default, and there should be more equal child support for single fathers.

Conclusion

Families are always changing, and people's expectations for families change, too. As recently as the early 1980s, newly marrying couples ranked sharing, caring, and responsibility for children number 11 out of 15 values they wanted to bring into their marriages. By the late 1990s, sharing was ranked number 2.[89] It is clear that today's couples want to share the caregiver role. This may explain why couples in which roles are more traditionally divided experience more conflict than do couples who more equally share providing and caring.[90] The change keeps happening. Today's fathers spend more time with their children than ever (at least for the time period for which we have data), and there are more and more families in which childcare is divided equally.[91]

This change may be particularly salient at a time when the economy is stagnant. Even before the current economic troubles, men's position in the labor market had been diminished by the decline in relatively high-paying and male-dominated sectors such as manufacturing.[92] The result is that more and more men are unable to fulfill the provider role. While men's diminished economic role may create instability for men and their families, it also offers an opportunity to reconsider strict gender roles that not only place the burden of housework and childcare mainly on women but also restrict men's time with children. Indeed, more egalitarian relationships can be developed when women step up to provide income for their families and men step up to take care of children and household needs.[93]

Just as we saw the trend toward more involved fathering and the proliferation of new dads, we may yet see the continued evolution of the role of fathers as more men become superdads. These superdads more closely resemble working mothers in their efforts to combine work and family. What happens to a society where family values and gender equality are long-term goals, one in which superdads are the norm rather than the exception? Men, women, children, and the society at large benefit. But fathers need help along the way. As noted at the beginning of this chapter, there has been much talk of a "stalled revolution" in which women were changing roles quickly while men (and workplaces) were lagging behind. I think today's "stalled revolution" has more to do with workers versus workplaces than men versus women. As I have tried to make clear, there are a growing number of men who are choosing family over work. These fathers have the potential of making work and family needs a parent issue rather than a women's issue. However, the problem lies in the fact that many dads see conflict between work and family as "personal troubles" rather than structural and systemic constraints. Without public policies that protect work-family balance for either fathers or mothers, men, like women, are left to figure things out on a case-by-case basis. So while fathers should do their part, government and employers need to take the lead role.

APPENDIX

Studying Fathers

While there is an increasing number of studies that focus on fathers, including ones that attempt to measure work-family conflict, there are few studies that explore in-depth fathers' feelings about work and family and their efforts to better balance the two. To really understand the work-family dilemmas that fathers face and their strategies for overcoming these challenges, I felt it was important to sit down and talk with real fathers about their feelings and experiences.

Selecting the Sample

In order to focus on fathers' experiences with work and family, I sought to interview a broad sample of working fathers. Logically, I started with the restrictions that the men I talked with must be employed and must be fathers. I further restricted my sample to adult men, who were at least 18 years old, and fathers who were living with at least one child under age 18. Stepfathers were included. Single fathers had to have custody of their child(ren) at least 25 percent of the time. California and North Carolina were chosen as data-collection sites in order to ensure a more representative American sample. Fathers were recruited through announcements and fliers placed in daycare centers, stores, churches, and community organizations, with some online solicitation. Special efforts were made to recruit single fathers through a single-parent support group. Some fathers were also recruited by word of mouth.

I used Terry Arendell's study of divorced fathers as a model in determining the sample size.[1] Previous studies on fathers have often used smaller samples. Nicholas Townsend's important study on family and work in men's lives was based on interviews with 39 men who graduated from a particular high school, though 18 men from other schools were interviewed as well.[2] Other studies have included smaller samples of fathers with special circumstances, such as low-income, noncustodial, African American fathers; Mexican-immigrant fathers; first-time fathers; stepfathers; professional fathers; and fathers of children with cancer.[3] The sample size of 70 fathers was chosen for three reasons. The first reason was to obtain racial and ethnic diversity. Conducting the interviews in California and North Carolina also helped achieve diversity since California has large numbers of Asian Americans and Hispanics, while North Carolina has large numbers of African Americans. The second reason was to represent a broad range of occupations. This was important given the focus on employment characteristics such as work schedules, travel, and bringing work home. The third reason was to allow for inclusion of a significant number of single fathers.

A Note on Class, Race, and Ethnicity

My sample represents a diverse range of class, race, and ethnicity, as well as age, marital status, number of children, and childhood region. While a majority of the sample is college educated, 8 stopped their education with a high school diploma, and 18 started but did not finish college. There is a great range of occupations among the fathers with whom I talked. There were working-class fathers, including a delivery driver, a bus driver, a warehouse worker, a security guard, a carpenter, a gardener, and several technicians. There were also professional fathers, including a bank executive, a lawyer, an engineer, a veterinarian, and a professor. But the majority of fathers were middle class, holding positions in education, design, planning, marketing, and middle management. While there were fathers of all class backgrounds represented among the "old" dads, "new" dads, and superdads, class seemed to influence fathers' experiences with family leave and work adjustments, which I elaborate on in the book. There is also a good deal of racial diversity in my sample, with a particularly high representation of African American fathers and a fair but small number of Asian American fathers. Unfortunately, my attempts to recruit Hispanic and Latino fathers, through community organizations and local establishments, were largely unsuccessful. Therefore, I cannot draw many conclusions about Hispanic fathers' experiences with work and family. I should also note that many of the African American fathers were recruited through their churches, which may affect their views of work and family. In particular, I did not find any racial or ethnic differences in men's experiences with family leave or work adjustments. The only thing to note is that all my single superdads were white, which is likely due to differences in marital status rather than type of father, as there were minority superdads who were married or cohabiting. This may again be a result of the disproportionate number of African American fathers who were recruited through their church.

Conducting Interviews

Interviews allow a more detailed examination of working fathers' experiences and their strategies for dealing with the challenges of combining work and family. As Shulamit Reinharz states, "Interviewing offers researchers access to people's ideas, thoughts, and memories in their own words rather than in the words of the researcher."[4] Previous research on work and family that has relied solely on quantitative data has been limited by the nature of close-ended survey questions. Interviews allow for a greater depth of understanding fathers' thought processes in relation to their decisions about work and family. Although there was some initial concern about the gender difference between researcher and participants, previous research has found that men are more willing to confide in female interviewers than in male interviewers. In conducting interviews with men about work and family, Kathleen Gerson reported that the men "disclosed openly and with enthusiasm."[5] Arendell conducted interviews with divorced fathers in New York and found that men were quite willing to talk about feelings they had not discussed with others prior to their interview. In fact, most of the divorced fathers did not feel comfortable sharing their feelings with other men but talked with Arendell, as she states, "*because* I am a woman."[6]

I conducted semistructured interviews with fathers from September 2005 to 2007 in California and North Carolina. An initial phone conversation was used to inform respondents of the purpose of the study, to ensure participants of the confidentiality of the interview data, and to arrange for an interview at a time and place that was convenient for the participant. Most interviews were conducted in my office, a friend's office (in the case of California), or a participant's workplace. Interviews were scheduled during weekdays, weeknights, and weekends, at the convenience of the participant. Before the interview, I went through the consent form drawn up for this project. The consent form includes a brief description of the project and information about confidentiality, compensation, and their right to refuse or withdraw. Participants were assured that their names would be changed in order to ensure confidentiality. Participation was voluntary, and respondents were told that they could stop the interview at any time or refuse to answer any questions. The participant and I each signed the form, and the participant was given a copy of the consent form. All interviews were tape-recorded or digitally recorded. Most interviews lasted between one hour and one and a half hours. Participants were given a brief questionnaire at the end of the interview. This questionnaire included basic demographic information such as age, race/ethnicity, highest level of education, current occupational title, relationship status, number of children, and state of birth or childhood residence. At the conclusion of the interview, participants were given $50. The interview questions focused on men's work lives, family lives, experiences with work-family conflict and adaptive strategies, and consequences of adaptive strategies for well-being:

Work characteristics: Questions about work life included job description, work hours, work schedule, travel, bringing work home, workplace environment, and job satisfaction.

Partner's work characteristics: Questions about partner's job, work hours, work schedule, travel, and career aspirations were included.

Family characteristics: Questions about family life included family description, partner status, relationship with partner, division of housework, number and ages of children, identity as a father, identity as a working father, childhood family experiences, division of childcare, relationship with child(ren), time spent with child(ren) on weekdays and weekends, and activities with child(ren).

Work-family conflict/strategies: Questions about work-family conflict and adaptive strategies included their experiences with conflict or strain, their efforts at adjusting to becoming a working father, their use of formal (e.g., flex-time, flex-place, condensed workweek, part-time work, job sharing, family leave) and informal work-family adaptive strategies, and their reasons for using or not using certain strategies.

Consequences of strategies: Questions about the consequences of using adaptive strategies included feelings about balancing work and family, satisfaction with work and family situation, feelings about how partner and child(ren) like or dislike adjustments, and thoughts on employers', co-workers', and friends' reactions to their use of adaptive strategies.

Future: Questions about the future included their personal plans for any future changes related to work and family and their suggestions about what employers might do and what policies might help working parents.

Data Analysis

The primary means of organizing and analyzing the interview data was coding. As Kathy Charmaz states, "Researchers use codes to pull together and categorize a series of otherwise discrete events, statements, and observations which they identify in the data. Researchers make the codes fit the data, rather than forcing the data into codes."[7] Coding was performed in two stages, initial coding and focused coding. Initial coding involves obtaining ideas from the data itself. Charmaz suggests four parts of initial coding. The first part involves examining participants' roles, important events in their lives, and the emphasis they give to certain roles and events. The second part involves paying attention to what participants ignore or deemphasize. The third part involves looking for particular words or phrases that participants use themselves that may apply beyond their individual situations. The fourth part involves comparing responses to detect similarities and differences in meanings.[8] I then used the codes developed in the initial coding stage in order to conduct the second stage of focused coding. Focused coding involves applying codes to the data. Charmaz states, "The purpose of focused coding is to build and clarify a category by examining all the data it covers and variations from it."[9] This process includes developing subcategories, clarifying codes based on the literature, and integrating categories through a "processual analysis." This allows the researcher to move beyond description to explanation.[10] The qualitative software program NVIVO was used to organize the coding schemes developed.

NOTES

NOTES TO CHAPTER ONE

1. All names have been changed.
2. Gerson 1993, ix.
3. Hochschild 1989.
4. Gerson 1993.
5. Deutsch 1999.
6. Holter 2007.
7. Ranson 2010.
8. Robinson & Hunter 2008; West 2002.
9. Galinsky, Aumann, & Bond 2009; U.S. Census Bureau 2010.
10. Galinsky, Aumann, & Bond 2009.
11. Galinsky, Aumann, & Bond 2009; Yeung et al. 2001.
12. Bernstein & Triger 2011.
13. Bianchi 2011.
14. Galinsky, Aumann, & Bond 2009.
15. Featherstone 2003.
16. Beck & Willms 2004, 71.
17. Hochschild 1989.
18. Hill et al. 2003.
19. Galinsky, Aumann, & Bond 2009; Marshall & Barnett 1993; Staines & Pleck 1983.
20. Galinsky, Aumann, & Bond 2009.
21. Milkie & Peltola 1999.
22. Bolger et al. 1989.
23. Schindler 2010.
24. Daly, Ashbourne, & Brown 2009.
25. Booth, Scott, & King 2010.
26. Pruett 2000.
27. Biblarz & Stacey 2010.
28. Blau, Ferber, & Winkler 2002.
29. Ibid.

30. DiMaggio & Powell 1991.

31. Roth 2006, 123–124.

32. Blair-Loy & Wharton 2004; Clarkberg & Moen 2001.

33. Blair-Loy 2003.

34. Roth 2006.

35. Collinson & Collinson 1997; Pleck 1993.

36. U.S. Census Bureau 2010.

37. Gornick & Meyers 2003; Mishel, Bernstein, & Schmitt 2001.

38. Fry 2010.

39. LaRossa 1997; Palkovitz & Palm 2009; Pleck & Mascaidrelli 2004.

40. Lamb 2000.

41. LaRossa 1988.

42. Lewis & O'Brien 1987.

43. Bianchi, Robinson, & Milkie 2006; Bond, Galinsky, & Swanberg 1998; Yeung et al. 2001.

44. Gerson 1993.

45. Hertz 1999.

46. Ranson 2001.

47. Stryker 1987, 90.

48. LaRossa & Reitzes 1993.

49. Stryker & Serpe 1994.

50. Altergott 1988; Palkovitz, Copes, & Woolfolk 2001; Rane & McBride 2000.

51. Ihinger-Tallman, Pasley, & Buehler 1995.

52. Lamb 1997; Lamb et al. 1987; Lamb, Pleck, & Levine 1985.

53. Palkovitz 1997.

54. Olmstead, Futris, & Pasley 2009.

55. Bernard 1981; Christiansen & Palkovitz 2001.

56. Bruce & Fox 1999; Goldberg 2011.

57. Rane & McBride, 2000.

58. Radin & Harold-Goldsmith 1989.

59. Palkovitz & Palm 2009.

60. Connell 1987, 183.

61. Connell 1987, 1995.

62. Connell & Messerschmidt 2005, 848.

63. Ibid., 852.

64. Ibid.

65. Bonney, Kelley, & Levant 1999; Harris & Marmer 1996; Radin & Harold-Goldsmith 1989.

66. While I describe some notable differences in family leave experiences between fathers living in California and North Carolina in chapter 2, the proportion of

dads in each group (old, new, and super) and their other work-family experiences are very similar for those living in the two states.

NOTES TO CHAPTER 2

1. Maurer, Pleck, & Rane 2001; Pleck & Pleck 1997; Townsend 2002.
2. Reed 2005.
3. Doucet 2006; Pleck and Pleck 1997; Sayer 2005.
4. Pasley, Futris, & Skinner 2002; Townsend 2002, 103–104.
5. Coltrane 1996, 235.
6. Gershuny 2001; O'Brien & Shemilt 2003; Pleck & Mascaidrelli 2004; Yeung et al. 2001.
7. Bianchi, Robinson, & Milkie 2006.
8. Bond, Galinsky, & Swanberg 1998.
9. Yeung et al. 2001.
10. O'Brien 2005.
11. Becker & Moen 1999.
12. Singley & Hynes 2005.
13. Becker & Moen 1999.
14. Eggebeen & Knoester 2001, 384.
15. Ray, Gornick, & Schmitt 2010.
16. Heyman, Earle, & Hayes 2007, 1.
17. Ibid.
18. Brandth & Kvande 2006.
19. Gislason 2007.
20. Moss & O'Brien 2006.
21. O'Brien, Brandth, & Kvande 2007.
22. Nepomnyaschy & Waldfogel 2007.
23. Grant, Hatchard, & Patel 2005.
24. Bond et al. 1991; Hyde, Essex, & Horton 1993; Pleck 1992.
25. Nepomnyaschy & Waldfogel 2007.
26. Hyde, Essex, & Horton 1993; Pleck 1992.
27. Nepomnyaschy & Waldfogel 2007.
28. Singley & Hynes 2005.
29. Seward et al. 2006.
30. Nepomnyaschy & Waldfogel 2007.
31. Haas & Hwang 2000.
32. Singley & Hynes 2005.
33. Nepomnyaschy & Waldfogel 2007.
34. Seward et al. 2006.
35. Cantor et al. 2001.

36. Bond et al. 1991.

37. Bond et al. 1991; Hyde, Essex, & Horton 1993; Pleck 1992.

38. Fried 1998.

39. Haas, Hwang, & Russell 2000.

40. Haas & Hwang 1995.

41. Kelly 2010.

42. Cantor et al. 2001.

43. Han, Ruhm, & Waldfogel 2009; Han & Waldfogel 2003.

44. Seward et al. 2006.

45. Baird & Reynolds 2004.

46. Andrews et al. 2004.

47. Bond et al. 1991.

48. Applebaum & Milkman 2011.

49. Ibid.

50. Nepomnyaschy & Waldfogel 2007.

51. O'Brien, Brandth, & Kvande 2007, 379.

52. Haas, Hwang, & Russell 2000.

53. Doucet 2009, 92.

54. Hyde, Essex, & Horton 1993; Seward et al. 2006.

1. Hochschild 1989.

2. Aumann, Galinsky, & Matos 2011, 1.

3. Voydanoff 2002, 147.

4. Brayfield 1995, 330.

5. Wight, Raley, & Bianchi 2008.

6. Greenhaus & Beutell 1985, 77.

7. Aumann, Galinsky, & Matos 2011.

8. Poposki 2011.

9. Frone 2003; Reynolds & Aletraris 2010.

10. Aumann, Galinsky, & Matos 2011; Frone 2003.

11. Reynolds & Aletraris 2010.

12. Golden 2006; Reynolds & Aletraris 2010.

13. Jacobs & Gerson 2004; Reynolds & Aletraris 2010.

14. Reynolds & Aletraris 2010.

15. Golden & Gebreselassie 2007; Reynolds & Aletraris 2006.

16. Clarkberg & Moen 2001.

17. Golden & Wiens-Tuers 2005.

18. Nomaguchi, Milkie, & Bianchi 2005.

19. Milkie et al. 2004; Nomaguchi, Milkie, & Bianchi 2005.

20. Milkie et al. 2010.
21. Aumann, Galinsky, & Matos 2011.
22. Reynolds & Aletraris 2010.
23. Aumann, Galinsky, & Matos 2011.
24. Milkie & Peltola 1999.
25. Bianchi, Robinson, & Milkie 2006.
26. Dew 2009.
27. Kingston & Nock 1987.
28. Nomaguchi, Milkie, & Bianchi 2005.
29. Presser 2000, 2005.
30. Nomaguchi, Milkie, & Bianchi 2005.
31. Poposki 2011.
32. Hill 2005.
33. Hochschild 1997.
34. Bolger et al. 1989.
35. Barnett 1998; Barnett & Baruch 1985.
36. Barnett & Hyde 2001.
37. Brayfield 1995; Crosby 1991.
38. Russell & Radin 1983.
39. Marks & MacDermid 1996.

NOTES TO CHAPTER 4

1. Parsons & Bales 1955.
2. Becker 1981.
3. Kanter 1977, 22.
4. Williams 2010.
5. Christiansen & Palkovitz 2001.
6. Ibid.
7. Lamont 2000; J. Pleck 1995.
8. Townsend 2002.
9. Ibid., 118.
10. Ibid.
11. Andrews et al. 2004.
12. American Heritage Stedman's Medical Dictionary 2002.
13. Christiansen & Palkovitz 2001.
14. Cooper 2000.
15. Jacobs & Gerson 2004.
16. Lundberg & Rose 2002.
17. Williams 1999.
18. Cooper 2000, 389.

19. Harpaz & Snir 2003.
20. Williams 2010.
21. Crouter et al. 2001.
22. Townsend 2002.
23. Lundberg & Rose 2000.
24. Seward 2010.
25. Townsend 2002.
26. Oppenheimer 1994, 1997.
27. Townsend 2002.
28. Seward 2010, 9.
29. Connell 1995.
30. Christiansen & Palkovitz 2001.

NOTES TO CHAPTER 5

1. Barnett 1998.
2. Moen & Wethington 1992, 234.
3. Voydanoff 2002.
4. Haddock et al. 2006.
5. Crouter & McHale 1993; Moen, Kelly, & Huang 2008.
6. Cooper 2000.
7. Haddock et al. 2006.
8. McDonald & Almeida 2004.
9. Becker & Moen 1999; Crompton & Lyonette 2010.
10. Kaufman, Lyonette, & Crompton 2011.
11. Armstrong & Squires 2002; Halford 2006.
12. Halford 2006.
13. Halford 2006; Sheller & Urry 2003.
14. Halford 2006, 386.
15. Schieman, Milkie, & Glavin 2009.
16. Bond, Galinsky, & Swanberg 1998.
17. Halford 2006, 398.
18. Shinn et al. 1989.
19. Hill et al. 2001.
20. Raley, Mattingly, & Bianchi 2006.
21. Bond, Galinsky, & Swanberg 1998.

NOTES TO CHAPTER 6

1. Lundberg & Rose 2002; Townsend 2002.
2. Lundberg & Rose 2002.
3. Loughran & Zissimopoulos 2007; Percheski & Wildeman 2008.

4. Kaufman & Uhlenberg 2000; Lundberg & Rose 2000.

5. Galinsky, Aumann, & Bond 2009.

6. Deutsch 1999; Galinsky, Aumann, & Bond, 2009.

7. Haddock et al. 2006.

8. U.S. Census Bureau 2009.

9. Gerson & Kraut 1988; Kraut & Grambsch 1987.

10. Daly, Ashbourne, & Brown 2009.

11. Ibid.

12. Kaufman & Uhlenberg 2000; Lundberg & Rose 2000.

13. Haddock et al. 2006.

14. Ibid.

15. Noonan, Estes, & Glass 2007.

16. Haddock et al. 2006.

17. Daly, Ashbourne, & Brown 2009.

18. Blair-Loy & Wharton 2002; Hochschild 1997; Moen, Kelly, & Huang 2008.

19. Gillies 2009; Shows & Gerstel 2009.

20. Waller 2009.

21. Shows & Gerstel 2009.

22. Gillies 2009.

23. Gerson 1993.

24. Waller 2009.

25. Brayfield 1995; Nock & Kingston 1988.

26. Grosswald 2002; Presser 1994.

27. Marsiglio & Cohan 2000; Waller 2009.

28. Gillies 2009, 398.

29. Galinsky & Bond 1998.

30. Bond, Galinsky, & Swanberg 1998; U.S. Bureau of Labor Statistics 2011b.

31. Hill et al. 2001.

32. Galinsky, Aumann, & Bond 2009.

NOTES TO CHAPTER 7

1. Amato, Meyers, & Emery 2009; Garasky et al. 2010; Guzzo 2009; Olmstead, Futris, & Pasley 2009.

2. Belkin 2011.

3. U.S. Census Bureau 2009.

4. Belkin 2011.

5. Bauserman 2002; Stamps, Kunen, & Rock-Facheux 1997.

6. Bauserman 2002.

7. Hawkins, Amato, & King 2006.

8. Hook & Chalasani 2008.

9. Dufur et al. 2010; Hawkins, Amato, & King 2006.

10. Brown 2000; Meyer & Garasky 1993.

11. Heath & Orthner 1999.

12. Greif, DeMaris, & Hood 1993.

13. DeGarmo 2010.

14. Coltrane 1996.

15. Kelly & Kalev 2006.

16. Stone 2007.

17. Kruk 2010.

18. Kanter 1977.

19. Waller 2009.

20. Ibid.

21. Chima 1999.

22. Ibid.; Nielsen 1999.

23. Stamps 2002.

24. Chima 1999.

25. Halford 2006.

26. Ibid.

27. Risman 1998, 48.

28. Doucet 2006, 123.

29. Daniels 1987.

30. Erickson 2005, 341.

31. Ibid.

32. Hilton & Kopera-Frye 2004.

33. Bauserman 2002; Bokker, Farley, & Bailey 2006.

1. Palkovitz & Palm 2009, 7.

2. Hochschild 1989; England 2010.

3. U.S. Bureau of Labor Statistics 2011a.

4. England 2010, 150.

5. Ibid.

6. Aumann, Galinsky, & Matos 2011.

7. Ibid.

8. Ibid.

9. Goldscheider & Waite 1993.

10. Ibid.

11. Aumann, Galinsky, & Matos, 2011.

12. Belkin 2003.

13. Stone 2007; Percheski 2008.
14. Palkovitz & Palm 2009.
15. Bernard 1975.
16. Dizard 1968.
17. Erikson 1968.
18. Palkovitz 2002.
19. Daly, Ashbourne, & Brown 2009.
20. Palkovitz, Copes, & Woolfolk 2001.
21. Daly, Ashbourne, & Brown 2009; Schindler 2010.
22. Ball & Moselle 2007.
23. Mansdotter & Lundin 2010.
24. Ball & Moselle 2007; Galinsky, Aumann, & Bond 2009.
25. Hill et al. 2003.
26. Craig 2006.
27. Gregg & Washbrook 2003, 54.
28. Ibid.
29. Coltrane 1988.
30. Olsen & Walby 2004.
31. Lambert 2008.
32. Coltrane 1996.
33. Chodorow 1999.
34. Silverstein & Auerbach 1999.
35. Lamb 1997.
36. Lamb & Tamis-LeMonda 2004.
37. Ruhm 2000.
38. Berger, Hill, & Waldfogel 2005; Fass 2009; Ruhm 2000.
39. Nepomnyaschy & Waldfogel 2007.
40. Flouri & Buchanan 2004.
41. Fagan & Iglesias 1999; National Center for Educational Statistics 1997; Pruett 2000.
42. Updegraff, McHale, & Crouter 1996.
43. Flouri & Buchanan 2004.
44. Lamb 1997.
45. Flouri & Buchanan 2003.
46. Barnett, Marshall, & Pleck 1992; Booth, Scott, & King 2010; Pruett 2000.
47. Amato 1994; Flouri & Buchanan 2003.
48. Ball & Moselle 2007; Flouri & Buchanan 2002.
49. Aldous & Mulligan 2002; Amato & Rivera 1999; Mosley & Thomson 1995.
50. Eggebeen 2002.

51. Knoester & Eggebeen 2006.
52. Eggebeen, Dew, & Knoester 2010; Knoester & Eggebeen 2006; Settersten & Cancel-Tirado 2010.
53. Coltrane 2007.
54. Kaufman 2000.
55. Coltrane 2007.
56. Fry & Cohn 2010.
57. Haas & Hwang 1995; Russell & Hwang 2004.
58. Allen & Hawkins 1999; Fagan & Barnett 2003; Schoppe-Sullivan et al. 2008.
59. Pleck 1993.
60. Correll, Benard, & Paik 2007.
61. Kelly, Moen, & Tranby 2011.
62. Daly, Ashbourne, & Brown 2009.
63. Fass 2009; Rudd 2004.
64. Reeves 2002.
65. O'Brien 2005.
66. Heyman, Earle, & Hayes 2007.
67. Gornick & Meyers 2003.
68. Bennhold 2010.
69. O'Brien 2005.
70. Fass 2009.
71. Ibid.
72. Ibid.
73. Ibid.
74. Nepomnyaschy & Waldfogel 2007; Kamerman 2006; Haas & Hwang 2008.
75. Chatterji & Markowitz 2005.
76. Fass 2009; Hofferth & Curtin 2006.
77. Gornick & Meyers 2003.
78. Ibid.
79. Williams & Boushey 2010.
80. Heyman, Earle, & Hayes 2007.
81. Gornick & Meyers 2003.
82. Heyman, Earle, & Hayes 2007.
83. Gornick & Meyers 2003.
84. Ibid.
85. Mason 1994.
86. Kruk 2005, 122.
87. Artis 2004, 797.
88. Bauserman 2002; Berger et al. 2008; Fabricius 2003; Kruk 2005.
89. J. Pleck 1997.

90. Cowan & Cowan 2000.
91. Coltrane 2007.
92. Edwards, Doucet, & Furstenberg 2009.
93. Settersten & Cancel-Tirado 2010.

NOTES TO APPENDIX

1. Arendell 1995.
2. Townsend 2002.
3. Clarke 2005; Dermott 2001; Gonzalez-Lopez 2004; Henwood & Procter 2003; Marsiglio 2004; Roy 2006.
4. Reinharz 1992, 18–19.
5. Gerson 1993, 291.
6. Arendell 1995, 8.
7. Charmaz 1983, 112.
8. Ibid.
9. Ibid., 117.
10. Ibid.

REFERENCES

Aldous, J., & Mulligan, G. M. 2002. Fathers' child care and children's behavior problems: A longitudinal study. *Journal of Family Issues, 23*, 624–647.

Allen, S. M., & Hawkins, A. J. 1999. Maternal gatekeeping: Mothers' beliefs and behaviors that inhibit greater father involvement in family work. *Journal of Marriage and Family, 61*, 199–212.

Altergott, K. 1988. Work and family: Understanding men's role evaluations. *Journal of Family and Economic Issues, 9*, 181–198.

Amato, P. R. 1994. Father-child relations, mother-child relations, and offspring psychological well-being in early adulthood. *Journal of Marriage and the Family, 56*, 1031–1042.

Amato, P. R., Meyers, C. E., & Emery, R. E. 2009. Changes in nonresident father-child contact from 1976 to 2002. *Family Relations, 58*, 41–53.

Amato, P. R., & Rivera, F. 1999. Paternal involvement and children's behavior problems. *Journal of Marriage and the Family, 61*, 375–384.

American Heritage Stedman's Medical Dictionary. 2002. Workaholic. Boston: Houghton Mifflin.

Andrews, A. B., Luckey, L., Bolden, E., Whiting-Fickling, J., & Lind, K. A. 2004. Public perceptions about father involvement: Results of a statewide household survey. *Journal of Family Issues, 25*, 603–633.

Applebaum, E., & Milkman, R. 2011. Leaves that pay: Employer and worker experiences with paid family leave in California. Center for Economic and Policy Research. Available at http://www.cepr.net/index.php/publications/reports/leaves-that-pay.

Arendell, T. 1995. *Fathers and divorce*. Thousand Oaks, CA: Sage.

Armstrong, C., & Squires, J. 2002. Beyond the public/private dichotomy: Relational space and sexual inequalities. *Contemporary Political Theory, 1*, 261–283.

Artis, J. E. 2004. Judging the best interests of the child: Judges' accounts of the tender years doctrine. *Law & Society Review, 38*, 769–806.

Aumann, K., Galinsky, E., & Matos, K. 2011. *The new male mystique*. Families and Work Institute, National Study of the Changing Workforce.

Baird, C. L., & Reynolds, J. R. 2004. Employee awareness of family leave benefits: The effects of family, work, and gender. *Sociological Quarterly*, 45, 325–353.

Ball, J., & Moselle, K. 2007. Fathers' contributions to children's well-being. Public Health Agency of Canada, Population Health Fund Project. http://www.fira.ca/cms/documents/123/PH_FI_Report_brief.pdf.

Barnett, R. C. 1998. Toward a review and reconceptualization of the work/family literature. *Genetic, Social & General Psychology Monographs*, 124, 125–182.

Barnett, R. C., & Baruch, G. K. 1985. Women's involvement in multiple roles and psychological distress. *Journal of Personality and Social Psychology*, 49, 135–145.

Barnett, R. C., & Hyde, J. S. 2001. Women, men, work, and family: An expansionist theory. *American Psychologist*, 56, 781–796.

Barnett, R. C., Marshall, N. L., & Pleck, J. H. 1992. Adult son-parent relationships and their associations with son's psychological distress. *Journal of Family Issues*, 13, 505–525.

Bauserman, R. 2002. Child adjustment in joint-custody versus sole-custody arrangements: A meta-analytic review. *Journal of Family Psychology*, 16, 91–102.

Beck, U., & Willms, J. 2004. *Conversations with Ulrich Beck*. Cambridge, UK: Polity.

Becker, G. 1981. *A treatise on the family*. Cambridge: Harvard University Press.

Becker, P. E., & Moen, P. 1999. Scaling back: Dual-earner couples' work-family strategies. *Journal of Marriage and the Family*, 61, 995–1007.

Belkin, L. 2003. The opt-out revolution. *New York Times Magazine*, October 26.

Belkin, L. 2011. With more single fathers, a changing family picture. *New York Times*, June 2.

Bennhold, K. 2010. In Sweden, men can have it all. *New York Times*, June 9.

Berger, L. M., Brown, P. R., Joung, E., Melli, M. S., & Wimer, L. 2008. The stability of child physical placements following divorce: Descriptive evidence from Wisconsin. *Journal of Marriage and Family*, 70, 273–283.

Berger, L. M., Hill, J., & Waldfogel, J. 2005. Maternity leave, early maternal employment and child health and development in the U.S. *Economic Journal*, 115, F29–F27.

Bernard, J. 1975. *Women, wives, mothers: Values and options*. Chicago: Aldine.

Bernard, J. 1981. The good provider role: Its rise and fall. *American Psychologist*, 36, 1–12.

Bernstein, G., & Triger, Z. H. 2011. Over-parenting. *UC Davis Law Review*, 44, 1221–1280.

Bianchi, S. 2011. Family change and time allocation in American families. *Annals of the American Academy of Political and Social Science*, 638, 21–44.

Bianchi, S., Robinson, J. P., & Milkie, M. 2006. *Changing rhythms of American family life*. New York: Russell Sage Foundation.

Biblarz, T. J., & Stacey, J. 2010. How does the gender of parents matter? *Journal of Marriage and Family, 72,* 3–22.

Blair-Loy, M. F. 2003. *Competing devotions: Career and family among women executives.* Cambridge: Harvard University Press.

Blair-Loy, M. F., & Wharton, A. S. 2002. Employees' use of work-family policies and the workplace social context. *Social Forces, 80,* 813–845.

Blair-Loy, M. F., & Wharton, A. S. 2004. Organizational commitment and constraints on work-family policy use: Corporate flexibility policies in a global firm. *Sociological Perspectives, 47,* 243–268.

Blau, F. D., Ferber, M. A., & Winkler, A. E. 2002. *The economics of women, men, and work.* Upper Saddle River, NJ: Prentice Hall.

Bokker, L. P., Farley, R. C., & Bailey, W. 2006. The relationship between custodial status and emotional well-being among recently divorced fathers. *Journal of Divorce and Remarriage, 44,* 83–98.

Bolger, N., DeLongis, A., Kessler, R. C., & Wethington, E. 1989. The contagion of stress across multiple roles. *Journal of Marriage and the Family, 51,* 175–183.

Bond, J. T., Galinsky, E., Lord, M., Staines, G. L., & Brown, K. R. 1991. *Beyond the parental leave debate: The impact of laws in four states.* New York: Families and Work Institute.

Bond, J. T., Galinsky, E., & Swanberg, J. E. 1998. *The 1997 National Study of the Changing Workforce.* New York: Families and Work Institute.

Bonney, J. F., Kelley, M. L., & Levant, R. F. 1999. A model of fathers' behavioral involvement in child care in dual-earner families. *Journal of Family Psychology, 13,* 401–415.

Booth, A., Scott, M. E., & King, V. 2010. Father residence and adolescent problem behavior: Are youth always better off in two-parent families? *Journal of Family Issues, 31,* 585–605.

Brandth, B., & Kvande, E. 2006. The Norway report. In M. Moss & M. O'Brien (Eds.), *International review of leave policies and related research.* London: Department of Trade and Industry, Employment Relations Research Series No. 57.

Brayfield, A. 1995. Juggling jobs and kids: The impact of employment schedules on fathers' caring for children. *Journal of Marriage and the Family, 57,* 321–332.

Brown, B. V. 2000. The single-father family: Demographic, economic, and public transfer use characteristics. *Marriage and Family Review, 29,* 203–220.

Bruce, C., & Fox, G. L. 1999. Accounting for patterns of father involvement: Age of child, father-child co-residence and father role salience. *Sociological Inquiry, 69,* 458–476.

Cantor, D., Waldfogel, J., Kerwin, J., Wright, M. M., Levin, K., & Rauch, J. 2001. *Balancing the needs of families and employers.* Rockville, MD: Westat.

Charmaz, K. 1983. The grounded theory method: An explication and interpretation. In R. M. Emerson (Ed.), *Contemporary field research: A collection of readings* (pp. 109–126). Prospect Heights, IL: Waveland.

Chatterji, P., & Markowitz, S. 2005. Does the length of maternity leave affect maternal health? *Southern Economic Journal, 72*, 16–41.

Chima, F. O. 1999. Fathers with single parenting roles: Perspectives on strengths, concerns and recommendations. *Free Inquiry in Creative Sociology, 27*, 3–13.

Chodorow, N. J. 1999. *The reproduction of mothering: Psychoanalysis and the Sociology of gender* (Updated ed.). Berkeley: University of California Press.

Christiansen, S. L., & Palkovitz, R. 2001. Why the "good provider" role still matters: Providing as a form of paternal involvement. *Journal of Family Issues, 22*, 84–106.

Clarkberg, M., & Moen, P. 2001. Understanding the time squeeze: Married couples' preferred and actual work-hour strategies. *American Behavioral Scientist, 44*, 1115–1135.

Clarke, J. N. 2005. Fathers' home health care work when a child has cancer. *Men and Masculinities, 7*, 385–404.

Collinson, D., & Collinson, M. 1997. "Delayering managers": Time-space surveillance and its gendered effects. *Organization, 4*, 375–407.

Coltrane, S. 1988. Father-child relationships and the status of women: A cross-cultural study. *American Journal of Sociology, 93*, 1060–1095.

Coltrane, S. 1996. *Family man: Fatherhood, housework, and gender equity*. New York: Oxford University Press.

Coltrane, S. 2007. What about fathers? Marriage, work, and family in men's lives. *American Prospect*, February 19. http://prospect.org/cs/articles?articleId=12490.

Connell, R. W. 1987. *Gender and power: Society, the person and sexual politics*. Stanford: Stanford University Press.

Connell, R. W. 1995. *Masculinities*. Berkeley: University of California Press.

Connell, R. W., & Messerschmidt, J. W. 2005. Hegemonic masculinity: Rethinking the concept. *Gender & Society, 19*, 829–859.

Cooper, M. 2000. Being the "go-to guy": Fatherhood, masculinity, and the organization of work in Silicon Valley. *Qualitative Sociology, 23*, 379–404.

Correll, S. J., Benard, S., & Paik, I. 2007. Getting a job: Is there a motherhood penalty? *American Journal of Sociology, 112*, 1297–1338.

Cowan, C. P., & Cowan, P. A. 2000. *When partners become parents*. Mahwah, NJ: Erlbaum.

Craig, L. 2006. Does father care mean fathers share? A comparison of how mothers and fathers in intact families spend time with children. *Gender & Society, 20*, 259–281.

Crompton, R., & Lyonette, C. 2010. Family, class and gender "strategies" in mothers' employment and childcare. In J. Scott, R. Crompton, & C. Lyonette (Eds.), *Gender inequalities in the 21st century: New barriers and continuing constraints* (pp. 174–192). Cheltenham, UK: Elgar.

Crosby, F. J. 1991. *Juggling: The unexpected advantages of balancing career and home for women and their families.* New York: Free Press.

Crouter, A. C., Bumpus, M. F., Head, M. R., & McHale, S. M. 2001. Implications of overwork and overload for the quality of men's family relationships. *Journal of Marriage and the Family, 63,* 404–416.

Crouter, A. C., & McHale, S. M. 1993. Temporal rhythms in family life: Seasonal variation in the relation between parental work and family processes. *Developmental Psychology, 29,* 198–205.

Daly, K. J., Ashbourne, L., & Brown, J. L. 2009. Fathers' perceptions of children's influence: Implications for involvement. *Annals of the American Academy of Political and Social Science, 624,* 61–77.

Daniels, A. K. 1987. Invisible work. *Social Problems, 34,* 403–415.

DeGarmo, D. S. 2010. A time varying evaluation of identity theory and father involvement for full custody, shared custody, and no custody divorced father. *Fathering, 8,* 181–202.

Dermott, E. 2001. New fatherhood in practice? Parental leave in the UK. *International Journal of Sociology and Social Policy, 21,* 145–164.

Deutsch, F. 1999. *Halving it all: How equally shared parenting works.* Cambridge: Harvard University Press.

Dew, J. 2009. Has the marital time cost of parenting changed over time? *Social Forces, 88,* 519–542.

DiMaggio, P., & Powell, W. 1991. Introduction. In W. Powell & P. DiMaggio (Eds.), *The New Institutionalism in Organizational Analysis* (pp. 1–38). Chicago: University of Chicago Press.

Dizard, J. 1968. *Social change in the family.* Chicago: University of Chicago Press.

Doucet, A. 2006. *Do men mother? Fathering, care and domestic responsibility.* Toronto: University of Toronto Press.

Doucet, A. 2009. Dad and baby in the first year: Gendered responsibilities and embodiment. *Annals of the American Academy of Political and Social Science, 624,* 78–98.

Dufur, M. J., Howell, N. C., Downey, D. B., Ainsworth, J. W., & Lapray, A. J. 2010. Sex differences in parenting behaviors in single-mother and single-father households. *Journal of Marriage and Family, 72,* 1092–1106.

Edwards, R., Doucet, A., & Furstenberg, F. F., Jr. 2009. Fathering across diversity and adversity: International perspectives and policy interventions. *Annals of the American Academy of Political and Social Science, 624,* 6–11.

Eggebeen, D. J. 2002. The changing course of fatherhood: Men's experiences with children in demographic perspective. *Journal of Family Issues*, *23*, 486–506.

Eggebeen, D. J., Dew, J., & Knoester, C. 2010. Fatherhood and men's lives at middle age. *Journal of Family Issues*, *31*, 113–130.

Eggebeen, D. J., & Knoester, C. 2001. Does fatherhood matter for men? *Journal of Marriage and the Family*, *63*, 381–393.

England, P. 2010. The gender revolution: Uneven and stalled. *Gender & Society*, *24*(2), 149–166.

Erickson, R. J. 2005. Why emotion work matters: Sex, gender, and the division of household labor. *Journal of Marriage and Family*, *67*, 337–351.

Erikson, E. 1968. *Identity, youth and crisis*. New York: Norton.

Fabricius, W. V. 2003. Listening to children of divorce: New findings that diverge from Wallerstein, Lewis, and Blakeslee. *Family Relations*, *52*, 385–396.

Fagan, J., & Barnett, M. 2003. The relationship between maternal gatekeeping, paternal competence, mothers' attitudes about the father role, and father involvement. *Journal of Family Issues*, *24*, 1020–1043.

Fagan, J., & Iglesias, A. 1999. Father involvement program effects on fathers, father figures, and their Head Start children: A quasi-experimental study. *Early Childhood Research Quarterly*, *14*, 243–269.

Fass, S. 2009. *Paid leave in the states: A critical support for low-wage workers and their families*. National Center for Children in Poverty Brief. Columbia University.

Featherstone, B. 2003. Taking fathers seriously. *British Journal of Social Work*, *33*, 239–254.

Flouri, E., & Buchanan, A. 2002. Life satisfaction in teenage boys: The moderating role of father involvement and bullying. *Aggressive Behavior*, *28*, 126–133.

Flouri, E., & Buchanan, A. 2003. The role of father involvement in children's later mental health. *Journal of Adolescence*, *26*, 63–78.

Flouri, E., & Buchanan, A. 2004. Early father's and mother's involvement and child's later educational outcomes. *British Journal of Educational Psychology*, *74*, 141–153.

Fried, M. 1998. *Taking time: Parental leave policy and corporate culture*. Philadelphia: Temple University Press.

Frone, M. R. 2003. Work-family balance. In J. C. Quick & L. E. Tetrick (Eds.), *Handbook of occupational health psychology* (pp. 143–162). Washington, DC: American Psychological Association.

Fry, R. 2010. *The reversal of the college marriage gap*. Washington, DC: Pew Research Center.

Fry, R., & Cohn, D. 2010. New economics of marriage: The rise of wives. Pew Research Center, http://pewresearch.org/pubs/1466/economics-marriage-rise-of-wives.

Galinsky, E., Aumann, K., & Bond, J. T. 2009. *Times are changing: Gender and generation at work and at home*. New York: Families and Work Institute.

Galinsky, E., & Bond, J. T. 1998. *The 1998 business work-life study: A sourcebook*. New York: Families and Work Institute.

Garasky, S., Stewart, S. D., Gundersen, C., and Lohman, B. J. 2010. Toward a fuller understanding of nonresident father involvement: An examination of child support, in-kind support, and visitation. *Population Research and Policy Review*, 29, 363–393.

Gershuny, J. I. 2001. *Changing times*. New York: Oxford University Press.

Gerson, K. 1993. *No man's land: Men's changing commitments to family and work*. New York: Basic Books.

Gerson, J., & Kraut, R. E. 1988. Clerical work at the home or in the office: The difference it makes. In K. E. Christensen (Ed.), *The new era of home-base work* (pp. 49–64). Boulder, CO: Westview.

Gillies, V. 2009. Understandings and experiences of involved fathering in the United Kingdom: Exploring classed dimensions. *Annals of the American Academy of Political and Social Science*, 624, 49–60.

Gislason, I. V. 2007. *Parental leave in Iceland: Bringing the fathers in; Developments in the wake of new legislation in 2000*. Ministry of Social Affairs and Centre for Gender Equality. Available at http://www.jafnretti.is/D10/_Files/parentalleave.pdf.

Goldberg, J. S. 2011. *Identity salience and involvement among resident and nonresident fathers* (Working Paper WP 11-14-FF). Princeton, NJ: Fragile Families.

Golden, L. 2006. Overemployment in the US: Which workers are willing to reduce their work hours and income? In J.-Y. Boulin, M. Lallement, J. C. Messenger, & F. Michon (Eds.), *Decent working time: New trends, new issues* (pp. 209–261). Geneva, Switzerland: International Labor Organization.

Golden, L., & Gebreselassie, T. 2007. Overemployment mismatches: The preference for fewer work hours. *Monthly Labor Review*, 130, 18–37.

Golden, L., & Wiens-Tuers, B. 2005. Mandatory overtime work in the United States: Who, where and what? *Labor Studies Journal*, 30, 1–26.

Goldscheider, F. K., & Waite, L. J. 1993. *New families, no families? The transformation of the American home*. Berkeley: University of California Press.

Gonzalez-Lopez, G. 2004. Fathering Latina sexualities: Mexican men and the virginity of their daughters. *Journal of Marriage and Family*, 66, 1118–1130.

Gornick, J. C., & Meyers, M. K. 2003. *Families that work: Policies for reconciling parenthood and employment*. New York: Russell Sage Foundation.

Grant, J., Hatchard, T., & Patel, N. 2005. *Expecting better: A state-by-state analysis of parental leave programs*. Washington, DC: National Partnership for

Women and Families. Available at http://www.nationalpartnership.org/por-tals/p3/library/PaidLeave/Parental-LeaveReportMay05.pdf.

Greenhaus, J., & Beutell, N. 1985. Sources of conflict between work and family roles. *Academy of Management Review, 10*, 76–88.

Gregg, P., & Washbrook, E. 2003. *The effects of early maternal employment on child development in the UK* (Working Paper Series No. 03/070). Centre for Market and Public Organisation, Department of Economics, University of Bristol.

Greif, G. L., DeMaris, A., and Hood, J. C. 1993. Balancing work and single fa-therhood. In J. C. Hood (Ed.), *Men, work, and family* (pp. 176–194). Thousand Oaks, CA: Sage.

Grosswald, B. 2002. "I raised my kids on the bus": Transit shift workers' coping strategies for parenting. *Journal of Sociology and Social Welfare, 29*, 29–49.

Guzzo, K. B. 2009. Men's visitation with nonresidential children. *Journal of Family Issues, 30*, 921–944.

Haas, L., & Hwang, P. 1995. Company culture and men's usage of family leave benefits in Sweden. *Family Relations, 44*, 28–36.

Haas, L., & Hwang, P. 2000. Programs and policies promoting women's economic equality and men's sharing of child care in Sweden. In L. Haas, P. Hwang, and G. Russell (Eds.), *Organizational change and gender equity: International per-spectives on fathers and mothers in the workplace*. Thousand Oaks, CA: Sage.

Haas, L., & Hwang, P. 2008. The impact of taking parental leave on fathers' par-ticipation in childcare and ties with children: Lessons from Sweden. *Commu-nity, Work & Family, 11*, 85–104.

Haas, L., Hwang, P, & Russell, G. 2000. *Organizational change and gender equity: International perspectives on fathers and mothers in the workplace*. Thousand Oaks, CA: Sage.

Haddock, S. A., Zimmerman, T. S., Lyness, K. P., & Ziemba, S. J. 2006. Prac-tices of dual earner couples successfully balancing work and family. *Journal of Family and Economic Issues, 27*, 207–234.

Halford, S. 2006. Collapsing the boundaries? Fatherhood, organization and home-working. *Gender, Work and Organization, 13*, 383–402.

Han, W. J., Ruhm, C., & Waldfogel, J. 2009. Parental leave policies and parents' employment and leave-taking. *Journal of Policy Analysis and Management, 28*, 29–54.

Han, W. J., & Waldfogel, J. 2003. Parental leave: The impact of recent legislation on parents' leave taking. *Demography, 40*, 191–200.

Harpaz, I., & Snir, R. 2003. Workaholism: Its definition and nature. *Human Re-lations, 56*, 291–319.

Harris, K. M., & Marmer, J. K. 1996. Poverty, paternal involvement, and adoles-cent well-being. *Journal of Family Issues, 17*, 614–640.

Hawkins, D. N., Amato, P. R., and King, V. 2006. Parent-adolescent involvement: The relative influence of parent gender and residence. *Journal of Marriage and Family*, 68, 125–136.

Heath, D. T., & Orthner, D. K. 1999. Stress and adaptation among male and female single parents. *Journal of Family Issues*, 20, 557–587.

Henwood, K., & Procter, J. 2003. The "good father": Reading men's accounts of paternal involvement during the transition to first-time fatherhood. *British Journal of Social Psychology*, 42, 337–355.

Hertz, R. 1999. Working to place family at the center of life: Dual-earner and single-parent strategies. *Annals of the American Academy of Political and Social Sciences*, 562, 16–31.

Heyman, J., Earle, A., & Hayes, J. 2007. *The work, family, and equity index: Where does the United States stand globally?* Boston: Project on Global Working Families. Available at http://www.hsph.harvard.edu/globalworkingfamilies/images/report.pdf.

Hill, E. J. 2005. Work-family facilitation and conflict, working fathers and mothers, work-family stressors and support. *Journal of Family Issues*, 26, 793–819.

Hill, E. J., Hawkins, A. J., Ferris, M., & Weitzman, M. 2001. Finding an extra day a week: The positive influence of perceived job flexibility on work and family life balance. *Family Relations*, 50, 49–58.

Hill, E. J., Hawkins, A. J., Martinson, V., & Ferris, M. 2003. Studying "working fathers": Comparing fathers' and mothers' work-family conflict, fit, and adaptive strategies in a global high-tech company. *Fathering*, 1, 239–261.

Hilton, J. M., & Kopera-Frye, K. 2004. Patterns of psychological adjustment among divorced custodial parents. *Journal of Divorce and Remarriage*, 41, 1–30.

Hochschild, A. R. 1997. *The time bind: When work becomes home and home becomes work*. New York: Metropolitan Books.

Hochschild, A. R., with Machung, A. 1989. *The second shift*. New York: HarperCollins.

Hofferth, S., & Curtin, S. 2006. Parental leave statutes and maternal return to work after childbirth in the United States. *Work and Occupation*, 33, 73–105.

Holter, O. G. 2007. Men's work and family reconciliation in Europe. *Men and Masculinities*, 9, 425–456.

Hook, J. L., & Chalasani, S. 2008. Gendered expectations? Reconsidering single fathers' child-care time. *Journal of Marriage and Family*, 70, 978–990.

Hyde, J. S., Essex, M. J., & Horton, F. 1993. Fathers and parental leave: Attitudes and experiences. *Journal of Family Issues*, 14, 616–641.

Ihinger-Tallman, M., Pasley, K., & Buehler, C. 1995. Developing a middle-range theory of father involvement post divorce. In W. Marsiglio (Ed.), *Fatherhood:*

Contemporary theory, research, and social policy (pp. 57–77). Thousand Oaks, CA: Sage.

Jacobs, J. A., & Gerson, K. 2004. *The time divide: Work, family, and gender inequality*. Cambridge: Harvard University Press.

Kamerman, S. B. 2006. Parental leave policies: The impact on child well-being. In P. Moss & M. O'Brien (Eds.), *International review of leave polices and related research, 2006*. London: Department for Trade and Industry.

Kanter, R. M. 1977. *Men and women of the corporation*. New York: Basic Books.

Kaufman, G. 2000. Do gender role attitudes matter? Family formation and dissolution among traditional and egalitarian men and women. *Journal of Family Issues, 21*, 128–144.

Kaufman, G., Lyonette, C., & Crompton, R. 2011. Fathers' work-family strategies in Britain and the U.S. Unpublished manuscript.

Kaufman, G., & Uhlenberg, P. 2000. The influence of parenthood on work effort of married men and women. *Social Forces, 78*, 931–947.

Kelly, E. L. 2010. Failure to update: An institutional perspective on noncompliance with the Family and Medical Leave Act. *Law & Society Review, 44*, 33–66.

Kelly, E. L., & Kalev, A. 2006. Managing flexible work arrangements in U.S. organizations: Formalized discretion or "a right to ask." *Socio-Economic Review, 4*, 379–416.

Kelly, E. L., Moen, P., & Tranby, E. 2011. Changing workplaces to reduce work-family conflict: Schedule control in a white-collar organization. *American Sociological Review, 76*, 265–290.

Kingston, P. W., & Nock, S. L. 1987. Time together among dual-earner couples. *American Sociological Review, 52*, 391–400.

Knoester, C., & Eggebeen, D. J. 2006. The effects of the transition to parenthood and subsequent children on men's well-being and social participation. *Journal of Family Issues, 27*, 1532–1560.

Kraut, R. E., & Grambsch, P. 1987. Home-based, white-collar work: Lessons from the 1980 census. *Social Forces, 66*, 410–426.

Kruk, E. 2005. Shared parental responsibility: A harm reduction-based approach to divorce law reform. *Journal of Divorce & Remarriage, 43*, 119–140.

Kruk, E. 2010. Parental and social institutional responsibilities to children's needs in the divorce transition: Fathers' perspectives. *Journal of Men's Studies, 18*, 159–178.

Lamb, M. E. 1997. *The role of the father in child development*. New York: Wiley.

Lamb, M. E. 2000. The history of research on father involvement: An overview. In E. Peters & R. D. Day (Eds.), *Fatherhood: Research, interventions and policies* (pp. 23–42). New York: Hawthorn.

Lamb, M. E., Pleck, J. H., Charnov, E. L., & Levine, J. A. 1987. A biosocial perspective on paternal behavior and involvement. In J. Lancaster, J. Altmann, A. Rossi, & L. Sherrod (Eds.), *Parenting across lifespan: Biosocial dimensions* (pp. 111–142). Hawthorne, NY: Aldine de Gruyter.

Lamb, M. E., Pleck, J. H., & Levine, J. A. 1985. The role of the father in child development: The effects of increased paternal involvement. In B. Lahey & A. Kazdin (Eds.), *Advances in clinical child psychology* (pp. 229–266). New York: Plenum.

Lamb, M. E., & Tamis-LeMonda, C. S. 2004. The role of the father: An introduction. In M. E. Lamb (Ed.), *The role of the father in child development* (pp. 1–31). Hoboken, NJ: Wiley.

Lambert, P. A. 2008. The comparative political economy of parental leave and child care: Evidence from twenty OECD countries. *Social Politics, 15*, 315–344.

Lamont, M. 2000. *The dignity of working men: Morality and the boundaries of race, class and immigration.* Cambridge: Harvard University Press.

LaRossa, R. 1988. Fatherhood and social change. *Family Relations, 37*, 451–457.

LaRossa, R. 1997. *The modernization of fatherhood: A social and political history.* Chicago: University of Chicago Press.

LaRossa, R., & Reitzes, D. C. 1993. Symbolic interactionism and family studies. In P. G. Boss, W. J. Doherty, R. LaRossa, W. R. Schumm, & S. K. Steinmetz (Eds.), *Sourcebook of family theories and methods: A contextual approach* (pp. 135–163). New York: Plenum.

Lewis, C., & O'Brien, M. 1987. *Reassessing fatherhood: New observations on fathers and the modern family.* Thousand Oaks, CA: Sage.

Loughran, D., & Zissimopoulos, J. 2007. *Why wait? The effect of marriage and childbearing on the wage growth of men and women* (Working Paper WR-482). Santa Barbara, CA: Rand.

Lundberg, S., & Rose, E. 2000. Parenthood and the earnings of married men and women. *Labour Economics, 7*, 689–710.

Lundberg, S., & Rose, E. 2002. The effects of sons and daughters on men's labor supply and wages. *Review of Economics and Statistics, 84*, 251–268.

Mansdotter, A., & Lundin, A. 2010. How do masculinity, paternity leave, and mortality associate? A study of fathers in the Swedish parental and child cohort of 1988/89. *Social Science & Medicine, 71*, 576–583.

Marks, S. R., & MacDermid, S. M. 1996. Multiple roles and the self: A theory of role balance. *Journal of Marriage and the Family, 58*, 417–432.

Marshall, N. L., & Barnett, R. C. 1993. Work-family strains and gains among two-earner couples. *Journal of Community Psychology, 21*, 64–78.

Marsiglio, W. 2004. When stepfathers claim stepchildren: A conceptual analysis. *Journal of Marriage and Family, 66*, 22–39.

Marsiglio, W., & Cohan, M. 2000. Contextualizing father involvement and paternal influence: Sociological and qualitative themes. *Marriage and Family Review*, 29, 75–95.

Mason, M. A. 1994. *From fathers' property to children's rights: The history of child custody in the United States*. New York: Columbia University Press.

Maurer, T. W., Pleck, J. H., & Rane, T. R. 2001. Parental identity and reflected-appraisals: Measurement and gender dynamics. *Journal of Marriage and the Family*, 63, 309–321.

McDonald, D. A., & Almeida, D. M. 2004. The interweave of fathers' daily work experiences and fathering behaviors. *Fathering*, 2, 235–251.

Meyer, D. R., & Garasky, S. 1993. Custodial fathers: Myths, realities, and child support policy. *Journal of Marriage and Family*, 55, 73–89.

Milkie, M. A., Kendig, S. M., Nomaguchi, K. M., & Denny, K. E. 2010. Time with children, children's well-being, and work-family balance among employees. *Journal of Marriage and the Family*, 72, 1329–1343.

Milkie, M. A., Mattingly, M. J., Nomaguchi, K. M., Bianchi, S. M., & Robinson, J. P. 2004. The time squeeze: Parental statuses and feelings about time with children. *Journal of Marriage and the Family*, 66, 738–760.

Milkie, M., & Peltola, P. 1999. Playing all the roles: Gender and the work-family balancing act. *Journal of Marriage and the Family*, 61, 476–490.

Mishel, L., Bernstein, J., & Schmitt, J. 2001. *The state of working America, 2000–2001*. Ithaca: Cornell University Press.

Moen, P., Kelly, E., & Huang, Q. 2008. Work, family and life-course fit: Does control over work time matter? *Journal of Vocational Behavior*, 73, 414–425.

Moen, P., & Wethington, E. 1992. The concept of family adaptive strategies. *Annual Review of Sociology*, 18, 233–251.

Mosley, J., & Thomson, E. 1995. Fathering behavior and child outcomes. In W. Marsiglio (Ed.), *Fatherhood: Contemporary theory, research, and social policy* (pp. 148–165). Thousand Oaks, CA: Sage.

Moss, M., & O'Brien, M. (Eds.). 2006. *International Review of Leave Policies and Related Research* (Employment Relations Research Series No. 57). Department of Trade and Industry, United Kingdom. Available at http://www.dti.gov.uk/files/file31948.pdf.

National Center for Educational Statistics. 1997. *Fathers' involvement in their children's schools* (NCES 98-091). Washington, DC: U.S. Department of Education.

Nepomnyaschy, L., & Waldfogel, J. 2007. Paternity leave and fathers' involvement with their young children: Evidence from the American ECLS-B. *Community, Work and Family*, 10, 427–453.

Nielsen, L. 1999. Demeaning, demoralizing, and disenfranchising divorced dads: A review of the literature. *Journal of Divorce and Remarriage*, 31, 139–177.

Nock, S. L., & Kingston, P. W. 1988. Time with children: The impact of couples' work-time commitments. *Social Forces, 67*, 59–85.

Nomaguchi, K. M., Milkie, M. A., & Bianchi, S. M. 2005. Time strains and psychological well-being: Do dual-earner mothers and fathers differ? *Journal of Family Issues, 26*, 756–792.

Noonan, M. C., Estes, S. B., & Glass, J. L. 2007. Do workplace flexibility policies influence time spent in domestic labor? *Journal of Family Issues, 28*, 263–288.

O'Brien, M. 2005. *Shared caring: Bringing fathers into the frame* (Working Paper Series No. 18). Manchester, UK: Equal Opportunities Commission. Available at http://www.eoc.org.uk/cseng/research/shared_caring.wp18.pdf.

O'Brien, M., Brandth, B., & Kvande, E. 2007. Fathers, work and family life: Global perspectives and new insights. *Community, Work and Family, 10*, 375–386.

O'Brien, M., & Shemilt, I. 2003. *Working fathers: Earning and caring.* Manchester, UK: Equal Opportunities Commission.

Olmstead, S. B., Futris, T. G., & Pasley, K. 2009. An exploration of married and divorced, nonresident men's perceptions and organization of their father role identity. *Fathering, 7*, 249–268.

Olsen, W., & Walby, S. 2004. *Modelling gender pay gaps* (Working Paper Series No. 17). Manchester, UK: Equal Opportunities Commission.

Oppenheimer, V. K. 1994. Women's rising employment and the future of the family in industrialized societies. *Population and Development Review, 20*, 293–342.

Oppenheimer, V. K. 1997. Women's employment and the gain to marriage: The specialization and trading models. *Annual Review of Sociology, 23*, 431–453.

Palkovitz, R. 1997. Reconstructing "involvement": Expanding conceptualizations of men's caring in contemporary families. In A. J. Hawkins & W. J. Doherty (Eds.), *Generative Fathering* (pp. 200–217). London: Sage.

Palkovitz, R. 2002. Involved fathering and child development: Advancing our understanding of good fathering. In C. Tamis-LeMonda & N. Cabrera (Eds.), *Handbook of father involvement* (pp. 119–140). Mahwah, NJ: Erlbaum.

Palkovitz, R., Copes, M., & Woolfolk, T. 2001. "It's like . . . you discover a sense of being": Involved fathering as an evoker of adult development. *Men and Masculinities, 4*, 49–69.

Palkovitz, R., & Palm, G. 2009. Transitions within fathering. *Fathering, 7*, 3–22.

Parsons, T., & Bales, R. F. 1955. *Family, socialization and interaction process.* New York: Free Press.

Pasley, K., Futris, T. G., & Skinner, M. L. 2002. Effects of commitment and psychological centrality on fathering. *Journal of Marriage and the Family, 64*, 130–138.

Percheski, C. 2008. Opting out? Cohort differences in professional women's employment rates from 1960 to 2005. *American Sociological Review*, 73, 487–517.

Percheski, C., & Wildeman, C. 2008. Becoming a dad: Employment trajectories of married, cohabiting, and nonresident fathers. *Social Science Quarterly*, 89, 482–501.

Pleck, E. H. 1993. Are "family-supportive" employer policies relevant to men? In J. Hood (Ed.), *Men, work and family* (pp. 217–237). Newbury Park, CA: Sage.

Pleck, E. H., & Pleck, J. H. 1997. Fatherhood ideals in the United States: Historical dimensions. In M. E. Lamb (Ed.), *The role of the father in child development* (pp. 33–48). New York: Wiley.

Pleck, J. H. 1992. Fathers and parental leave: A perspective. In D. E. Friedman, E. Galinsky, & V. Plowden (Eds.), *Parental leave and productivity: Current research*. New York: Families and Work Institute.

Pleck, J. H. 1995. Men's power with women, other men, and society: A men's movement analysis. In M. Kimmel & M. A. Messner (Eds.), *Men's lives* (pp. 5–12). Boston: Allyn and Bacon.

Pleck, J. H. 1997. Paternal involvement: Levels, sources, and consequences. In M. E. Lamb (ed.), *The role of the father in child development*. New York: Wiley.

Pleck, J. H., & Mascaidrelli, B. P. 2004. Parental involvement: Levels, sources and consequences. In M. E. Lamb (Ed.), *The role of the father in child development*. New York: Wiley.

Poposki, E. M. 2011. The blame game: Exploring the nature and correlates of attributions following work-family conflict. *Group & Organization Management*, 36, 499–525.

Presser, H. B. 1994. Employment schedules among dual-earner spouses and the division of household labor by gender. *American Sociological Review*, 59, 348–364.

Presser, H. B. 2000. Nonstandard work schedules and marital instability. *Journal of Marriage and the Family*, 62, 93–110.

Presser, H. B. 2005. *Working in a 24/7 economy: Challenges for American families*. New York: Russell Sage Foundation.

Pruett, K. D. 2000. *Fatherneed: Why father care is as essential as mother care for your child*. New York: Free Press.

Radin, N., & Harold-Goldsmith, R. 1989. The involvement of selected unemployed and employed men with their children. *Child Development*, 60, 454–459.

Raley, S. B., Mattingly, M. J., & Bianchi, S. M. 2006. How dual are dual-income couples? Documenting change from 1970 to 2001. *Journal of Marriage and Family*, 68(1), 11–28.

Rane, T. R., & McBride, B. A. 2000. Identity theory as a guide to understanding fathers' involvement with their children. *Journal of Family Issues*, 21, 347–366.

Ranson, G. 2001. Men at work: Change—or no change?—in the era of the "new father." *Men and Masculinities, 4*, 3–26.

Ranson, G. 2010. Working fathers. Paper presented at the International Sociological Association's World Congress of Sociology, Gothenburg, Sweden, July.

Ray, R., Gornick, J. C., & Schmitt, J. 2010. Who cares? Assessing generosity and gender equality in parental leave policy designs in 21 countries. *Journal of European Social Policy, 20*, 196–216.

Reed, R. K. 2005. *Birthing fathers: The transformation of men in American rites of birth.* New Brunswick: Rutgers University Press.

Reeves, R. 2002. Dad's army: The case for father friendly workplaces. London: Work Foundation.

Reinharz, S. 1992. *Feminist methods in social research.* Oxford: Oxford University Press.

Reynolds, J., & Aletraris, L. 2006. Pursuing preferences: The creation and resolution of work hour mismatches. *American Sociological Review, 71*, 618–638.

Reynolds, J., & Aletraris, L. 2010. Mostly mismatched with a chance of settling: Tracking work hour mismatches in the United States. *Work and Occupations, 37*, 476–511.

Risman, B. J. 1998. *Gender vertigo: American families in transition.* New Haven: Yale University Press.

Robinson, B. K., & Hunter, E. 2008. Is mom still doing it all? Reexamining depictions of family work in popular advertising. *Journal of Family Issues, 29,* 465–486.

Roth, L. M. 2006. *Selling women short: Gender inequality on Wall Street.* Princeton: Princeton University Press.

Roy, K. M. 2006. Father stories: A life course examination of paternal identity among low-income African American men. *Journal of Family Issues, 27*, 31–54.

Rudd, E. 2004. *Family leave: A policy concept made in America.* Boston: Sloan Work and Family Research Network.

Ruhm, C. J. 2000. Parental leave and child health. *Journal of Health, 19*, 931–960.

Russell, G., & Hwang, C. P. 2004. The impact of workplace practices on father involvement. In M. E. Lamb (ed.), *The Role of the Father in Child Development* (4th ed.). Hoboken, NJ: Wiley.

Russell, G., & Radin, N. 1983. Increased paternal participation: The fathers' perspective. In M. E. Lamb & A. Sagi (Eds.), *Fatherhood and family policy* (pp. 139–166). Hillsdale, NJ: Erlbaum.

Sayer, L. C. 2005. Gender, time and inequality: Trends in women's and men's paid work, unpaid work and free time. *Social Forces, 84*, 285–303.

Schieman, S., Milkie, M. A., & Glavin, P. 2009. When work interferes with life: Work-nonwork interference and the influence of work-related demands and resources. *American Sociological Review, 74*, 966–988.

Schindler, H. S. 2010. The importance of parenting and financial contributions in promoting fathers' psychological health. *Journal of Marriage and Family, 72*, 318–332.

Schoppe-Sullivan, S. J., Brown, G. L., Cannon, E. A., Mangelsdorf, S. C., & Sokolowski, M. S. 2008. Maternal gatekeeping, coparenting quality, and fathering behavior in families with infants. *Journal of Family Psychology, 22*, 389–398.

Settersten, R. A., & Cancel-Tirado, D. 2010. Fatherhood as a hidden variable in men's development and life course. *Research in Human Development, 7*, 83–102.

Seward, R. R. 2010. Exploring fathers' involvement with children: Concepts, clusters, and inclusive theoretical model. Paper presented at the International Sociological Association's World Congress of Sociology, Gothenburg, Sweden.

Seward, R. R., Yeatts, D. E., Zottarelli, L. K., & Fletcher, R. G. 2006. Fathers taking parental leave and their involvement with children: An exploratory study. *Community, Work and Family, 9*, 1–9.

Sheller, M., & Urry, J. 2003. Mobile transformations of "public" and "private" life. *Theory, Culture and Society, 20*, 107–125.

Shinn, M., Wong, N. W., Simko, P. A., & Ortiz-Torres, B. 1989. Promoting the wellbeing of working parents: Coping, social supports, and flexible job schedules. *American Journal of Community Psychology, 17*, 31–55.

Shows, C., & Gerstel, N. 2009. Fathering, class, and gender: A comparison of physicians and EMTs. *Gender and Society, 23*, 161–187.

Silverstein, L. B., & Auerbach, C. F. 1999. Deconstructing the essential father. *American Psychologist, 54*, 397–407.

Singley, S. G., & Hynes, K. 2005. Transitions to parenthood: Work-family policies, gender, and the couple context. *Gender & Society, 19*, 376–397.

Staines, G. L., & Pleck, J. H. 1983. *The impact of work schedules on the family.* Ann Arbor: University of Michigan, Institute for Social Research.

Stamps, L. E. 2002. Maternal preference in child custody decisions. *Journal of Divorce and Remarriage, 37*, 1–11.

Stamps, L. E., Kunen, S., & Rock-Facheux, A. 1997. Judges' beliefs dealing with child custody decisions. *Journal of Divorce and Remarriage, 27*, 105–122.

Stone, P. 2007. *Opting out? Why women really quit careers and head home.* Berkeley: University of California Press.

Stryker, S. 1987. Identity theory: Developments and extensions. In K. Yardley & T. Honess (Eds.), *Self and identity: Psychosocial perspectives* (pp. 89–103). New York: Wiley.

Stryker, S., & Serpe, R. T. 1994. Identity salience and psychological centrality: Equivalent, overlapping, or complementary concepts? *Social Psychology Quarterly, 57*, 16–35.

Townsend, N. W. 2002. *The package deal: Marriage, work, and fatherhood in men's lives*. Philadelphia: Temple University Press.

Updegraff, K. A., McHale, S. M., & Crouter, A. C. 1996. Gender roles in marriage: What do they mean for girls' and boys' school achievement? *Journal of Youth and Adolescence, 25*, 73–88.

U.S. Bureau of Labor Statistics. 2011a. America's young adults at 23: School enrollment, training, and employment transitions between ages 22 and 23. News release. Washington, DC: U.S. Department of Labor.

U.S. Bureau of Labor Statistics. 2011b. Work at home and in the workplace, 2010. http://bls.gov/opub/ted/2011/ted_20110624.htm.

U.S. Census Bureau. 2009. *Father's day: June 21, 2009*. Washington, DC: U.S. Department of Commerce.

U.S. Census Bureau. 2010. *Statistical abstract of the United States: 2010*. Washington, DC: U.S. Department of Commerce.

Voydanoff, P. 2002. Linkages between the work-family interface and work, family, and individual outcomes: An integrative model. *Journal of Family Issues, 23*, 138–164.

Waller, M. R. 2009. Family man in the other America: New opportunities, motivations, and supports for paternal caregiving. *Annals of the American Academy of Political and Social Science, 624*, 156–176.

West, L. P. 2002. *Soccer moms, welfare queens, waitress moms, and super moms: Myths of motherhood in state media coverage of child care* (MARIAL Working Paper 16). MARIAL Center, Emory University.

Wight, V. R., Raley, S. B., & Bianchi, S. M. 2008. Time for children, one's spouse and oneself among parents who work nonstandard hours. *Social Forces, 87*, 243–271.

Williams, J. C. 1999. *Unbending gender: Why family and work conflict and what to do about it*. New York: Oxford University Press.

Williams, J. C. 2010. *Reshaping the work-family debate: Why men and class matter*. Cambridge: Harvard University Press.

Williams, J. C., & Boushey, H. 2010. *The three faces of work-family conflict: The poor, the professionals, and the missing middle*. Washington, DC: Center for American Progress.

Yeung, W. J., Sandberg, J. F., Davis-Kean, P. E., & Hofferth, S. L. 2001. Children's time with fathers in intact families. *Journal of Marriage and the Family, 63*, 136–154.

INDEX

ABOUT THE AUTHOR

Gayle Kaufman is Professor of Sociology at Davidson College. She is a 2012–13 Fulbright Award recipient.